Not in *Our* Town
The Queen City vs. The King of Smut

PETER BRONSON

Author of:

Forbidden Fruit
Sin City's Underworld and the Supper Club Inferno

Behind the Lines
The Untold Stories of the Cincinnati Riots

Cincinnati... For Pete's Sake
A Collection of Cincinnati Enquirer Columnist
Peter Bronson's Greatest Hits

Not in Our Town
The Queen City vs. the King of Smut

© 2022 Peter Bronson

All rights reserved. No portion of this book may be reproduced in any fashion, print, facsimile, digital or electronic, or by any method yet to be developed, without express permission by the copyright holder.

ISBN: 978-1-7359194-9-2

For information, contact the author:

Peter Bronson
1488 Greystone Lane
Milford, Ohio 45150
Pbronson1253@gmail.com
513-287-0001

Published by:

Chilidog Press LLC
pbronson@chilidogpress.com

Chilidog Press
Milford, Ohio
www.chilidogpress.com

Cover photo of protest: Glenn Hartong, *The Cincinnati Enquirer*
Cover photo of broken glass: S. Bonaime/Shutterstock.com

Cover design, interior design and typesetting:
Craig Ramsdell
RamsdellDesign.com

Contents

Introduction ... v

Prologue: The Raiding Constable ... 1
1. How Soaptown Stayed Ivory Clean ... 15
2. 'Not in Our Town' ... 35
3. Chief of What? ... 43
4. Putting the Sin in *Sin*cinnati ... 63
5. 'Do You Take Checks for That?' ... 79
6. 'Boot the Hogs' ... 89
7. Busted Heads and Breaking News ... 97
8. The Other Charlie Keating ... 107
9. Rotten in Denmark ... 115
10. Getting Wise to the Wiseguys ... 127
11. Butchie, Rocco and Meese ... 143
12. In Walked Jesus ... 161
13. The Wizard of Odds ... 171
14. The Smut King and the Mafia ... 183
15. Kamikaze Larry: The FBI File ... 195
16. Flynt vs. Falwell ... 209
17. Meet the New Boss ... 219
18. The Devil Went Down to Georgia ... 229
19. Political Porn ... 249
20. Serpent's Tooth ... 257
21. The Mapplethorpe Meltdown ... 269
22. What Were Once Vices Now Are Habits ... 281

Last Word ... 297
Selected Reading ... 301
Acknowledgements ... 303

Introduction

This story began with a question. I was signing my first book about the Mob in Northern Kentucky, *Forbidden Fruit: Sin City's Underworld and the Supper Club Inferno,*[1] when someone asked: "What was going on in Cincinnati while Newport was run by organized crime right across the river?"

Well, you could say Cincinnati didn't need a Mob because it had Newport. They had an unwritten agreement:

The adult playground of bootleg booze, gambling, prostitution and corruption stayed on the south side of the Ohio River, where Cincinnati residents streamed across the bridges for a wild time in "Sin City." The Mob was happy to get the business, especially from conventions that were lured to Cincinnati hotels with a wink and an elbow nudge about wild, wide-open Newport.

Meanwhile, Cincinnati could advertise itself as a clean, family-friendly city and shake a finger of shame at the wickedness in Newport.

That's all true. But as I researched the history of the Mob in Cincinnati and Ohio, it turned out the answer was more complicated. I was surprised to discover that it took a dangerous and constant battle to keep the underworld from opening a franchise in the Blue Chip City.

Stopping the Mob was a dirty game, and Cincinnati did not stay as "Ivory clean" as the soap products it sold.

- Like Newport, Cincinnati had its own brand of police corruption, including payoffs, intimidation and a sensational sex scandal.
- Mob boss Frank "Screw" Andrews ran his hugely profitable numbers racket from his Sportsman's Club in Newport. But Screw

---

1 www.chilidogpress.com, bookstores and Amazon

and his crime family lived in Cincinnati,[2] and most of his numbers customers came from Cincinnati's black neighborhoods. Many in Cincinnati had no idea that the underworld boss who reported to the Genovese crime family in New York was a neighbor, until his "hoodlums" started dynamiting each other's cars and houses in a 1958 rackets gang war.

- The Gambino crime family of New York moved into Cincinnati in the 1960s with the Blue Angel Mob, led by "Little Al" Anastasia, who ran the biggest heroin network in the Midwest until it was busted by Cincinnati Police.
- Politicians, police and city leaders were compromised, threatened, bribed and disgraced. Even an Ohio governor was linked to the Mob, and cities throughout the state had hidden, well-established branches of LCN (La Cosa Nostra).

And much more in the pages that follow. As I followed the footprints of the Mob, the research took me to Cleveland, Miami, Los Angeles, Dayton, Columbus and back to Cincinnati.

But there was never a "Cincinnati Mob" the way there was a Kansas City Mob, Cleveland Mob, Detroit Mob and Newport Mob. Organized crime in Cincinnati never compared to the brazen underworld empire run by the Cleveland Four Syndicate in Northern Kentucky—an incredible history told in *Forbidden Fruit*.

One reason for that was a handful of Cincinnati leaders over the years who risked their lives, their families, their careers and their reputations to vow, "Not in our town."

They fought back with Tommy guns, shotguns, lawsuits, protests and prosecutions. Cincinnati is cleaner than most cities today because those leaders were not afraid to pay the price to make sure their city stayed off-limits to the underworld.

But the Mob never stopped trying. They just learned new tricks.

---

2   Residences in Cincinnati: Screw Andrews - 2301 Boone Street; Albert "White Smitty" Schmidt – Miles Road, Mt. Healthy; Willard Whitley - 2629 Melrose; Peter "Junior" Andrews – 3555 Eppley Avenue.

Cincinnati could not be easily bribed or threatened like small-town prosecutors, judges and cops in Newport and Covington. So the Mob chose sex.

A common theme running through the Mob's battle with Cincinnati is the sex trade and porn industry, which grew like cellar mold in the 1960s, as organized crime took over and expanded it nationwide.

The Mob was always resourceful. When repeal of Prohibition ended their monopoly on bootleg booze in 1933, they moved into gambling. And when Attorney General Bobby Kennedy closed down the Mob's national illegal gambling network in Newport in 1961, the Mob spread like rats running from a burning barn.

Some, like Cleveland Mob boss Moe Dalitz, relocated to Las Vegas, where gambling and prostitution were legal and he was hailed as the "Godfather" of casinos. Others branched out into seedy, crime-magnet "sin strips" in cities all over the country. Newport was typical: After the Cleveland Mob left for Las Vegas, their glamorous "carpet joint" casinos, rough "bust-out joints" and underworld hangouts were replaced by a gaudy carnival midway of strippers, topless bars, massage parlors, "gentlemen's clubs," adult bookstores, peep shows and X-rated movies. The FBI reported in the 1970s that 90 percent of the multibillion-dollar porn industry was owned by the Mafia.

The face of the Mob that came to Cincinnati in 1965 did not look like movie gangster goons wearing fedoras and pinstriped suits. It was a stable of "dancers" at Larry Flynt's Hustler Club, who wore almost nothing.

When Charlie Keating and Citizens for Decency Through Law (CDL) fought back against the Mob's latest "forbidden fruit," he was scorned as a prude and ridiculed for his old-fashioned, uncool Catholic morals. His daughter was assaulted at the urging of Cincinnati's Smut King. But Keating did not give up. He moved to Arizona and turned up the heat. His warnings about the hazards of porn were prophetic.

When Hamilton County Prosecutor Simon Leis indicted porn peddler Larry Flynt for obscenity and included charges of organized crime, critics mocked and scoffed. Even the *Wall Street Journal* said he was being "vindictive." They were wrong. Reports would later show Leis was right: Flynt was bankrolled by the Mob.

As I followed the winding trail through FBI documents, police records, news reports, books, interviews, magazines, websites, White House records, trial transcripts and long-forgotten reports by several state attorney generals' commissions on organized crime, Flynt kept popping up like a repeat sex offender lurking around a playground. No matter how he hated the city, he was shackled to Cincinnati like the handcuffs he wore to jail after his first obscenity conviction in 1976. Even the man who shot him was tied directly to Cincinnati.

Flynt eagerly courted his role as the face of the porn business, so he makes a useful symbol of how it has corroded our culture, entertainment, morality, innocence and relationships.

On the flipside, the battle against Flynt defined Cincinnati as one of the very few cities that drew a bright red line against porn and obscenity and said, "Not in our town." Like a straight kid at a kegger, Cincinnati was pressured to go along, then ridiculed for saying no.

Looking back at the past sixty years, it now seems obvious that Cincinnati was right: Larry Flynt was the lowest of the low, a super-spreader of depravity who destroyed women, degraded men as animals and poisoned our society. The battle to keep the Smut King out of Cincinnati was valiant, not embarrassing, as many seemed to think at the time. To those who still blush about it: Try to filter Larry Flynt through the "Me Too" machine of 2022 and see how that works out.

Yet for six decades, most of the media have stubbornly defended him and allowed him to wrap himself in the First Amendment, even celebrating him as a "martyr" and "patriot."

For the record:

As a career newsman, reporter, editor and columnist at the *Cincinnati Enquirer* and the *Tucson Citizen*, among others, I spent some of the best years of my life in newsrooms and loved the profession.

As I wrote this book I used those newsrooms as fodder for fictional scenes that help move the story along. But none of my fictional newsroom characters are meant to be individuals I knew and worked with.

INTRODUCTION

I hope I captured the spirit of cynical humor I enjoyed so much. And also, the helpless dismay I felt as I watched the steady decay of a profession I loved. I watched the news business take a lemming leap into political bias; objectivity and fairness were left behind as relics of the "unenlightened" past.

The credibility of the media is now crippled by the same ideology that insisted obscenity without any redeeming value was protected "free speech." I wonder how much trust in the press was squandered to spin that fable and defend porn gangsters such as Flynt.

Respect for the First Amendment—which is first because it protects the rest without resort to the Second—has never been lower. Where are the defenders of free speech today? Where is the ACLU that staged rallies for porn? Where are the editors and reporters who understood that there can be no free press without free speech? Where are the college faculties that invited Flynt to speak and held him up to students as a hero?

One answer: At Ohio State University (and many others) they are busy organizing Sex Week, including: a "Freaky Friday" beginner's guide to masturbation; an expo of sex toys from those creepy truck-stop Lions Den adult stores; how-to sessions on BDSM (binding, dominance, sadomasochism—I had to look it up); "Valentines" donations to abortion providers; and sessions to sell college kids on "gender affirmation surgery" like time-shares in a bizarro-world universe.

If pep rallies to promote sex on campus sound as ridiculous as teaching dogs to chase cats, believe me, I am not making it up.

The only thing more amazing than Sex Week on campus is how parents who pay six-figure tuition shrug it off. When my kids were growing up, I often asked, "How did we get to this?"—as I wanted to cover their ears and eyes during ads, movies and TV shows. How did we get to a coarsened culture that doesn't even blink when F-bombs are dropped anywhere in public? How did we get to "entertainers" who cover their lack of talent by uncovering themselves? How did we get to lazy writers who substitute obscenity for creativity? If you have wondered too, read on.

This is not the history of the Porn Wars that you thought you knew, with the predictable heroes and villains. If my career in newsrooms taught me anything, it was that stories are far more complicated than "Film at 11," and are invariably filtered through the political lens of the left. I made a successful career of running against the media herd, not with it.

So please, bring an open mind and you may be as surprised as I was to discover "the other side of the story."

This book started with that question, as a sequel to *Forbidden Fruit*, Part Two of the Mob history in the Midwest. But it soon became more. It became a story about how organized crime exploited the dark side of human nature with help from an unwitting media; the erosion of free speech and freedom of the press; the end of sexual innocence and cultural standards; and the horrible things done to women, children—and men—to satisfy fallen mankind's lust for forbidden fruit.

Cincinnati won some battles. But you can be the judge if America is losing the war for decency.

To my daughter, Elizabeth, who shares my love of writing.

The greatest trick the Devil ever pulled was convincing the world that he doesn't exist. – CHARLES BAUDELAIRE

His second greatest trick was convincing the world that he is the good guy. – ANONYMOUS

Man of Constant Sorrow

PROLOGUE
The Raiding Constable

Campbell County Courthouse in the 1920s. Kenton County Library archives.

Carl Besse must have felt like a bald tire just one nail shy of a blowout. His life had swerved off the highway a dozen times, skidding into the weeds of theft, shakedowns, armed robbery and bootleg liquor. But he had always managed to wrestle it back onto the pavement—back between the straight lines where his badge as a Campbell County Constable gave him an unrestricted hunting license to do almost anything.

And in Newport, Kentucky, there was *so much* to do. "Sin City" had it all. Blackjack, poker, slots, dice and dope were all as common as drunks staggering down sidewalks on a Saturday night. More "bawdy houses" than churches. More "sporting girls" than teachers. And enough bootleg whiskey to float a riverboat down the Licking River.

AUCTION SALE

Entire Housefurnishings of

GEORGE REMUS,

Eighth and Hermosa Avs.,
PRICE HILL.

To be sold at auction, without limit or reserve, on

WEDNESDAY, JULY 2, 1924

AT 10 A. M.

The most magnificent collection of House Furnishings, Oriental and Domestic Rugs, Oil Paintings, Pictures, Bric-a-Brac, etc., ever sold at auction in Cincinnati.

Also, a number of Mahogany Desks, with glass tops; several Pianos, including Baby Grands, Uprights and Players.

Statues, including "Three Graces," formerly owned by the Duke of Tuscany.

Dogs, including the brother of "Laddie Boy," owned by the late President Harding.

A few of the numerous items are: Solarium Furniture, Lamps and Shades, Couches, Pedestals, Paintings, Bedroom Suites, Clothing, Tables, Desks Living Room Suites and many other items too numerous to mention.

☛ There will be no inspection until the day of the sale Doors of the mansion will be open at 8 A. M.

TERMS OF THE SALE ARE CASH OR CERTIFIED CHECKS.

GORDON CO,

Auctioneers—Complete Home Furnishers

335 MAIN ST. PHONE MAIN 5920

HALF MILLION IS OFFER MADE TO DRY DIRECTOR

Bert Morgan, of Indiana, Gives Testimony In Geo. Remus Liquor Case At Cincinnati.

Cincinnati, May 24.—George E. Remus, attorney, and seven codefendants were found guilty by a jury in U. S. District court late tonight on charges or having set up and maintained a nuisance on the Dater Farm, near this city. The government charged that liquor in large quantities had changed hands at the farm in violation of the federal prohibition law. Immediately following conviction, Judge John W. Peck sentenced the defendants to serve terms in prison ranging from one year to three months and imposed fines of $1,000 each.

Things began to unravel for George Remus in May 1922 when a U.S. Prohibition Director Bert Morgan testified that Remus had offered him a bribe of $500,000 for permits to get stockpiled liquor in Indiana. The agent said Remus claimed other officials "high in Washington circles" had been bribed and he was the last "stumbling block." By 1924 he had a $74,000 tax lien for violations of the Volstead Act (Prohibition) and had to sell everything in his lavish Price Hill mansion. From the *Owensboro* (Kentucky) *Messenger,* May 25, 1922.

Best of all, most of the cops were so crooked you couldn't straighten them out with a fence stretcher. George Remus and his bootlegging gang had bought all the lawmen in the county before the Treasury feds finally sent Remus to prison in 1922.[3] The Remus Syndicate owned beat

---

3   While George Remus was in prison, his wife, Imogene ran off with a former federal agent, Franklin Dodge, who was prosecuting her husband. Together, Imogene and Dodge looted his home and squandered his vast fortune. When he got out, Remus shot and killed Imogene in Eden Park, then defended himself on grounds of temporary insanity and was set free after a short stay in an asylum.

cops, detectives, police chiefs, sheriffs, prosecutors, judges—all the way up the ladder to governors and senators. Some said he had a mortgage on the White House. Anyone who was not on the Mob payroll was too scared to complain. And enamel-eyed enforcers like Red Masterson made sure they stayed scared. Rumor had it Red had killed enough people to fill a small church. Red carried two .38s, but he also liked the "Newport Nightgown"—wrap a guy in chains and make him fly off the Roebling Suspension Bridge into the deep, green Ohio River.

Remus, "The Bootleg King," was as proud of the politicians he bought as he was of his Price Hill mansion with the indoor swimming pool. He liked to brag, "There's not enough money in the world to buy up all the public officials who demand their share." But he still managed to purchase nearly all the inventory. And when the Remus gangsters got out of prison, they came back to Newport and Covington to reopen the spigot on the payola pipeline. They didn't just take a nibble of forbidden fruit. They shook the tree until all the vices known to fallen man covered the ground like rotting apples.

Pete Schmidt, second from right, was a tough George Remus gangster who opened illegal gambling and bootleg booze nightclubs in Newport, starting in the 1930s. Here he is in 1948, surrounded by police during a raid of his Glenn Rendezvous Club after he was muscled out of his swank Beverly Hills Country Club by the Cleveland Mob.
The Cincinnati Enquirer.

And now even Carl had a badge. The wild delinquent kid who ran away to join the circus when he was fifteen, and had to be dragged back by the sheriff; the blackest of black sheep in a flock of nine children—Carl was now a lawman with nearly all the authority of a county sheriff.[4]

That was a shock to his brothers who were training to be Jesuit priests. Suddenly, they had to ride in the backseat. Now it was Carl who was the pride of his father. "Mr. Besse," the German immigrant who owned the feed and grain elevator, was an upstanding, respected community leader. And he almost popped the buttons off his vest when he talked about his son the Constable. Crazy Carl was getting the last laugh. Before he was done, he would have more money in his mattress than his old man had in the bank.

But he was not about to follow the deep footprints of Remus. "Pigs get fat, hogs get butchered," he reminded himself. No, he was content to wet his nose in the trough now and then, quietly, while cultivating his growing reputation as a fearless crime fighter. "The Raiding Constable," they called him in headlines. If they only knew....

And then those damned farmers had to show up. Since that day—April 1, 1929—his life was like one big April Fool's prank. Everything was going sideways, right into a ditch.

The farmers came to Newport in dusty pickups and muddy old Ford sedans, driving twenty miles up from Melbourne, winding along the old Mary Ingles Highway named after that crazy woman who followed the river to escape Shawnee scalp hunters in the old frontier days. The farmers' parade was a "delegation," the newspaper said.[5] They parked at the old red-stone Campbell County Courthouse on York Street and marched into court wearing bib overalls, starched high collars and manure-crusted work boots, like they owned the place.

"We're here to lodge a complaint and demand the arrest of Constable

---

[4] Kentucky constables were created even before police, in 1792. As of 2022, they were still allowed by law to charge $3 for killing and burying a sick horse, and $1 for shooting a mad dog.

[5] "Deputy Riddled Car of Youth; Delegation of Farmers Demand Arrest of Carl Besse, Former informer For Government," *The Cincinnati Enquirer*, April 2, 1929.

Carl Besse," they said. And then that farm boy Otto Good—had to be a name like that, the way things were going—told the judge a story.

One Sunday afternoon as he was driving down River Road with three of his teen-age friends in his car, Good told the judge, they were run right off the road. They thought it might be a holdup, so Otto yanked his car around and poured on the gas heading the other way. And that's when the lunatic in the other car jumped out and started shooting at them.

He emptied his gun right at them. A big gun. Loud like a blowout tire. Five shots hit their car. One bullet smashed the windshield and narrowly missed their heads. Two more shots hit the left front tire. One hit the spare on the back and another went into the rumble-seat and the left rear wheel—luckily stopped before it killed one of them.

The farmers brought along witnesses who said the gunman strolled into a drugstore in nearby Silver Grove a little while later and asked everyone if they had seen anyone with bullet wounds. The witnesses were certain: The guy flashing his badge and asking questions was Carl Besse, "The Raiding Constable."

Walter Lukens, the magistrate who had hired Besse to bust up stills and crack down on bootleggers and speeders, told the judge he was riding with Besse that day and they only stopped the boys for speeding. "Those young men nearly ran over the Constable," Lukens said. "And Carl only fired once into the air, not at the car." He told the judge that Besse had been an "undercover man" for the feds.

But everyone knew Lukens was as bent as a bucket of snakes. Besse and Lukens were widely known to supplement their income with "wayside courts." Carl would pull someone over and show them his badge. Then Lukens would step up to the driver's window and offer a choice: "Listen, Mister, you can lose a day of work to come to court, or we can settle this in more friendly way, right now."

"Friendly" meant $20 or more, depending on the "court's" liquor supply. Cash only.

Campbell County Judge William Buten did everything but roll his eyes at Lukens' testimony. And Otto Good's bullet-riddled car was very persuasive evidence. One bullet "fired in the air" would have to be quite a trick shot to make all those holes.

Judge Buten shook his head at Lukens' lies, banged his gavel like a slammed door and issued a warrant for Carl's arrest. And from there on, everything snowballed.

A week later, Carl got a tip from one of the gangs that were waging another moonshine war, and took his wife, Loretta, on a midnight raid to bust a still in Dayton, Kentucky. Maybe a big bust could win some public support and shine up his tarnished badge, he figured.

He broke down the door at the address he was given and found a 100-gallon still and thirty barrels of mash. Then he spotted men with shotguns watching in the yard next door and took after them. But when he jumped a locked gate, he snagged a shoe on the gate and fell hard. As he hit the ground, one of his .38s went off, shooting him clean through the calf.[6]

"Besse's body shows the mark of at least one other gun battle," a coroner would note a year later when he examined the scar. "The man was a dope fiend, and his arms appear to have felt the thrust of a dope-filled hypodermic needle many times." The "gun battle," like the needle marks, was self-inflicted.

Bleeding from his leg wound as the bootleggers escaped, Carl limped back to his car. Loretta took him to the hospital that night and boasted to reporters how she went along on raids and packed a pistol to protect her husband. "I know how to use it," she crowed. The newsmen lapped it up. Carl and Loretta were Bonnie and Clyde before Bonnie met Clyde.

A week after that, the bootlegger-snitch who had tipped him off to the rival's 100-gallon still was shot, dragging Carl's name into the papers again. And then a Campbell County Grand Jury went out of its way to chastise Lukens and Besse. "We have investigated the roadside court held by Lukens in Fort Thomas and we condemn it," the honorable citizens said. "Nor do we approve of Lukens accompanying a Constable in an automobile, hunting petting parties and speeders."

---

6 "Constable Suffers Wound in Leg," *The Kentucky Enquirer,* April 9, 1929.

PROLOGUE • THE RAIDING CONSTABLE

Carl had to laugh when the same grand jury also declared on June 22 that Newport was "a spotless town," completely exonerating the Newport Police. Even the mayor knew better. He had recently said, "We could not have conditions in Newport, which appears to be a hideout for murderers, criminals and gangsters, unless there was some understanding."

"The answer to it all," the mayor had said, "is graft."

The mayor's statement about crooked cops and graft, the citizen jury said, was "just another puff of ill wind."[7]

The mayor backed down and retracted his statement. But he was right the first time. The grand jury found no "gambling, slot machines, disorderly houses or other evils" because it had the "Newport Eye"— blind to corruption, with one eye squinted shut like a wino seeing double.

The only problem in Newport, their report said, was "no-account, worthless white men and negroes, floaters and non-residents."

Besse had to laugh at that, too.

But then his name made the papers again while he was waiting for his trial on the Otto Good complaint. Harry Cohane, proprietor of E.Z. Credit Clothing Store, sued him for failing to pay the remaining $80 owed for two suits at $50 each. Carl had to keep up his appearance. The Raiding Constable couldn't be seen in threadbare, shabby suits. He needed to be at least as sharp-dressed as the gangsters he chased.

When his trial for the "malicious shooting" complaint by Otto Good finally went to court on November 12, the farmers came to Newport again, but Besse didn't show up. He had skipped town and was somewhere in Virginia, the judge was told. The next day, Loretta filed for divorce, claiming cruelty, drunkenness and a violent temper.

On December 4, Besse finally came back from San Antonio, Texas. He was arrested and released on bond.[8] Two months later, on February 10, 1930, he was arrested again, for highway robbery. His criminal career escalated as America sank deep into the Great Depression. Many would follow: John Dillinger, Pretty Boy Floyd, Baby Face Nelson. They

---

7   "Lily White! Is City of Newport," *The Cincinnati Enquirer*, June 23, 1929.

8   "Former Officer is Released on Bond," *The Cincinnati Enquirer,* December 5, 1929.

became criminal celebrities, almost heroes for robbing the banks that failed and foreclosed on the American dream. But Besse was no hero, just a lawman gone bad.

Planning to steal slot machines and cash, Besse and a friend busted into a gambling house on Southgate Street in a black neighborhood near the Licking River. They waved their guns around and pistol-whipped some of the men there who asked too many questions. Alice Covington, who ran the house, thought at first that it was a legit raid and asked if she was being arrested.

"Everything is all right," Besse said on his way out. "Everyone is trying to make a living and I am also."

He was released on bond again, but now he had the Otto Good shooting, the highway robbery charges and Loretta's divorce all hanging over him like a purple storm cloud. He could almost feel the prison walls leaning in on him. And then he had an idea that could only make sense to a desperate dope addict. He had to die. Or at least make it look that way.

The *Louisville Courier-Journal* headline on May 8, 1930 said:

> **RIDE VICTIM STATE CONSTABLE**
>
> Belief that the body of a man, murdered and found several days ago on the banks of the Big Miami River at Lost Bridge, may be that of his son, was expressed today by Charles Besse of Belleview, Ky.
>
> The son referred to is Carl Besse, twenty-four years old, who gained notoriety in Northern Kentucky through his activities as a Raiding Constable. Police said the victim had been "taken for a ride." The Raiding Constable was known to have many enemies and his father said he had not heard from Carl for six weeks.
>
> The day the body was located, Besse said he received a telephone call and a voice said, "Well we got your son for good."

But the burned corpse found floating in the river was not Carl Robert Besse. It was some poor unknown vagrant Carl had killed or found dead, then burned beyond recognition. Then he spread the word that the Raiding Constable had been "taken for a ride" by the Mob in Newport. And the old man backed it up.

Carl was not dead but he was in purgatory, hiding out in Cleveland. He visited a friend in the hospital there and met a cute, sassy nurse, Alice Blackburn of Hamilton, Ohio, formerly of Champaign, Illinois. On June 12 they were married in Hamilton. The newlyweds started their honeymoon the next day with a wild crime spree.

Besse and his gang, with Alice riding along, robbed a poolroom in Franklin, Ohio at gunpoint, slugged the manager and took $900. They stole a Chrysler and a Buick and headed south to Cincinnati, home to most of the gang.

That night, Besse was back in Newport again, flush with cash and a ravenous heroin habit to feed.

* * *

Newport Patrolman Gus Schoo. Cincinnati Police Museum.

Newport Patrolman August "Gus" Schoo felt like a lucky man. After twenty-one years of hard labor as a "shearman" in the Newport Rolling Mill, cutting red-hot steel with a huge hydraulic pincer, sweating his life away drop by drop, he had been hired by the Newport Police. At an age when bankers, cab drivers and store clerks start daydreaming of retirement, Gus became a cop. He was 48.

After surviving that molten-hot steel mill, walking a beat was light work. Gus and his wife, Maria, had a nice little white house at 526 Lindsey Street. Life was good.

The night of June 14, 1930 was quiet. Gus's partner went off to investigate reports of a fistfight, and Gus continue walking their beat alone. At about 11:30, Patrolman Schoo got off a streetcar and walked up Saratoga Street, where he spotted Carl Besse leaning against a light pole. Maybe Schoo was surprised to see a "ghost." Newport Police still thought Besse was dead, and they were not heartbroken about it. But here was Carl, very much alive. There were no warrants out for him, so Schoo chatted with Besse as they walked east on Third Street toward Washington Avenue. Maybe Gus offered some friendly advice. Or maybe he asked too many questions.

Besse tried to stay calm, but inside he was on the ragged edge of panic. What if Schoo had been alerted to the stolen car ditched behind the Glenn Hotel, that linked him to the pool room robbery? What if the old cop was walking him into an ambush by more cops waiting around the next corner? And what would happen when the courts found out he was not dead, but still very much alive enough to go to prison for the highway robbery and malicious shooting charges?

As they approached 328 Washington Street, Besse suddenly stopped, stepped back and pulled a .45 caliber semi-automatic pistol, firing three shots before Schoo could reach for his gun. He hit the patrolman in the head, shoulder and upper body. The big .45 sounded like a cannon. Its legendary stopping power was attributed to hydrostatic shock: the impact of a high-caliber round creates pressure waves that spread through the body like ripples from throwing a rock in a pond, causing incapacitating nerve damage and instant death. Used with hollow-point rounds, the .45 ACP (Automatic Colt Pistol) can leave an entrance wound the size of a cigarette burn and exit like a grapefruit.

Patrolman Schoo was probably dead before he hit the ground, and Carl Beese was off running for the river, sprinting so fast his hat flew off his head as he barreled past stunned witnesses. At the riverfront he found a man on a houseboat and ordered him to take him across the river. "I just knocked off a probation officer," the panting gunman announced to the frightened boat owner.

Schoo was long dead when police got to the scene. They found Besse's straw hat on the ground near the policeman's body. It was traced to Champaign, Illinois. Detectives didn't know it at the time, but that was the hometown of Besse's new wife, Alice. The hat shop in Champaign had no records of the buyer, though, so the trail of the killer went cold. Besse, meanwhile, was in the wind, still dead, as far as detectives knew.

Then the newspapers reported on June 25 that the First National Bank was robbed in the tiny town of Noble in southeast Illinois. A gang of four men and a woman came in waving pistols and shotguns and made off with more than $30,000. Five counties joined the manhunt with a 200-man posse of farmers, lawmen and local businessmen—their

PROLOGUE • THE RAIDING CONSTABLE

biggest search ever in those parts. As the posse closed in, Alice Besse quickly surrendered with two Cincinnati men, Harry Adams and Eddie Myers, who were carrying five guns. Alice's clothes and jewelry all had been stolen. She claimed her husband told her he was a jewelry salesman.

The remaining two bank robbers, "Jack Dunken" (Francis Bunnieu of Cincinnati) and Besse, kept running. When their car broke down, they jumped out and ran into the woods, where they were quickly surrounded. Besse, using the pulp-fiction alias "Jim Dane," was determined he would not be taken alive.

"They're not going to take me unless they haul me in on a stretcher," Besse told Dunken as the exhausted, desperate fugitives realized they were cornered after a 60-mile chase.

Asked about it later, Dunken raised his eyebrows and said, "Me? No, I didn't want to be a target for any of those bullets so I just stuck my hands up like a good boy and came along."

But Besse could never be a good boy. As they left the woods to approach a farmhouse, the posse was waiting in the road. Besse started shooting and hit Special Deputy Sheriff Everett Woolen, a small-town druggist, in the knee. It was Besse's last mistake. Woolen took the bullet as he stood on the running board of his car, then calmly returned fire and shot Besse through the right eyebrow. The Raiding Constable's circus of crime was over. He was left lying in the road, barely clinging to life, as the posse rushed Woolen to the nearest hospital. When they returned for Besse, they were surprised to find he was still breathing. He was dead within hours.

As police put the story together, they traced Besse to the straw hat. He was identified by the houseboat owner and other witnesses who saw him walking with Schoo before the patrolman was murdered.

Besse's father, Charles Besse, a former Bellevue City Councilman, refused to believe it. "I know that my son was not guilty of any murder, bank robbery, whatever they want to pin on him. They are ready to jump at the chance to blame him for everything," he railed bitterly. His wandering prodigal son could do no wrong.[9]

---

9   "Father Defends Son," *The Cincinnati Enquirer,* June 28, 1930.

"Dead men tell no tales and for that reason they are framing Carl," the old man told *The Cincinnati Enquirer* on June 28. "The boy got the blame for everything since the day he was appointed Constable. He attempted to enforce the laws but instead of receiving praise he received criticism. Carl was the victim of rotten politics. He was the victim of the gambling fraternities," he said darkly.

Some people probably believed it. Newport politics was rotten enough, and the Mob that ran Newport was certainly violent enough. But Carl was gunned down by a small-town Illinois Methodist who ran a drugstore—not a Newport gangster.

Newspapers gave Carl his epitaph in printer's ink: "all around crook."

His body went unclaimed for days, waiting for "the first member of the Besse family who raises sufficient money to pay the undertaker's bill," the *Journal Gazette* in Matoon, Illinois reported. Besse's father "is said to have been well off financially at one time, but lost most of his money through the conduct of his son."

> **BESSE SERVICES TOMORROW.**
> Funeral services for Carl Besse, 24 years old, former raiding constable of Bellevue, Ky., are to be conducted tomorrow morning at 9 o'clock at the home of his father, Charles Besse, 413 Fairfield Avenue, Bellevue. Besse was shot and killed at Noble, Ill., last week by police who were pursuing bank robbers. Newport police recently charged the slaying of Patrolman August Schoo, two weeks ago, to Besse.

Charles Besse finally retrieved the body of his son. Carl was buried in Bellevue after a funeral at his father's home.

Twelve years later there was a postscript.

> **SHOT FATAL**
> Charles Besse, retired hay and grain dealer who shot himself above the heart Thursday at his home, 413 Fairfield Avenue, Bellevue, died yesterday at Speers Hospital, Dayton. He was sixty-four years old.

The old man was found in bed with a .38 revolver next to him. His obituary said he had seven sons and two daughters. Two of his sons went to seminary. One became a councilman. Another became a priest. His sons and daughters gave him a houseful of grandchildren and a big, successful family in which he could take great pride and satisfaction.

But Charles Besse poured his money and his love into one wild son named Carl, who crossed the line from constable to criminal and killed a good cop named Gus Schoo. Carl drove his father to the grave as surely as if he had shot him with that .38 revolver.

Carl Besse was rotten to his shoes. His father had to know that. But there is no explaining a father's stubborn love.

What man of you, having a hundred sheep, if he loses one of them, doth not leave the ninety and nine in the wilderness, and go after that which is lost, until he find it? —LUKE 15:4

Born to be Wild

1
How Soaptown Stayed Ivory Clean

THE CINCINNATI ENQUIRER, DEC. 18, 1972—Screw Andrews, the "Numbers King" of Cincinnati, a brawler, bully and coldblooded killer who bossed the Mob on both sides of the river, got clean away with murder in 1955. But his last roll of the dice came up snake eyes yesterday when he fell—or was pushed—from a fourth-story window at St. Luke's Hospital in Falmouth, Ky.

His life was an X-rated parable of the rise and fall of the underworld in Cincinnati and Newport.

When he was growing up as a street fighter in Mount Auburn and Walnut Hills, he was Frank Andriola. By the time he made the top-40 list of Attorney General Robert Kennedy's most-wanted underworld kingpins in 1962, he was going by Frank Andrews, known on the streets as "Screw," for his favorite hobby.

One of Kennedy's top prosecutors once boasted that, finally, they had targeted a kingpin named Andrews, who was not Italian. "His real name is Andriola," someone corrected. He was as Italian as an anchovy pizza, and just as subtle.

In 1946, he was the first man sent to an Ohio prison for running a numbers racket. When he got out, he immediately went back to the rackets, and moved in on the reigning Cincinnati Numbers King, black gangster Marvin Clark.

On August 18, 1955, Clark was shot nine times behind the Alibi Club in Newport—coincidentally owned by Screw Andrews. A witness said she watched as Clark was ambushed and killed. But then the woman suddenly changed her story and refused to testify. After meeting some of Screw's friends, her husband also decided his wife was lying and didn't see anything. Murder? What murder?

Another witness, Clark's girlfriend, was given police protection because she feared for her life. She said Clark was unarmed when he went to the Alibi Club to buy some slot machines from Screw. She told detectives she watched from Clark's car as he walked up to the back door. Suddenly, she heard gunshots and saw him fall. Several more gunshots followed as she ran to a nearby club to call the police. As she hid, she saw Andrews with a gun, standing in the street, yelling, "Where is that b---- that was with Clark?"

The back door of the Alibi Club where 'Numbers King' Marvin Clark was shot nine times by Screw Andrews and his gang. *The Cincinnati Enquirer*

She was literally a "smoking gun" witness.

But curiously, Newport Police said her version was "impossible." Detective Pat Ciafardini—the same crooked cop who helped the Mob frame Campbell County Sheriff George Ratterman—said the girl was lying. He testified that when he arrived on the scene, he found a gun clutched in Clark's right hand. That was very convenient for Screw.

Andrews pleaded self-defense and claimed he was ambushed by Clark as he exited the back door of the Alibi Club. Clark fired first, Screw claimed, so he ran to his car, grabbed a gun and shot Clark four times. Apparently, Clark waited politely while Screw armed himself. After Clark was shot four times by Screw, someone else apparently fired five more bullets into Clark. Screw wouldn't say who, and the police were not interested.

The jury deliberated just forty-five minutes. The headline the next day was played above "Red A-Blast Biggest Ever." Screw's verdict was bigger than an atomic bomb: Not guilty. It was the best the jury could do without giving Screw a medal.

Clark was not mourned. He was the terror of the West End of Cincinnati. He took over the Cincinnati "policy" racket in the 1950s and quickly earned a reputation as a fast and accurate gunman, known for "numerous shootings, bombings and knifings" in turf wars. To boost his racket he also took over the Cincinnati Leader, which was "the negro newspaper" in the West End, published in a building owned by former councilman Theodore Berry, who was elected as Cincinnati's first black mayor in 1972.

After he murdered Clark, Andrews announced that he was the new King of the Numbers, ruling Cincinnati and the Newport underworld with a gang that had more mobbed-up nicknames than a Damon Runyan script. Gus "Whiskey" Postel, Russel "Kid" Malone, Daniel "Spider" Andrews, Albert "White Smitty" Schmidt....

For the past thirty years the numbers racket has had its "bank" in Newport, but most bets came from Cincinnati's black neighborhoods. When RFK fumigated Newport in 1961 after the botched Ratterman scandal, he put Screw at the top of his list as a prime example of gambling rackets that he said were the "life-blood" of the Mob in America.

The Ratterman case drew all the headlines. As prosecutors told the jury, it had more drama than a gangster movie: "politics, intrigue, mystery, false alibi, sex."

But quietly, the IRS and the Kennedy "Mob Squad" infiltrated Screw's headquarters at the Sportsman's Club in Newport. In late August of 1961, even before Ratterman was elected Sheriff of Campbell County in a landslide for reform, 33 IRS agents raided the Sportsman's Club and spent fifteen hours searching it. They found guns, $50,000 in cash, secret rooms, a hidden closet that could only be opened by touching two nails together, slot machines and "barrels of numbers records." Three phones rang constantly as players asked for the daily winners.

And that was just scraping the surface of the underworld in Newport.

That raid was the beginning of the end for Screw. In a 17-day trial, the feds revealed that his racket hauled in more than $5 million between 1959 and 1961—about $2 million a year. But he only reported and paid the 10 percent gambling tax on about $1 million. They also wanted the public to know that the game was fixed: Winning numbers were carefully picked to limit losses to the Mob.

The jury deliberated for four days, but this time the verdict was "guilty." Andrews and his gang were sentenced to five years in prison and $10,000 fines.

"This trial was a sequel to large-scale, illegal but wide-open gambling operations in Newport," said the Sixth Circuit Court of Appeals in affirming the sentence. "There is no indication of public shock in this community over the crime of federal tax evasion being charged. This community has indeed been quite tolerant of defendant's 'business.'"

That was an understatement. A local weekly spoke for many in Cincinnati and Newport when it urged the federal prosecutors to go back to Washington because they were making Cincinnati look like "the outskirts of Gomorrah."

We like our Sin City playground—as long as none of the dirt rubs off on the Queen City's skirts. But we miss a lot when we look the other way to cover up corruption. Such as:

Screw's partner and lawyer was Morris Weintraub—former speaker of the Kentucky House, former judge, founder and president of Yavneh Day School in Roselawn, showered with honors and prestigious board memberships by the Jewish community, here and nationally.

The City of Newport was entangled in deals with Andrews and bought his Sportsman's Club property for $475,000 just before the IRS raid. Surprise: The Newport Housing Commission that approved the purchase was led by Morris Weintraub.

Newport inspectors noticed that Andrews violated building permits to put five hidden rooms in the basement of his new $90,000 nightclub at Second and York streets, but the city did nothing to enforce the codes. What stories those rooms could tell now.

When Ratterman ticketed Andrews for shouting profanities at the sheriff that could be heard blocks away, the Louisville Courier-Journal shook its finger and scolded... Sheriff Ratterman.

By the time the IRS was finished with him, Screw had next to nothing. But he was still the brawler, the bully full of... bluster. When he was identified as an "undesirable" and asked to leave Miles Park Race Track in Louisville in 1964, he told a security

CHAPTER 1 • HOW SOAPTOWN STAYED IVORY CLEAN

The new Sportsman's Club built by Screw Andrews in Newport had secret rooms and hidden doors. It was the headquarters of his multi-million dollar numbers racket, but Screw's crime family and most of his customers lived in Cincinnati. Taken in 1963. *The Cincinnati Enquirer.*

guard, "I'll be back Thursday and I don't think you have enough men to keep me off, and we'll see if you are big enough to keep me off."

That's the same Screw Andrews who claimed that Bobby Kennedy had "a vendetta against me because I talked back to him at a meeting in Las Vegas. He said we were all going to have to do time."

RFK turned out to be right, but he's gone now. Some of his top prosecutors in the war on organized crime believe he and his brother paid the ultimate, tragic price for squashing underworld cockroaches like Screw Andrews.

But most people missed that. It's hard to see with one eye closed.

* * *

"That's good," Jake said to himself. "All the good stuff is in there, and I still came in right at a thousand words."

"Copy!" he shouted. He looked at his watch. It was 7:05 p.m. Still plenty of time for Jim to review it and get it in tomorrow's edition before the eleven o'clock press run in the basement. He pushed back from his cluttered desk and stretched his arms over the big, black Royal typewriter. He looked for the remains of a Birdie's Deli pastrami on rye under all the papers, notebooks and ballpoint scribbles on curling sheets torn from a yellow legal pad.

There were photos under there somewhere. He already had one picked out to run with his column. It showed Screw Andrews, knees bent, legs spread out like a Reds batter swinging for the Seibler Tailoring

Cincinnati Post and Times Star photographer Byron Schumaker was knocked to the ground by Screw Andrews outside the Flamingo Club in Newport in April 1962. Schumaker had gone with Sheriff George Ratterman, who was collecting delinquent taxes from Andrews. Newport Police arrived just in time to ticket *the sheriff's* car for a parking violation. *The Cincinnati Enquirer.*

sign in centerfield ("Win a Free Suit"). In the photo, Screw wore an expensive gray suit with a sharkskin shine, over a three-button white shirt. His right arm was cocked back for a roundhouse right, aimed at the head of a flinching photographer who had his eyes closed. Jake wrote a quick cutline.

"Got something for Jim?" the copyboy interrupted his thoughts.

"Yeah, here you go." Jake pulled the cutline out of the typewriter carriage with a satisfying zip of tiny gears and handed it to the copyboy, with the column and photo. It was the time Jake liked best. The newsroom symphony was building to an urgent, deadline crescendo. Phones rang. Voices ebbed and flowed like surf in a background wash of questions and answers. And over it all the clackety clacking of typewriters made that mechanical, news factory sound of metal keys pounding ink into paper, making streams of words that flowed downhill into the City Desk and the Copydesk, where they became a flooding river of stories for tomorrow morning's edition of *The Cincinnati Enquirer*.

In a few hours the newsroom would be as quiet as a courtroom on Sunday. He took a bite of the cold sandwich and thought about getting a cup of coffee from one of the machines in "Vendeville" on the first floor. Instead, he lit a cigarette and watched the smoke mingle with the gray cloud hovering over the ranks of desks and typewriters that filled the newsroom. The walls, originally cream or off-white, were an anemic yellow, like the death-pallor of a dying kidney patient, stained by years of accumulated nicotine. On closer inspection, the wall behind his desk was streaked with brownish drip lines where the summer humidity had reconstituted all that tobacco smoke into something like grasshopper spit—

"Jim wants to talk to you." The copyboy had snuck up and startled him, and seemed pleased about it. He acted like he knew a secret that Jake would not like to hear. "He said now."

Jake got that sinking feeling. If Jim liked one of his columns that ran four times a week, he would hear nothing. Jim would make a few changes, correct some errors, write a headline, then hand it off to the Copydesk where it would get a quick readthrough and a headline, then be slotted for the next day's edition, front of the Local Section.

But every now and then, City Editor Jim Gardner would summon him for more intense editing that felt like something between a traffic stop and a bad day at the dentist.

"Have a seat," Jim said, hardly looking up. Jake took what everyone called "the hotseat" in front of the City Desk. Gardner finished reading the police roundup, shouted, "Cops coming your way, Punch," to the copy chief and pulled a cigarette out of a pack of Chesterfields. He lit one, shook the match out, dropped it into an overflowing ashtray and shook his head as if he had just witnessed another sorrowful act of what he called "felony stupid" writing.

Jake hoped it was not his column that was about to be indicted.

"Can you believe it," Jim said, "our city hall reporter turned in a story quoting a 'commentator,' but spelled it 'c-o-m-m-o-n-t-a-t-e-r.' Punch objected that a talking potato is not common at all."

Common tater. Jake laughed.

Jim seemed to smile. Maybe. It was hard to tell. Unless he was in a high state of pissivity, he always looked like he was silently chuckling about a private joke that nobody else would get. Jake couldn't decide if it was just the way the lines on his face naturally hinted at a smile, or if it was the look of amused disbelief that Jim wore no matter what was going on around him.

"Lord save us from *journalism* schools and their fresh out of the box graduates," Jim said, rolling his eyes at the smoke-fogged ceiling. "If they are going to teach these kids to save the world from injustice, they could at least teach them to spell it." As usual, Jim said the pretentious French word "journalism" like he was spitting loose tobacco from his tongue. In his world, there was no such thing. Only reporters and editors. Good ones and bad ones.

For Jim there was only one news business and that was newspapering. Radio and TV were "rip and read" pretenders who would be speechless if they couldn't steal headlines and copy from the daily paper. And Jim believed newspapering was going to hell since the trade became a college-credentialed degree called "journalism." Reporters began to have delusions of grandeur, he would say over drinks at the Cricket Bar. Pretty soon everyone who overstayed in college would call themselves "Doctor." Jim would point to the stylebook: "If you can't write a prescription or remove an appendix, you're not a doctor," he would say, "especially if you're a professor or a school superintendent." And each step closer to the professional class took newsrooms farther from the readers they served, Jim believed.

Most reporters feared Jim the way horses fear a barn fire. For good reason. Jim had once been awarded a pair of gold-painted pliers by the copy desk, to memorialize the time he brought a pair to work and used them to pry loose the exclamation point from a sportswriter's typewriter.

Jim was different. Nearly all of the men in the newsroom were "hip." Hair over the collar and long sideburns for the young guys and at least a mustache on most older guys. They wore garish neckties that looked like something left behind by the life squad at the scene of an accident. Their shirts were made of "silk-like" polyester and had stripes like beach umbrellas, or prints like Aunt Betty's drapes from the 1940s. Their high-waisted slacks poured over their shoes like miracle-fabric syrup. Some had even started wearing blue jeans to work. Not Jim. His idea of long hair was letting his Marine Corps buzzcut grow into a graying flattop. He wore plain chinos and ordinary blue or white oxford shirts with simple ties in black, blue or dark red. In short-sleeve weather, the Marine Corps globe and anchor made an appearance, tattooed on his right bicep.

He crushed his cigarette and pushed Jake's column across the desk. "Sorry, Jake, we can't use this," he said.

Jake opened his mouth to protest, but Jim held up a hand to cut him off, then spoke in a low voice to spare Jake from being embarrassed in front of the nearby editors and reporters. "Before you start talking, just listen. Neither one of us will last long in this business by making the man upstairs spill his coffee tomorrow morning."

Jim meant the Enquirer president, Bill Keating, or perhaps the owner, Carl Lindner, or maybe both. Whatever he meant, there was no arguing when Jim started talking about "the man upstairs" who signed the paychecks.

"What do I do to fix it?" Jake asked.

"Let's talk about that after the press run. Do you have something else for tomorrow?"

Jake's heart sank. "I can work up something on the anniversary of the Wright brothers' first flight. It was seventy years ago." He was half joking. Jim was not.

"Do it. Just get it to me in an hour. We can talk at eleven after they push the red button in the pressroom."

Jake scrambled to write a replacement column, turned it in, felt crappy about it, then returned to the City Desk at 11:15 and took the hotseat again. Jim was sorting unused photos and tapping the ash from another unfiltered Chesterfield. They could both feel the hum of the big presses in the basement. They made the whole building jitter enough to create tiny ripples in the cold cup of coffee on Jim's desk.

"So where do I start, boss?" Jake asked. "I put a lot of research into that column. Can it be saved?"

Jim leaned back, ran a hand through his short, graying hair and blew a cloud of smoke at the ceiling. He took off his black-framed glasses, massaged the bridge of his nose and leaned forward to square up the typed column in the middle of his now-clean desk. "Fiiiiirst," he said slowly, drawing it out to signal that this would not be a quick discussion. "Your lead says 'Numbers King of Cincinnati.' That needs to be 'Numbers King of Newport.'"

Jake opened his mouth, but Jim cut him off: "I know, I know, the bets come from Cincinnati, but we have a deal. We don't throw rocks at the junkyard dogs across the river, and they don't lift a leg in Cincinnati. Cincinnati gets to lure conventions with a wink and a nudge about the exciting adult *amusements* in Newport, and meanwhile the Cincinnati chamber of commerce can brag about being a model city. Hell, this is the world capital of soap. Clean towns don't have numbers kings."

"So we're not going to mention the Mob on both sides of the river? Screw Andrews *lived* in Cincinnati. I've met people whose daughters babysat for the guy...."

"As far as we're concerned there is no Mob on both sides of the river. Only in Newport."

"But that guy in Louisville beat us silly on coverage of the Mob in Newport."

"Last time I checked, Hank Messick doesn't live or work in Cincinnati, and he sure as hell would not live long in Newport. He doesn't have to deal with the fallout. And from what I've heard, even his own newspaper wants to put a muzzle on him. Some very important people in Louisville enjoy nightclubs, dice and hookers too."

"Okay," Jake said, "what else?" He had a feeling there would be a lot more "else."

"As much as Punch is itching to use 'defenestrated' in a headline," he said, pointing his cigarette at the copy chief a few desks away, "you can't say Screw was pushed out of the hospital window unless you have evidence."

"I heard from a nurse who works there that two big goons showed up and told everyone to leave. Then, abracadabra, Screw flew out the window like Peter Pan."

Jim paused. "My little boy was crushed to find out Peter Pan was a woman named Mary Martin," he muttered half to himself. He looked back at Jake, "So, this nurse. On the record?"

"No. Everyone over there is scared the goons will come back. But what about the AP story that put his 'accidental fall' in quotes?"

"Okay, do that, and leave it to the readers to figure it out. But this line about his favorite hobby, that has to go. Anyone can add the dice to guess how he got a nickname like Screw." Jim paused and ran his finger down the copy that was marked up by heavy blue pencil.

"This 'B-blank-blank-blank,' change it to 'woman.' We're not one of those hippie weeklies, we have standards. Make it read that Andrews says 'Where is that *woman* that was with Clark?' And that stuff about Ted Berry. Unless you can prove he was a knowing partner with that gangster Clark, we can't use it. Same for Weintraub and the Jewish community."

"But it's all part of the public record."

"Jake, there's true and there's stupid. Go ahead and roast Screw, I'm with you, but picking fights you can't win with no payoff even if you do is felony stupid. In case you haven't noticed, publishers also get awards from the Jewish community, and Ted Berry is the most popular black man in Cincinnati since Ezzard Charles defeated Joe Louis. You can look it up."

Jim put down the column, sucked on his cigarette and knocked off an ash that rolled out of the full ashtray onto his clean desktop. He blew it off onto the carpet that was a blend of 80 percent wool and 20 percent cigarette ashes.

"Is that all?" Jake said. He respected Jim more than any editor. But he was feeling discouraged and it showed.

"No. Look, I like your style or you would not be writing columns. There are lots of people in the newsroom who would walk over your dying body in track shoes to get a column. It's a good column, mostly. But have you thought about what this would do to your dad?"

It took Jake by surprise. He didn't think Jim even knew who his father was. Apparently, Jim noticed his reaction.

"Relax. I knew Knuckles in the Alibi Club back when I was working the cop shops on both sides of the river. Outside of Red Masterson, and maybe Trigger Mike Coppola, nobody was feared—and respected— more than your dad. Take a look sometime in the morgue for clips on the Carl Besse story. Your dad couldn't stand the guy and helped me with background. Some of the stuff he told me didn't make the paper, but it did help the cops.

"What I'm trying to tell you is that Screw Andrews still has friends in Newport. There are some very bad hombres over there. If some of those mangy peep-show Mafiosos think your father put you up to this, it could get rough. And just for the record, I like him."

Jake didn't know what to say. He cleared his throat. Finally, he said, "So tell me more about this unwritten agreement to leave the Newport gangsters alone."

"Okay, so you understand that the Cleveland Mob owned and ran Newport as a gangster's paradise for thirty years, until Bobby Kennedy chased Moe Dalitz and his friends to Las Vegas in 1961, right? That's when Screw stepped up to be the boss. The classy carpet joints closed and Newport was left with seedy dives like the Sportsman's Club, the Flamingo, the Tropicana.

"But during all those years, with all the murder and mayhem across the river, Cincinnati never had much of a problem with that underworld trash. That's how the Mob wanted it, and that's how Cincinnati wanted it."

"I thought I heard about Capone gangsters killing a cop?" Jake said.

"That was in the late 1920s. Ask for the folder on Peter Dumele, a town marshal in North College Hill. He was murdered during a bank robbery by members of the Capone gang. Guys who had been in on the Valentine's Day massacre. Names like 'Crane Neck' Nugent, 'Killer' Burke, and a George Remus gangster called 'The Fox.' One of them went to the chair.

"But that was about it. And the reason is guys like Machinegun Meldon." Jim saw Jake's eyebrows raise. "No, I'm not pulling your leg. He was a Cincinnati Police detective. Robert Meldon, nicknamed 'Machinegun Meldon.' I think he was involved in at least a dozen shootouts. He used a Thompson like the ones movie gangsters carry in violin cases. Hell of a weapon for close range combat. I had one for a while in Korea."

Jim paused and lit another cigarette. Jake could tell a story was coming.

"Meldon had a very deep pipeline into the Newport Mob. Maybe several. Back in 1957, he got word from one of his informants that some out-of-town freelance hoodlums were planning to rob a Thriftway Supermarket in Anderson Township. The Mob didn't want the heat it would bring, and Cincinnati Police were glad to roll out the unwelcome mat for any syndicate types.

"So Meldon and his crew smuggled Thompsons into the back of the store in boxes that said 'Lettuce' and 'Toilet Paper,' and set up an ambush. Sure enough, the guys broke in as advertised by the Mob informant, and they were stupid enough to shoot it out. When it was over, there was nothing left of those guys. When I got there you could still smell the gun smoke and blood. Nothing was cleaned up yet. And I still can't pass the meat department at Kroger without a flop in my stomach."

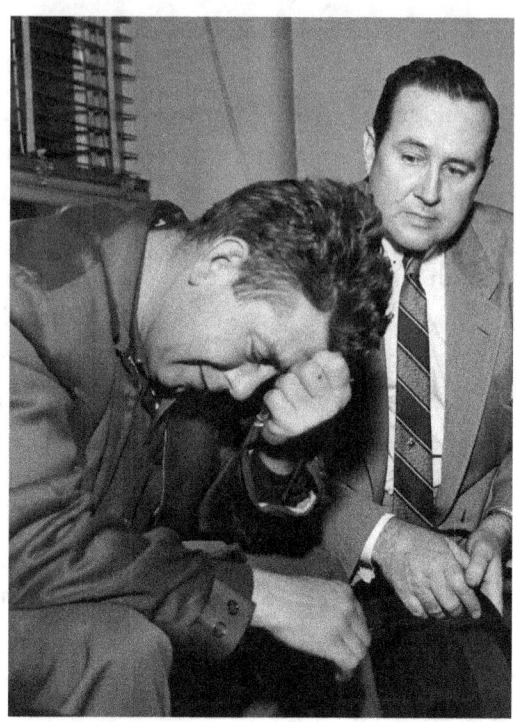

Detective Robert Meldon interviews an unidentified man in 1958. Ran Cochran, *The Cincinnati Enquirer.*

"I guess that sent a message," Jake said.

"It must have, because that unwritten agreement has worked pretty well over the years. Except for some bombings in 1958, the Mob wants no part of Cincinnati PD and the FBI on this side of the river, and Cincinnati likes its Ivory Soap reputation and the convention visitors who flock to Newport."

"Bombings?"

"Yeah, it was part of a numbers racket war between Screw and 'White Smitty' Schmidt. I think three people were injured. Two houses were blown up with dynamite. One target was a black woman whose sister was murdered a few months before, and the other target was Screw's nephew, Peter "Junior" Andrews. All of them were in the rackets. Cincinnati Police arrested 266 people, then hauled in the gang bosses—Screw, Smitty, Junior, Gus Postel, the whole bunch. Junior talked just enough to say it was all part of a much bigger outfit—meaning the East Coast crime families. But the penalty for running numbers was only a $50 fine,

CHAPTER 1 • HOW SOAPTOWN STAYED IVORY CLEAN

Screw Andrews and 'Whiskey Gus' Postel, kings of the Cincinnati and Newport Numbers racket, in 1962. *The Cincinnati Enquirer.*

and the Mob paid it like leaving a tip. You should've seen the crater in the driveway of that bombed house."

"I guess you got around in those days," Jake said. He was still stung by the rejection of his column, but the stories from Jim made it easier to take, knowing that his boss had been a tough street reporter.

"I saw a few things," Jim said. "Then, like all reporters who finally get good at working their beat, I got promoted to a desk. And my stories are just near-beer compared to the ones your dad could tell. Now there's a genuine tough guy. Does he still raise a shot glass at the Alibi?"

Jake got the point. That was his dad's favorite hangout with his friends Myron the Cabbie, Gus the Bookie, Frank the Wiedemann's driver and Slow-Foot Bill the bartender. It was also one of the clubs owned by Screw Andrews before the IRS cleaned him out. The same place where Andrews emptied a gun into Marvin Clark to take over the rackets. And Jake never talked much to his dad about his "work," because neither of them really wanted to open that locked drawer.

"Yeah," Jake said. "You should stop by and tip a few sometime."

"Maybe I will do that." He crushed his last cigarette and said, "Let's do it all again tomorrow, kid. It's time to call it a night. Remember, never have a bad day over something that costs a dime."

• • •

The next day, Jake pulled the clips on Besse, Dumele and Meldon.

"Bob Meldon, Mob Menace, Will Case Gun and Retire," said the headline on a story dated October 2, 1962.

> "Fellow officers like to recall Meldon's answer to threatening calls made to his home after the Thriftway shootings. The message was that Midwestern mobsters had brought in professional killers from New Jersey to 'get him.'
>
> "Detective Meldon sent word to the Newport underworld that he would appear alone, at the corner of Sixth and York Streets, Newport, at 10 p.m. on a certain date. He would be carrying a pistol on the side and the familiar little suitcase that contained his submachine gun. No one showed."

'Machinegun Bob' Meldon examines a revolver taken from a suspect in 1958. Ran Cochran, *The Cincinnati Enquirer.*

CHAPTER 1 • HOW SOAPTOWN STAYED IVORY CLEAN

... Finds the Mark

10/21/49

Bob Meldon, in his days as a detective, once machine gunned a suspect who holed up in a coal cellar on West Sixth Street. The photograph was picked as one of the 10 best in the nation in 1949.

Spectators Watch Police Rout Suspect With Tommy Guns, Gas on Sixth Street

Machine-gun bullets and tear gas wounded and drove a gunman from his West End cellar hideout early Tuesday as scores of gaping spectators watched. The gunman was shot in the left leg.

The gunman, Sidney Morris, 38, of 530 W. Sixth street, was snatched, terrified, from the cellar at 528 W. Sixth street, where he had hidden after firing a shot at two policemen.

Nearly 100 shots were poured into the cellar on the heels of a police tear gas barrage. Morris had fled to the cellar after threatening a drinking companion, William Mosely, 53, of 820 W. Fourth street, with a pistol.

"He snapped it three times in my face, but it didn't go off," the terrified Mosely told Patrolmen Winston Gibson and Robert Edwards.

The patrolmen chased Morris to the cellar, where he ducked into a tunnel and fired at them. They

withdrew and called for reinforcements.

Capt. Walter Martin and District 4 police arrived. They covered all exits, and ordered Morris to surrender. There was no answer.

Lt. Jacob Schott started the gunplay by firing a tear gas shell into the basement.

When the gas drove Morris into view, Detective Robert Meldon raked the basement with machine gun bursts. Morris retreated into the tunnel again, but was routed by the gas as Detective Meldon continued to spray bullets into the cellar.

Finally, struck in the leg, the fugitive shouted "I'm coming out," during a lull in the firing.

As he came up the stairs, he was seized, hurled to the sidewalk and searched by the policemen. A dozen arms, including pistols, shotguns and machine guns covered him. They found no weapon. "I buried it in a hole in the cellar," he told the officers. He was

unable to direct police to it and they could not find the hole.

Morris told police later that he and Mr. Mosely had been drinking "sweet Lucy," slang for any cheap, sweet wine, all night, and that an argument had broken out over having "just one more drink."

The Life Squad task unit was summoned to ventilate the gas-filled cellar before police could enter to search the rubble-strewn cellar for Morris' gun.

Morris was taken to General Hospital for treatment, and was to be booked on shooting charges. He said he came here several months ago from Jackson, Miss.

The Weather

HOURLY TEMPERATURES AT THE FEDERAL BUILDING.

Midnight	32	8 a. m.	27
1 a. m.	30	9 a. m.	28
2 a. m.	30	10 a. m.	31
3 a. m.	30	11 a. m.	34
4 a. m.	29	12 noon	36
5 a. m.	27	1 p. m.	38
6 a. m.	28	2 p. m.	39
7 a. m.	27	3 p. m.	40

Sunset Tuesday 5:20 p. m.; sunrise Wednesday 7:29 a. m.

Jake spread out the clips to find the Thriftway Supermarket shootings and smiled at the headline: **Two Yeggmen Die.** An old-time gangland name for safecrackers.

"Police were hiding behind cartons of groceries and sundries piled seven feet high. The first gangster to fall was cut down by more than twenty bullets from Detective Robert Meldon's machine gun."

Another 'yeggman' had tried to make himself small behind a meat counter, so two more detectives opened fire on him with Thompsons. At least a dozen bullets went through the case and killed him, mingling his remains with the mangled steaks, porkchops and pot roasts in the case.

So that's what Jim was talking about, Jake thought. No wonder his stomach flops in the meat department.

Pictures showed Detective Meldon in a fedora: a hard-looking big man with kind eyes, casually holding a .38 taken from a suspect. Men like him enforced the unwritten law that kept "Soaptown" Ivory clean and bottled up all the dirt across the river.

The files on Besse and Dumele were like something from Elliot Ness battling gangsters in black and white. Jake wondered: What did my dad know about these stories? What if he had been the undercover

Detectives Lawrence Cogliano, with Thompson submachinegun, and Gene O'Brien, with shotgun, respond to a call in 1957. The Mob had machineguns and the police were not about to be outgunned. Their arsenal also included a Gatling Gun. By 1979, after three cops were shot to death, Cincinnati Police protested at city hall that their .38 revolvers were obsolete in the crime arms race. Cincinnati Police Museum.

informant in the Sportsman's Club? He decided Jim was right: That column about Screw Andrews could wait.

Another set of clips suggested by Jim was more recent: the Blue Angel and the Cravens bust. "Police disturbed by connection to Anastasia," said one story from 1960 about the purchase of the Blue Angel nightclub. At first the buyers denied the underworld connection, but then they were forced to admit the money came from the son of New York Mob boss "Big Al" Anastasia, who had been executed by Mob hit men as he sat for a haircut in a classy Manhattan hotel.

Another folder of clips showed a table covered with rows and rows of shotguns, rifles and handguns taken in the arrest of one James Perry Cravens. The raid on April 30, 1971 netted twenty-seven ounces of heroin, raw cocaine, 36 rifles and shotguns, 2 machineguns, 41 handguns and $50,000 in cash. Cravens showed up in court wearing a tailored mink coat. He had two Lincolns, two Cadillacs, three women and four homes. On paper he owned a cleaning service and several pony kegs and bars.

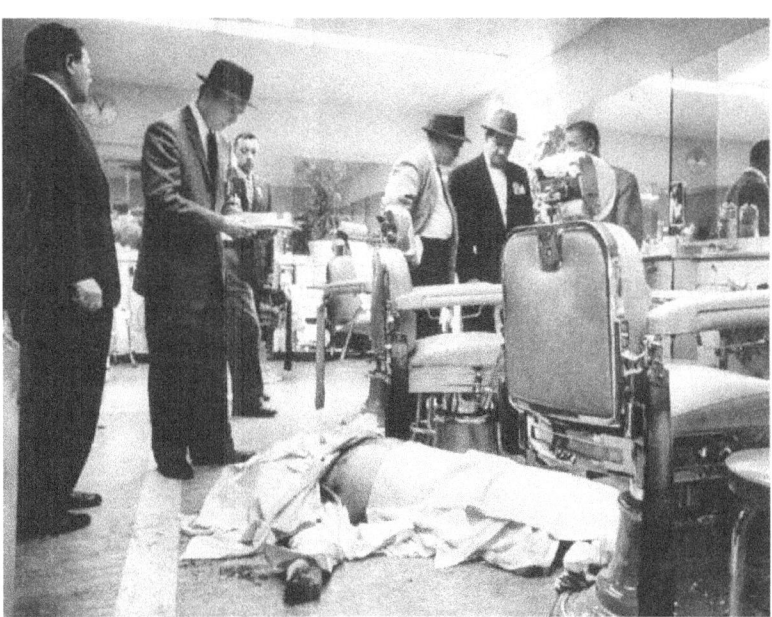

The body of 'Big Albert' Anastasia, known as the Mob's 'Lord high Executioner,' was shot ten times by two masked gunmen as he sat in a Manhattan barbershop in 1957. The Mob hit was never solved. Wikimedia Commons/public domain.

He worked as manager of the Crown Bar on McMillan Avenue.

"J.P. Cravens was the main man in Cincinnati," an unnamed drug dealer told the *Cincinnati Post*. "This guy was no one to fool with—he kept machine-guns around to keep him warm. He had three radios on, 24 hours a day, all tuned to police bands in Ohio, Kentucky, Indiana and Illinois."[10]

Vice officers connected the dots to "Little Al" Anastasia of the New York Gambino crime family, who owned a Cincinnati restaurant where Cravens claimed to work as a short-order cook. Jake thought, "So the Mafia capital of narcotics in the Midwest was Cincinnati."

Jake went to the morgue and requested another clip suggested by Jim. Dave, who supervised the newspaper archives, raised an eyebrow when he saw what Jake wanted, but said nothing. Dave had an almost photographic memory and probably knew more than anyone in town about the long-forgotten secrets of Cincinnati.

A prominent citizen with enough pull or wealth could get his court records expunged, but the news clips stayed on, deep in the files, turning yellow, unknown to nearly everyone but Dave and his "J. Edgar Hoover Library." Stories changed. People forgot. But ink on newsprint was forever.

"Most of these are from the *Post*," Dave said, passing the folder of clips across the counter. "They covered it a lot better than we did."

As soon as he looked at the clips, Jake could see that there could not be a better example of the "unwritten code" that kept the underworld trash out of Cincinnati.

Jim was right. The "Valentine's Day Bookstore Massacre" was a great story.

---

[10] "Smack in the middle of the street," John Eliot, the *Cincinnati Post*, June 16, 1972.

2
'Not in Our Town'

It was the dregs of a long Saturday night, staggering into the too-early hours of Sunday morning, February 14, 1971—Valentine's Day. At 2:30 a.m., two beat cops were patrolling the icy deserted streets of downtown Cincinnati. The bars were all closed. The last few drunks had been herded out the doors and were now home, sleeping it off. The city was cemetery quiet.

As their patrol car cruised slowly past empty office buildings, their headlights flashed on the dark windows of Shillito's Department Store, where store-window manikins held their frozen poses in the dark, like burglars caught in a spotlight. Then suddenly the still winter night was broken by gunshots. They heard the big boom of a shotgun and the more piercing crack of a revolver.

It sounded like the shots were coming from somewhere up around Seventh, so the cops hit the accelerator, disregarded one-way streets and sped north on Race Street. As their squad car turned east on Seventh, a pair of headlights came glaring out of the darkness and a carload of men roared past.

The patrol cops didn't see much, but they saw enough to recognize it as one of the unmarked cars used by Cincinnati Police detectives. As they passed, they glimpsed four or five men in the car. One was wearing a brown, narrow-brimmed "porkpie" hat, sitting next to a rear window that was rolled down. That was odd. It was only five degrees above zero.

As they came to the intersection of Seventh and Main, just past the Olympic Parking Garage, they saw broken glass on the sidewalk and gaping, jagged holes where big plate glass windows were shattered in the storefront at 134 Seventh. The Seventh Street News Shop. An "adult bookstore."

The cops nodded to each other. Another one. It was the twenty-fifth time adult bookstores had been attacked with guns, bricks and rocks in the past seven weeks. The broken glass could fill a swimming pool. They split up and checked out the store. Empty. As they returned to their car, a spent twelve-gauge shotgun shell was laying on the snow-covered ground near the sidewalk.

When they got back to the station, they filed a report:

"Two eight-by-ten-foot glass front windows, one three-by-seven-foot glass door and one six-by-seven-foot foyer window were damaged by shotgun and revolver shots," they noted for the record.[11]

Their incident report was kicked up the chain of command to their district commander at police headquarters, Captain Orville Barkhaus. He read it and leaned back, thinking. The presence of an unmarked police car leaving the scene was puzzling. So he checked the motor pool records and traced the car to Sgt. Thomas Streicher of the vice squad, who was on duty that night.

Barkhaus found Streicher's unmarked car and looked inside. It was still warm. There were wet footprints on the floorboards from at least four men. In the trunk was the standard police-issue twelve-gauge shotgun and an open box of shells. One empty shell was in the chamber. Barkhaus wiped the inside of the gun barrel with a finger and sniffed it. No doubt. It had been fired that night. He could still smell the gunpowder and see black traces of it on his finger.

He bagged the shotgun shell and compared it to the one that was found in the snow and broken glass at the crime scene. They matched, and ballistics analysis confirmed it: Both were fired by the same shotgun in the unmarked car that was issued to Sgt. Streicher.

Barkhaus realized the investigation had to be bumped up the chain of command and handed off carefully, like a grenade with the pin pulled out. A few days later they brought Sgt. Streicher in for questioning. It

---

[11] "Adult books store 'mystery': Acts of violence remain unsolved," *The Cincinnati Post*, March 15, 1971.

CHAPTER 2 • 'NOT IN OUR TOWN'

Vice Squad detectives Sgt. Thomas Streicher and Gene O'Brien load shotguns in 1957.
Cincinnati Police Museum.

went nowhere. He denied shooting out the porn shop windows and refused to talk. But he was responsible for the car and the gun, so he was charged by Police Chief Carl Goodin with violating police regulations:

"No member shall intentionally fire any weapon except as authorized."

If prosecuted for criminal property damage, the vice detective could face up to a year in jail, and the department would be embarrassed. One of their own highly respected vice detectives shooting up adult bookstores? That would be hard to explain.

A board of inquiry was convened, led by Chief Carl Goodin and two police captains. Sgt. Streicher "declined" to participate. So he was suspended by the chief. Finally, he was summoned to a hearing in the office of Safety Director Henry Sandman, who had been a detective himself, partnered with "Machinegun Bob" Meldon.

They met in Sandman's office. The top brass asked their questions, and Streicher still refused to talk, giving the same reason each time: "I refuse to answer on the grounds it may incriminate me." They offered him a deal to keep his job if he would just give up the other men in the car. He admitted he picked up friends that night, but would not reveal who was with him. Most believed it was other members of the vice squad.[12]

The case landed on the desk of City Manager Richard Krabach, who suspended Sgt. Streicher for thirty days without pay and demoted him to Police Specialist—back to the beat. Sandman had made his own recommendation. Asked if it was the same decision Krabach announced, he refused to comment—meaning it was not.

The punishment cost Sgt. Streicher $1,000 for a month's pay and $1,000 in annual wages for the demotion in rank. His 24-year unblemished record and hard-earned promotion to detective were gone.

That was not enough for some. A *Cincinnati Post* editorial called the incident "vigilante tactics" and said the outcome "strikes us as a whitewash."

"The Post believes that Sgt. Streicher has lost his usefulness as a member of the Cincinnati Police force," it said. "A Policeman who will not say freely and frankly all that he knows about the commission of a crime has no business working as a defender and upholder of law and order."[13]

Letters to the editor responded with anger—at the self-righteous *Post* editorial.

"I would appreciate an editorial on the number of windows broken ... since the riots of 1967, also how many arrests were made and the number of convictions," said one letter, pointing out that invoking the Fifth Amendment against self-incrimination was a civil right used by "U.S. Senators, judges, Black Panthers, Weathermen and numerous other members of society," including radical Yippie Jerry Rubin, a Walnut Hills High School graduate and former reporter for the *Post*.[14]

A woman who said she knew, respected and admired Streicher wrote, "To quote (your editorial), you say 'There are legal ways to attack every problem.' Really, now, is there? At times the legal way is slow, if it moves

---

12 "Policeman is suspended, demoted after probe of shot-out windows," *The Cincinnati Post & Times Star,* March 2, 1971.

13 "The police and the law," *The Cincinnati Post,* March 17, 1971.

14 "Our Readers Write," *The Cincinnati Post,* March 22, 1971.

at all, in reference to adult bookshops."

Her letter asked why none of the stories mentioned that Sgt. Streicher "goes to church with his family, is active in athletic sports for children, works at church and civic activities and is a good family man."[15]

Cincinnati was fed up. Adult bookstores were creeping into town like poison ivy, sprouting through cracks in the sidewalk. There had been two dozen attacks on the stores while efforts to legally put them out of business were glacially slow and ineffective. "Pornography is a complicated matter," the press tried to explain, "bound up in community standards and individual tastes, the constitutional freedom to publish, the right to do business, and the frustrations that police and judges have in keeping up with a growing phenomenon."[16]

But most parents didn't think it was complicated at all. Some picketed the stores for weeks at a time and forced a few out of business. Others would gladly buy the shotgun shells or pick up bricks to smash store windows if that's what it took.

At least one of the attacks seemed to be solved by the suspension of Sgt. Streicher, while the previous twenty-four attacks on adult bookstores remained a mystery, as far as the press was concerned. But it didn't take a vice detective in a porkpie hat to follow the clues.

Sgt. Streicher, who retired from the Cincinnati Police after twenty-nine years in 1978—still as a beat cop—was representative of his generation. He was a World War II Navy veteran, past commander of his VFW Post 5354 and had been given numerous community awards, especially for his coaching of Knothole Baseball. He was a lifelong Westside man, raised in the conservative, German-Irish neighborhoods that produced Cincinnati's police, prosecutors and judges. He was a devout Catholic, past president of the Police Holy Name Society.

Things were changing in Cincinnati. The retirement of Machinegun Bob Meldon in 1962 had marked the end of an era when tough Cincinnati cops were willing to take on the Mob in Newport with a Thompson

---

15 ibid

16 "On 'adult' bookstores," *The Cincinnati Post*, December 11, 1970.

submachine gun, if necessary, to keep the gangsters from contaminating Cincinnati like they had polluted Newport with organized crime, illegal gambling, prostitution and murder.

But the invisible wall over the Ohio River that separated "Sin City" and Cincinnati was not entirely gone. Sgt. Streicher and his friends knew how important it was to send a message: "Not in our town." Their generation survived the Depression and then went off to Europe and the Pacific to defeat the two most powerful empires of evil on earth. They were not going to stand by while the courts, the ACLU and the pipe-smokers in the press said it was too "complicated" to keep porn shops, X-rated movie theaters and strip clubs off the streets where their sons and daughters were growing up.

"These were tough old World War II veteran cops," said Roger Hildebrand, who served as a Cincinnati Police officer for thirty years, from 1965 to 1995. He summed up the attitude: "They thought that what guys like Larry Flynt were bringing to their city was nasty."

Sgt. Thomas Streicher did not live long enough to see his son Thomas Streicher Jr. become Cincinnati's police chief in 1999.[17] He died suddenly of a heart attack in 1985 at 61, while working as a welfare fraud investigator for Hamilton County.

"We talked about it some," said his son, the former chief. "But as for who was in the car, he took the secret to his grave. The rumor was, one of them was a priest, and it was the priest who pulled the trigger."

When the news about his dad was reported on TV, he was 16. "I was upset, and my dad came into my bedroom and asked, 'Are you mad at me?' I said, 'No. When people did the same thing at the Boston Tea Party they were heroes, but now you're the bad guy.' I was in high school. It was different times."

---

17 Police Chief Tom Streicher Jr. was one of the few local leaders who emerged from the 2001 race riots with his honor intact. Politicians ran for cover; business leaders scrambled to appease protesters; the media incited violence with sensational, sloppy reporting; federal intervention crippled law enforcement and spawned a wave of black-on-black killings. Chief Streicher disciplined officers who deserved it, and defended the good cops who were slandered as "racists" by a flock of hustlers and anti-police activists. *Behind the Lines: The Untold Stories of the Cincinnati Riots*, Peter Bronson, Chilidog Press, 2005.

CHAPTER 2 • 'NOT IN OUR TOWN'

Thomas Streicher Jr. followed his father's path to the Cincinnati Police Division. As Cincinnati Police Chief, he guided the city through the turbulent riots of 2001 and restored morale among discouraged cops who were unfairly smeared as racists and handcuffed by political attacks. Michael Keating, *The Cincinnati Enquirer*, 2010.

It's hard to even imagine anything like it taking place now. But in 1971? Sure. For anyone who lived through the wild and turbulent late 60s and early 70s, with violent riots, anti-war protests, assassinations, drugs, "Love-ins" and bitter family battles over the "generation gap," it's easy to picture: A carload of vice cops who have seen the gritty underworld and know what smut peddlers can do to a town. Tough veterans, proud of keeping their city clean. A few drinks on a Saturday night. A priest to offer his benediction for the war on porn. And a message written in broken glass with twelve-gauge buckshot: "Not in our town."

Most in Cincinnati cheered for them.

While Sgt. Streicher was suspended, anti-porn crusader Charlie Keating got in touch and arranged for him to take a temporary job with UDF, his son recalled. And Cincinnati cops passed a hat to raise enough cash to equal the weeks of pay he lost. The support for what they did was quiet, but unflinching.

Tom Streicher Jr. remembered, "One day we drove past one of those bookstores near St. Lawrence Corners (West Price Hill) and my dad said, 'You'll understand this later. I have six daughters. The perverts who are drawn to those places hurt children. I'll be a sonofabitch if they hurt my daughters. They're not coming here.'"

Now retired in South Carolina, he believes most of the two dozen hits on adult bookstores and porn shops were done by his father and his friends. "There may have been a couple of copycats, but those guys were pretty active. I have a good idea of who they were by who was coming to the house. But they're all gone now. They never talked. They all took that secret with them.

"It was different times. Very different times."

In spite of being suspended, Sgt. Streicher and Chief Goodin remained very close friends.

Both would be casualties of Cincinnati's porn battles. The Valentine's Day Bookstore Massacre of 1971 was just the first skirmish.

A Little Help From My Friends

3
Chief of What?

As the weekend approached in early March 1975, three Cincinnati vice cops in an unmarked car pulled up at the curb in front of J&J Fruit Market and went in to stock up on supplies for the weekend. The market was almost in the shadow of City Hall on West 8th Street. It was also home to an illegal bookmaking operation.

But the bookie who ran the market had no worries about brazenly breaking the law right under the nose of the mayor's office next door. He was a little man with big connections. He had the best kind of protection, provided by the Cincinnati Police.

The three vice cops emerged from the market fifteen minutes later carrying three bottles of whiskey in brown paper bags. Compliments of the bookie. They had a good deal: free liquor payoffs to "overlook" criminal gambling violations that vice cops are supposed to investigate.

The freebies were not unusual in those days. But as they got back in their car and drove off, the vice detectives were being watched by another carload of Cincinnati cops who were actually doing what the vice squad would not do. CPD officers from District One were "surveilling" the bookie's market as part of an undercover investigation. They were looking for illegal gamblers and organized crime figures. Instead, they netted three fellow officers making a liquor run at 11:30 a.m.

"Are you seeing what I'm seeing?" they wondered, looking at each other in amazement as they recognized the vice cops and videotaped them with a camcorder. They knew something wasn't right. But they had no idea just how wrong it was.

They were about to pry the lid off a barrel of police corruption that would spill out indictments for robbery, extortion, bribery, sex parties, soliciting prostitutes, obstruction of justice, perjury and destruction of evidence—the worst police scandal Cincinnati had seen.[18]

Before it was over, corrupt Newport looked almost clean by comparison... almost. The ensuing investigation would destroy the careers of vice squad detectives, force top police officials to hastily retire, and force the removal in disgrace of the city's popular and promising young police chief, Carl Goodin, a rising star who had graduated at the top of his police academy class and was on the very short list to replace FBI Director J. Edgar Hoover.[19]

The District One cops who staked out the bookie's fruit market took their videotape back to their commander and reported what they had seen. He took one look and tossed it to Lt. Richard Beyer, commander of the vice squad at police headquarters, also known as "carpetland," where the top brass occupied plusher offices than the bare-linoleum districts.

The tape landed on Beyer's desk, flagged as evidence for disciplinary actions. Lt. Beyer took action immediately—to destroy the tape. No evidence, no crimes, no problem. Abracadabra, the problem disappeared. As far as he was concerned, that was the end of it.

But then a few months later, at the end of October 1975, an anonymous letter was sent to top city officials and the local press. Six paragraphs, written on city interoffice stationery, rocked Cincinnati the way Mob-town Newport had been shocked by the attempted sex frame-up of reform sheriff George Ratterman in 1960.

At first, news stories did not publish the letter because of the incendiary accusations it contained. Then on November 2, *The Cincinnati Enquirer* published it halfway down the page on the front of the Local and Area News section:

> **City of Cincinnati**
> **Interdepartmental Correspondence**
> There are nine police officers present and aware that this is being typed, one captain, one lieutenant, one sergeant and six patrolmen,

---

[18] "32 Charges: Bribery," *The Cincinnati Enquirer*, December 19, 1975.

[19] "Police Career Lifelong Goal," *The Cincinnati Enquirer*, February 10, 1971.

and we have the blessing of 47 other police officers we can name of all ranks.

There is presently an investigation being made by the Internal Investigation Department of the Cincinnati Police Division. It indicates that two captains have used their command for personal gain. The one insisting on kickbacks being made for paid details given his men AND for instituting a hands-off policy in enforcing the law at the Clock Bar, merely because he and other police officers could eat free there. Men who were active in trying to enforce the law in and around this bar were quickly transferred to less desirable assignments. The fact that this bar was allowed to remain open was indirectly responsible for the loss of Ptn. William Lofton's life. The second captain is guilty of employing on-duty police personnel to renovate his home. Both captains are also guilty of maintaining a close social relationship with a convicted felon. Both of these men may and must be called to account.

The reason this is being written, however, is that unfortunately the likelihood exists that they and they alone will be made to suffer.

The entire police division is aware that they are guilty of nothing more than that which Colonel Goodin and Assistant Police Chief [Embry] Grimes have been guilty of on a far greater scale. On duty personnel have for some time been employed on Col. Goodin's property in Kentucky, and Col. Grimes property in Cincinnati at a staggering expense to the taxpayers of the city. These men have been given additional time off at a later date, which incurs and even greater expense. The Police Division is aware of those locations which feed these two chiefs free, and these are off limits to enforcement policy. The Police Division is also aware of the hands-off policy in enforcing vice control, while money flows through the vice squad into the hands of the chief. We write this with the full knowledge that if and when these facts are brought to light every police officer will be branded a thief in the eyes of the public, but we have been silent long enough. We are afraid this investigation will be swept under the rug. We address this letter to you five men in the hopes that these four men can be removed from their command with as little publicity as possible. If not, within 30 days we will

> call a news conference. And those men who have done the work of carpenters and electricians for the chief's personal gain will step forward and identify themselves. We pray, sincerely pray, this does not become necessary.[20]

More than fifty cops were so fed up with corruption they decided to risk their careers to blow the "Stop, police!" whistle on their own bosses.

"Most cops like being part of a clean organization," said Roger Hildebrand, a 30-year Cincinnati Police officer who was a young patrolman at the time. "What was going on outraged some of us, but we couldn't report it to anybody because it was the police chief. The vice squad was a closed unit, very close to Goodin and others in command. They had their own way of doing business."

Many of the patrol cops knew the fix was in for certain businesses, he said. "When cops could see that there were certain places you couldn't enforce, they knew. There would be a subtle word to leave that place alone. Bars were allowed to run after hours. We'd call and say there are cars there at 2:00 a.m. and we'd be told, 'Never mind, leave it alone. Go find some real crime.' We had a feeling that something was going on. So when that stuff (with Goodin) hit the fan, I don't think anybody was shocked."

Former Cincinnati Police Chief Tom Streicher Jr. was a rookie cop in District 7 in those years. He remembers a sharp divide between the younger cops and the older "captain's bagmen" cops who had the district captain's approval to take bribes, fix tickets and block enforcement of afterhours gambling spots in black neighborhoods, called "house joints."

"The captain's bagmen would pull tickets written around certain bars and rip them up and flush them down the toilet. They'd say, 'You must not like working in District Seven. You're not going to be police much longer.' It was veiled threats," Streicher said.

"If we busted a house joint and seized all the crap tables and dice and liquor, these bagmen cops would take it all back the next day and

---

20 "Letter Contains Charges Against Goodin: Misuse of Personnel Claimed," *The Cincinnati Enquirer*, November 2, 1975.

even set it up for them. I was utterly amazed by it. I would guess that was going on for years and years. We used to joke about the captain's car on Christmas. He'd pull in and we'd say, 'If he puts anything else in the trunk, the front wheels will come off the ground.' It was just stuffed in there with hams and whiskey and all the stuff he was given by the bars and house joints. He would share that with his bagmen."

After the indictments of Goodin hit the news, the younger cops retaliated by wallpapering the District 7 office with xeroxed tickets that the bagmen were tearing up, Streicher said. "We told them, 'All these have gone to the prosecutor. Your ass is going to jail for destroying property.'"

They raided house joints and took the dice tables and crates of liquor and dumped it all in their captain's office overnight. The battle was on.

Cops had taken sides in 1971, Streicher said: for and against the old ways of corruption. The anonymous letter was the first shot fired by the new generation to fumigate the crooked bagmen, all the way to the chief's office.

The accusations were serious: on-duty cops working on the chief's private property in Kentucky; cops paying the chief kickbacks in return for permission to take off-duty jobs; and a "hands off" policy at some notorious bars, including the Clock Bar in Avondale, which remained in business despite twenty-five arrests and seizures of more than 600 bags of heroin there in less than a year.[21]

The letter also was motivated by what happened at the Clock Bar that summer of 1975. Vice Officer William Loftin was shot to death outside the bar on August 26 by a man who had walked into the bar and asked for a gun to "shoot a cop."[22] Lofton was the fourth cop killed in three years. Mayor Ted Berry rubbed salt in the wounds by blaming the murder on handguns and saying the killer "simply had too much to drink."[23] Many cops were furious.

Once the letter went public, any hope that corrupt commanders

---

21 "Clock Bar Policy Surprise to Manager," *The Cincinnati Enquirer,* November 4, 1975.

22 The cop-killer was sentenced to death twice in two trials but his death penalty was commuted. He died in prison.

23 Cincinnati Police Museum.

"can be removed from their command with as little publicity as possible"[24] was hopeless.

City Manager William Donaldson immediately announced that the allegations would be investigated, but rushed to assure the public that Chief Goodin was "one of the straight arrows of this world." Donaldson said he would be "very surprised to find out he'd done anything other than to conduct himself in a very good way."

If he really believed that, the city manager was in for a big surprise.

Meanwhile, letters to the editor criticized *The Cincinnati Enquirer* for publishing the anonymous letter and called it unfair "garbage" and "slander of a good man."

Cincinnati had caught an infection of Newport Eye—temporary blindness to corruption and organized crime.

While Donaldson publicly insisted Goodin was a Boy Scout, he was more concerned than he let on. The city manager summoned Goodin to a November 6 breakfast meeting at the Queen City Club with Donaldson, Safety Director Richard Castellini and Assistant City Manager Henry Sandman, a former cop.

Later in court, Donaldson recalled how Goodin was very "emotional" during the meeting and had threatened to resign if vice squad cops were transferred to other assignments. Sandman and Castellini verified Goodin's puzzling overreaction and stubborn defense of the vice officers.

Only later did it become obvious that the chief couldn't transfer vice officers. He needed them to keep a tight lid on the scandal. But it was too late. Donaldson and his team had already met with Hamilton County Prosecutor Si Leis.

"The city manager and Henry Sandman came to me and asked me to get involved," Leis recalled forty-seven years later. "Sandman was a straight shooter. What many people didn't understand was that I was a close friend of Carl Goodin. I thought I could prove the letter was slander and prosecute the letter writer."

It was well known that Leis and Goodin were close. Cynics thought

---

[24] "Officials Dispute Goodin Testimony," *The Cincinnati Enquirer*, June 24, 1976.

CHAPTER 3 • CHIEF OF WHAT?

Carl Goodin became the city's youngest police chief in 1971 at age 37. *The Cincinnati Enquirer.*

the investigation was only a formality, and would be "swept under a rug," as the anonymous letter put it. But that was not how Si Leis operated.

The city loaned three Cincinnati Police investigators to the prosecutor's investigation and Leis impaneled a special grand jury to use as an investigatory tool.

"To my surprise, all of the allegations were true," Leis said. And much more. The footprints of corruption led back to an old nemesis of the prosecutor: Larry Flynt, whose Hustler Club on Walnut Street was a source of chronic obscenity complaints and criminal violations.

Leis was shocked to find out his friend Carl Goodin was corrupt, but he was not surprised to find out that Flynt was the source of bribes and prostitution for crooked cops.

The prosecutor's epic battle with Flynt had ignited three years earlier, in 1972. "It started at the Hustler bar on Walnut. Flynt took this girl to a bar called Caesar's Palace for 'entertainment.' The entertainment was having the girl give him (oral sex), and when he reached climax, Flynt fired a weapon into the ceiling."

The woman was Flynt's wife or girlfriend at the time, Flora Ravenna Griffith-Flynt. The incident occurred at 1 a.m. on March 16, 1972. At first, Flora and Larry Flynt testified under oath that the gun went off accidentally in her purse. But witnesses said Flynt had the gun and fired it deliberately. The Flynts were charged and convicted of perjury.[25]

Leis also charged Flynt with sodomy and discharging a weapon.

---

25 "Two Guilty in Perjury Trial Here," *The Cincinnati Enquirer,* April 24, 1973.

When he learned of the criminal charges, Flynt ran to his lawyer and told him to go "buy my way out of this." When the lawyer said it couldn't be done, Flynt told him, "Yes, it can be done," and offered to prove it. "You come by tomorrow at three o'clock and I will have the police chief sitting there."

As Leis tells it, sure enough, Chief Goodin showed up on time at the Hustler Club, summoned by Larry Flynt. Troubled by his conscience, Flynt's lawyer had gone to Hamilton County Democratic Party Chairman Socco Wiethe. Socco, a former football coach, took the story to the prosecutor, Si Leis.

It looked like Cincinnati's police chief was in the pocket of the sleaziest porn pusher in town, Larry Flynt.

Flynt was convicted of perjury and on the firearms and sodomy charges. He served twenty-one days in the Workhouse. After that, Leis thought that nothing Larry Flynt did could shock him. "He was the absolute lowest of the low," he said. But as the investigation of the vice squad unfolded, he was surprised by what he learned. "I thought Chief Goodin was a nice, friendly, good guy, someone I knew because I had worked with him many times."

On December 19, 1975, the grand jury indictments were released and the city was stunned by the headline:

> **Chief Goodin, six Others Indicted in Grand Jury Probe**

In fact, the grand jury indicted ten individuals—seven police and three civilians, including Larry Flynt, a "dancer" who worked for him, and a vice-detective's brother who was accused of robbing a man who was in town for the World Series.

The indictments confirmed what the anonymous letter said. The grand jury revealed kickbacks to Goodin: Two helicopter cops hired by radio stations WLW and WKRC for off-duty traffic reports each paid the police chief $15 a week. They were told by Goodin that it was for a fund to entertain "visiting dignitaries."

Leis and the grand jury were convinced that the only "dignitary" who was entertained was Chief Goodin.

But Goodin insisted under oath that the money went into "Informant Fund C," which he said was used by the vice squad to pay confidential informants and make drug busts. Backing him up, one of the vice cops, Jimmy Simon, testified that he had used the "regular payments" for specific drug informants—who had to be protected and couldn't be named. When Goodin was challenged for proof, he hurried back to police headquarters and returned with seven pages of records that listed payments from "Informant Fund C."[26]

"I knew that was BS," Leis said. "But my whole career depended on it being proved."

The city was sharply divided. "Half of the city supported me, and half hated me for it. To this day there are CPD officers who won't talk to me because of that case," he recalled in 2022. "So I took a hell of a gamble."

The animosity toward Leis was thick in the courtroom, as friends of the police on trial cheered and applauded when the prosecutors stumbled or defense lawyers scored a point. After the trial, First Assistant Prosecutor Fred Cartolano, who helped Leis prosecute the police chief, said, "Goodin was a tremendously respected individual. He was a part of the establishment here. It was a hell of a courageous move by Si."[27]

He added, "There was a personal, very personal risk in the Goodin trial. After all, we knew the man, and it's a hell of a lot harder to prosecute someone you know."

Hildebrand offered the beat cop view: "Most cops probably just thought the prosecutor was doing his job," he said. "Remember, we had just come off the (Chief Stanley) Schrotel era."

Schrotel was featured in *Life Magazine* in 1957 as America's most professional police chief with the model department for the nation.[28]

---

26 "Public Release of Particulars Unusual, Says Defense," *The Cincinnati Enquirer,* January 23, 1976.

27 "Tough Guy in the Courtroom," Gary Grace, *The Cincinnati Post,* March 5, 1977. Cartolano abruptly refused further interviews for the story after learning that the story was a hit piece to undermine his boss, Si Leis.

28 "What a City Should Expect From Police: Chief of Cincinnati's Model Police Force," *Life Magazine,* September 16, 1957.

"Goodin seemed to fit right in—smart, sharp, progressive polices for community policing. We were ready for the same clean police department we'd had. So we weren't offended when Si Leis took action," Hildebrand said.

Leis and his investigators sent Goodin's "Informant Fund C" records to Washington's FBI lab for analysis. "We were able to ascertain that the entries for informant payments were dated *before* the ink was manufactured," Leis recalled.

That proved the records were forgeries, cooked up by Goodin and the vice squad to cover up the kickbacks and growing scandal.

"Thank God the FBI proved it or my career would have been in the sewer," Leis said.

Cartolano agreed. "The whole turning point, really, a stroke of luck, was the ink. Once we had the ink, we knew (the case) was there."

Goodin was indicted for bribery, extortion, soliciting and perjury. The indictment document was published verbatim in *The Cincinnati Enquirer* on December 19, 1975. It listed thirty-two charges against the chief, his top brass and vice cops.

The chief, out of uniform, was caught outside the courthouse after his arraignment on Christmas Eve, 1975. He pleaded innocent to all of the charges. Gerry Wolterman, *The Cincinnati Enquirer.*

CHAPTER 3 • CHIEF OF WHAT?

One of the indictments of Goodin could have been a script for an episode of *Green Acres*, a popular TV comedy in the 1970s.

The police chief owned a farm in Sadieville, Kentucky, about an hour south of Cincinnati. He had purchased eighty acres for $17,000 in cash in 1974. A tax assessor said it had a dilapidated log cabin on it that everyone expected would be torn down by the new owner. Instead, Goodin had the shack carefully taken apart, nail by nail, log by log, and reassembled it twenty-five yards farther up the hillside—with help from on-duty Cincinnati Police officers who were being paid by taxpayers to be laborers for the chief.

Investigators also noted a conflict of interest: Goodin bought the farm from a relative of Elmer Dunaway, the colorful Fraternal Order of Police union president who wore a cowboy hat and gave city hall more heartburn than Tex-Mex chili with a chaser of jalapeños. The conflict: Goodin had benefited from a deal that indirectly involved his adversary in police union negotiations.

With the help of free labor by Cincinnati Police, Goodin had turned that tumble-down Snuffy Smith log cabin into a "pleasant, rustic, two-story home," *The Cincinnati Enquirer* reported.[29]

The 'rustic, two-story' hideaway of Police Chief Carl Goodin, June 27, 1976.
The Cincinnati Enquirer.

---

29   "City Knew of Police Misuse," Tom Brinkmoeller and Ed Bedinghaus, *The Cincinnati enquirer*, June 27, 1976.

The police chief's topless caboose. June 27, 1976. *The Cincinnati Enquirer.*

Then, like the shady "Mr. Haney" on *Green Acres,* Chief Goodin had a another bright idea.

Thanks to a friend who ran the railroad police for the Chessie System, Goodin was given a worn-out caboose—another troubling, unethical gift. He loaded it on a garish red-white-and-blue flatbed truck that rural neighbors said "looked like a big American flag," and hauled it down to his Kentucky farm.

But the caboose was too tall to squeeze under an I-75 overpass on a country road near the farm. So Goodin and his crew of cops unloaded heavy equipment from a second flatbed and began to excavate the gravel road to fit the caboose under the bridge.

"You can't bulldoze our road up here," a neighbor complained to Goodin, as traffic backed up for hours. Goodin ignored him and kept digging. So the neighbor called the Kentucky State Police.

The state troopers "were nice" to the Cincinnati Chief, the neighbor said, but told him to get his caboose off the road.

Undaunted, the chief and his crew of cops fired up chainsaws and cut the top off the caboose to squeeze it under the overpass. A year later, the abandoned caboose roof was still sitting alongside the gravel road where Goodin left it, while the rest of it was on his farm, still listed on property records of the Chessie System.

The next indictments changed the channel from *Green Acres* to the Playboy network. They alleged that even six months before Goodin was promoted to police chief at age 37, in 1971, he was participating in sex parties with several other top CPD officers and local civilians.

Ironically, in his first interview with *The Cincinnati Enquirer*, the city's youngest new chief had said one of his biggest concerns was declining respect for the police department. "It's a reflection of the loss of respect for authority in general," he said. "It's manifested against the police because they are a visible representative of an orderly society and government."

He made those remarks in February 1971. But as early as the summer of 1970, the indictment said, prostitutes provided by Larry Flynt had been sent to hotel "stag parties" to provide sex to "high-ranking police officials." In return, the vice cops who delivered the hookers promised Flynt and others that they would ignore criminal violations.

Also named in the indictments was William Poulos, owner of the Tender Trap in Roselawn, who provided two "go-go dancers" to stag parties in return for police "overlooking" complaints, beginning in late 1971. One of the prostitutes he sent had worked for Flynt as a police party girl.

She said she was working off a $1,000 debt to Poulos, and was told the parties were "good for all of us."

Poulos, who owned dozens of bars in Cincinnati, claimed he knew nothing about the parties, but then told reporters he was working on a book that would "tell it all" and "make Watergate look like nothing."

While some citizens angrily defended Goodin and the vice cops, others demanded to know who those unnamed high-ranking officers were. It didn't take *Kojak* to figure it out. Three police commanders resigned or retired immediately after the indictments were published; one of them was Assistant Chief Embry Grimes, who was named in the anonymous letter.

In July 1976, another letter was published in the *Enquirer*: It was the resignation letter by Chief Goodin. "The morale in the Police Division is at an all-time low," he wrote, but blamed it on layoffs, not the scandal. "It is obvious to me that I was the target from the very beginning of the police probe." He urged the city and county to drop the "frivolous indictments against the other officers."

"I want to reiterate that I have not extracted money (from kickbacks), I have not lied about it, I have not violated the law, nor have I solicited anyone to violate the law on my behalf. I will be vindicated in the courts and my name will be cleared."

Then in September, the wheels of justice finally began to turn. Vice cop Jimmy Simon pleaded guilty to providing false information and resigned; as part of the deal, a theft charge against his brother was dismissed.

Three other cops were eventually acquitted also. A crowd of their families and supporters in the courtroom cheered. Two of them stayed on the force; one retired early and opened a bar, where they all went to celebrate.

Goodin and Vice Squad Commander Beyer had already been convicted in June of perjury and tampering with evidence, but they also went to the celebration.

On September 21, more news made it clear that their party was over. Details that emerged in court made it almost impossible to defend Goodin anymore.

The headline: **Goodin Linked to Sex Parties**[30]

A go-go dancer at the Hustler bar testified that she had attended two parties at the direction of Larry Flynt: one in the summer of 1970, before Goodin was chief, and another in the spring of 1971 at the Marriott Hotel in Sharonville,[31] after he was promoted. Other "dancers" told similar stories, adding up to at least four sex parties.

Suddenly it was obvious to anyone with a calendar why Goodin would have appeared at the Hustler Club for Larry Flynt, and why Flynt was so brazen he had his "go-go girls" dancing in windows that

---

30 "Goodin Linked to Sex Parties," Margaret Josten, *The Cincinnati Enquirer*, September 21, 1976.

31 "6 Subpoenas Reissued in Hummeldorf Dismissal," Dennis Cusick, *The Cincinnati Enquirer*, November 5, 1976.

faced busy downtown sidewalks on Walnut Street.

All of the hookers said Goodin was there among the men who were "entertained" with sex as they watched stag films in hotel rooms. One of the women said Larry Flynt compensated her for the extra duty with $100 and an extra night off. He told her it was "a very important mission."[32]

All of them said they were taken to the hotels by a vice cop nicknamed "Boxhead." One said she was told in 1970 by Boxhead that it was a very important party for both of them because one of the men there would be the next chief.

She asked, "Chief of what?"

"Chief of police," she was told.

"Chief of police where?"

"*City of Cincinnati!*" Boxhead said.

She testified, "They told us if we could keep close to the police force, we wouldn't have any trouble."

They couldn't get any closer.

The woman also said Boxhead told her that Flynt needed to remove the window dancers because increasing complaints were causing problems. She relayed the message and Flynt removed them immediately, she said.

As Boxhead fought his suspension, it was rumored around the courthouse that he would never go to trial because he knew too much. City and court officials were indeed curiously unenthusiastic. He was allowed to plead to a misdemeanor of obstructing justice after he threatened to bring the hookers back for testimony that might have revealed more names from more hotel stag parties.

At one point, Boxhead could be heard through the door of an interrogation room shouting, "WHY DO I HAVE TO BE THE FALL GUY?"

Finally, in November 1977, two years after the anonymous letter ignited the police corruption bonfire, the Ohio Court of Appeals showed up with a fire hose. The court stunned the city by reversing

---

[32] "Investigator Recalls Dancer's Confession," Margaret Josten, *The Cincinnati Enquirer*, September 21, 1976.

the conviction of Goodin, citing courtroom errors by the prosecutor and the highly respected judge, Gilbert Bettman.[33]

The news stories said the Appeals Court gave a "sharp rebuke" to Leis, but even a thousand words of newsprint could not clearly explain the grounds for reversal. The supposed "errors" were obscure and convoluted. The Appeals Court opinion said perjury was not adequately proved, although the evidence was as clear as forged ink on paper that the records of "Informant Fund C" were a coverup, proving perjury under oath to the grand jury.

The appeals court ruled that testimony by Donaldson and Sandman about Goodin's bad character was "improper." Even his immediate bosses were not allowed to judge the chief they supervised.

"There is a presumption that one told the truth under oath," the appeals court said, ignoring abundant evidence of perjury. And presto, with a magic "presumption," his crimes vanished and Goodin was set free without a day in jail.

Goodin was vindicated, as he predicted he would be. "I think it was a disservice to the city," he said. "I am not the person I was two years ago." By then he was working for Frisch's. He vowed, "But you have not heard the last of Carl Goodin."[34]

Sympathetic news stories told of Chief Goodin's "long ordeal," and scolded Leis with accusations that he indicted and prosecuted his good friend only because he was "seeking publicity."

"The appeals court decision was BS," Leis recalled. "All I can say is there was politics involved."

What did Goodin know that might be more embarrassing? Who else was among the "civilians" at the parties? Judges? Lawyers? Party officials?

On September 15, 1976, after Hummeldorf's plea bargain, an editorial in *The Enquirer* raised that question: "Throughout the proceedings, implications have been made regarding the possibility that other Cincinnati officials are involved. The full impact of the events behind

---

[33] "Prosecution Errors a Focal Point," Jim Delaney, *The Cincinnati Enquirer*, November 24, 1977.

[34] "I Am Not the Person I Was," Jim Delaney, *The Cincinnati Enquirer*, November 24, 1977.

the Hummeldorf verdict are still unknown to this community. ... Hummeldorf's attorney stated in court that his client was 'protecting other people.'"

The editorial said, "In reality, nothing has been settled."[35]

Jimmy Simon was the vice cop who resigned from the Cincinnati Police to spare his brother from being prosecuted for theft. He was born in The Bottoms, a poor neighborhood on the riverbank, one of seven children living in a three-room apartment with his mother and father. After leaving CPD he rose to become CEO of Reading Central Mixed Concrete, one of the biggest construction suppliers in the Midwest. After that, he started a successful private investigations firm, Business Intelligence Inc., that does a variety of confidential work for celebrities, politicians, business leaders and Cincinnati's biggest corporations.

Among the services listed by BII are homicide investigations, executive protection, counter-surveillance, skip tracing, undercover work and vice. Nobody knows more of Cincinnati's secrets than Jimmy Simon.

But he still misses being the rising star narcotics detective on the vice squad. "I treasured my days with the police," he said. "I miss it every day."

And he remains loyal to Goodin. "The smartest guy I ever met. Carl Goodin is a damned good guy. I was at many parties with the chief and I never saw Flynt's prostitutes there. Never. Never."

He recalls one party when Jimmy Flynt brought up a case of free liquor and Goodin angrily threw him out and told him to take his "bleeping" booze with him.

Everyone knew Flynt was crooked, Simon said. "They did everything they could to ingratiate themselves with the vice squad, I can tell you that."

But he remains convinced that Goodin was treated unfairly. Simon said friends of the chief may have taken kickbacks in the chief's name without informing Goodin. "Carl was so loyal he wouldn't believe anyone was doing that."

---

35 "The Case Is Not Closed," *The Cincinnati Enquirer,* September 15, 1976.

Simon said, "I know Informant Fund C was real because I used it to pay informants. If I had revealed their names, they would have been dead almost immediately. But they (vice commanders) didn't keep good records. I heard later that they did try to re-create records for it, but it was not an attempt at fraud."

"All of Chief Goodin's convictions were overturned," Simon points out. He believes Goodin was prosecuted because he had angered powerful political leaders, and the chief provided the excuse by using free labor from on-duty cops. "They got him because guys from the vice squad helped him with the damned caboose."

But even if true, Goodin put the target on his own back and gave his enemies a trainload of ammunition. The former chief moved to Northern Kentucky. He was unable to comment after a having a stroke in 2022. In 1976 he insisted, "I will be vindicated. I have done nothing illegal, unethical or immoral." The appeals court decision to overturn his conviction was affirmed by the Ohio Supreme Court in 1978 by a vote of two to one. One of the justices on the panel wanted a retrial.

Back in 1975, Cincinnati just wanted it all to go away. For years, the Queen City was praised as a clean, family-friendly town with a tough, professional, model police department—especially in contrast to corrupt Newport across the river, where the Cleveland Mob owned police, judges, prosecutors and politicians the way kids collected marbles.

The truth was, Cincinnati was not as clean as advertised. There was corruption that spread from afterhours bars and gambling all the way to the top of the Police Division and probably judges and city hall. "If they prosecuted everyone who took freebies like liquor, meals and gifts, they could have busted eighty percent of the police department at the time," said Simon.

But after the Goodin scandal, Cincinnati got national attention for police corruption, prostitution and a "Smut King" who compromised the police chief and the vice squad for less than $500 and a few nights off for his go-go dancers.

It was embarrassing, said letters to the editor. "Penny ante charges," said city officials who knew better.

CHAPTER 3 • CHIEF OF WHAT?

A stinging wet-towel snap came from a January 1976 story in *Time Magazine* that quoted city leaders:

"People were kind of horrified," said City Manager Donaldson.

"It has been a tremendous shock to the city," said Mayor Bobbie Stern.

The article described the seedy side of Cincinnati for all the world to see, like some rude paparazzi passing around an unflattering shot of the wide-eyed Queen City in her skivvies. The *Time* article said:

> "Flynt, who claims 1.5 million circulation for his monumentally vulgar magazine … runs three Hustler Clubs in Ohio, tacky rip-offs of the Playboy Clubs…. His Cincinnati dive has been in and out of trouble with police and the state's liquor commission for several years."
>
> "Both Cincinnati's city hall and its two daily newspapers were tame watchdogs. Said one dismayed patrolman, 'The top man has been indicted. It couldn't be much worse. There is a dark cloud hanging over all of us.'"

When the gavel finally banged to end a two-week jury trial with a conviction of Police Chief Carl Goodin on June 25, 1976, it looked like Cincinnati's dark cloud of shame would be blown away by the city's collective huge sigh of relief. But the case dragged on for more than a year. Then, just in time for Thanksgiving in 1977, the Appeals Court declared it was all a mistake. The convictions were overturned. As the editorial said, "In reality, nothing has been settled."

Goodin was gone. Contrary to his vow, it was the last Cincinnati heard from him. Acting Chief Myron Leistler immediately replaced the entire vice squad.

But it was not over for Cincinnati.

The cloud would linger for years like a bad odor around the Hustler Club. The feud between Prosecutor Simon Leis and Larry Flynt was just getting started.

4

Putting the Sin in *Sin*cinnati

The first month of 1977 was the coldest January ever recorded in Cincinnati. The temperature fell hard past zero and could not get back up. It finally bottomed out at 25-below on January 18. The Ohio River froze solid for the first time since 1958, allowing hundreds of people to walk on water across the Ohio River from Kentucky to Ohio. At least one foolhardy driver even drove his VW Beetle on the frozen river.

In Judge William Morrissey's courtroom in the Hamilton County Courthouse, jurors shivered and rubbed their hands to stay warm as the deep cold crept in around the leaky old tall windows. But the drafty old courtroom was about to warm up in a hurry.

Prosecutor Simon Leis stood in front of the jury box and held up a copy of *Hustler Magazine*. He opened it to a centerfold of Althea Leasure, and let the page unfold. The "life-size" picture did not quite reach the floor, but the jaws of a few jury members did.

"Their eyes kinda popped," Leis recalled years later. "The picture was an unusual pose."

"Unusual pose" was an understatement on a scale with calling twenty-five below zero "brisk."

Adding to the drama, the woman in that unusual centerfold pose was sitting right there in court just twenty feet away with her husband, *Hustler Magazine* Publisher Larry Flynt. Both were being prosecuted for pandering obscenity, along with a second charge that raised eyebrows all over Ohio: organized crime.

Leis had just won a conviction of Police Chief Carl Goodin in the police corruption trial that shook up the city and drew uncomfortable national attention. And now scandal-weary Cincinnati hardly had a

Larry Flynt, flanked by wife, Althea, and his lawyer, talks to the press during a break in his 1977 trial on obscenity and organized crime charges. Ed Reinke, *The Cincinnati Enquirer.*

chance to catch its breath before another sensational trial drew an even more intense national media spotlight. The Flynt obscenity case had the potential to redefine "community standards" on obscenity for cities across the nation.

And once again, Larry Flynt was in the middle of it. He sat in court wearing long sideburns, shaggy, uncombed hair and his trademark smirk. He had traded his usual flared slacks, colorful open shirt and leather jacket for a dark, lawyerly three-piece suit, the uniform of executives at Procter & Gamble, Kroger, Chiquita and other Fortune 500 companies in the "Blue Chip City."

But the sharpest dressers were among Flynt's four defense lawyers: two from New York, one from Columbus and one from Cincinnati. They called the charges a "kamikaze attack" and "a stampede" to censor his freedom of speech and First Amendment rights. They buried the judge in a blizzard of delays and motions, hoping to ice the case like the frozen Ohio River—then complained that Flynt's right to a speedy trial was being denied. They attacked the prosecutor personally as a neanderthal prude who was imposing his "hang-ups" about sex on the whole community. *Hustler* was just another harmless "girlie magazine" that presented an "honest, humorous discussion of sex," they told the jury.[36]

A letter to the editor from an unabashed *Hustler* subscriber quoted a "prestigious international group of Catholic theologians" to support Flynt. "The importance of the erotic element, that is, instinctual desire for pleasure and gratification, deserves to be affirmed and encouraged," the letter said, quoting the alleged theologians. "Human sexual expression is meant to be enjoyed without guilt or remorse."[37] It was so 70s.

On the other side of the courtroom aisle, seated at a big wooden table, Leis prosecuted the case himself, with his chief assistant, Fred Cartolano. Leis wore a charcoal two-piece suit with a tightly knotted black tie and a plain, snow-white shirt—a sort of conservative protest against the garish prints, exaggerated kite collars and floppy bellbottom sailor pants that divided the hip from the square. Leis was as proudly square as those new Rubik's Cubes that everyone was buying, but far less complicated.

He had no grandiose "philosophy" like *Playboy* publisher Hugh Hefner, whose glossy photo spreads and foldouts mainstreamed "girlie magazines" by wrapping soft-core porn around famous authors, interviews and culture. The Si Leis philosophy was simple: God, country, family, morality and swift justice for anyone who violated the law.

He replied to Flynt's New York lawyers by telling the five women and seven men in the jury box that he was sorry they would be required to go through eleven issues of *Hustler Magazine*. It was not the typical jury duty of sorting out fender benders, business disputes and felonies. To review the evidence of obscenity, they would have to wade knee-deep into a cesspool of smut, bestiality, sadism, bondage, orgies, cartoons about pedophilia and incest and graphic close-up photos that were seldom seen outside of medical textbooks for training in the specialty of gynecology.

---

36 "Sex Exploiter," Peggy Lane, *The Cincinnati Enquirer*, January 25, 1977.
37 "Reed and Heed," *The Cincinnati Enquirer*, June 3, 1977.

Then he opened the magazine and let the centerfold of Larry Flynt's wife unfold. The picture was worth a thousand words of protest from Flynt's lawyers.

* * *

Until the police corruption indictments for sodomy, bribery, perjury and sex parties broke, followed by the obscenity trial, Cincinnati did not know much about Larry Flynt.

It was not for lack of trying on Flynt's part. He put almost-nude go-go dancers in the windows of his Walnut Street Hustler Club, mailed pornographic and offensive postcards to thousands of residents of Hamilton County, picked public battles by making outrageous statements and buying full-page newspaper ads, and made international news when he paid $100,000 for nude pictures of Jacqueline Kennedy-Onassis and published them in his magazine in 1975.

But the local press showed little interest.

His first mention in *The Cincinnati Enquirer* was a rape charge in 1972, the same year he fired a pistol into the ceiling during a sex act at Caesar's Underground, across the street from his own bar. For whatever reason—intimidation, threats, embarrassment, payoff—the rape charges were apparently dismissed.

Flynt showed up again in a relatively flattering profile in early 1975. The headline called him a "Man on the Go."

"Hustler to me means a man on the go, a man trying to accomplish something," Flynt said, pointedly avoiding the more common use of "hustler" to mean prostitute. He was "a poor man's Hugh Hefner" the story said, comparing him to the pseudo-intellectual publisher of glamour nudes. "I'd rather sell to ten truck drivers than one college professor," Flynt said.

Larry Flynt was a skilled and prolific liar who camouflaged his deceit behind a screen of statements that sounded honest because they seemed too crude to be clever. He would brag about being a "male chauvinist" pig one day, then pretend his magazine was really about changing the world by helping "uptight" America get over its sexual repression.

His cheap motel version of the "Hustler Philosophy" preached that sexual liberation was a panacea that would eliminate the "need for a barbaric approach to abortion, toward violence, toward all the ills involved in our prisons and ghettos."

"Mr. Flynt may be a toad of a man," said an incisive 2011 profile. "But in his way, he was a more morally honest man than Hugh Hefner. ... He knew that the (*Playboy*) smoking jackets and fancy parties and A-list short stories were all a cynical act to make men feel classy" as they indulged their sexual fantasies.

By comparison, Flynt "was upfront with his contention that man is a degraded animal who cares about nothing except carnal lust and his own ego."[38]

It was always all about making a buck any way he could. He didn't care if he was prosecuted and put in jail for obscenity because, "I'll get it all back in sales" from the national attention, he said.

The Hillbilly

He was the oldest of three children of a hard-drinking sharecropper. In an interview on TV's *60 Minutes* in 1977, he said his father forged a birth certificate to help him join the Army at age 14 so he could escape the dirt-floor poverty in Magoffin County, Kentucky.

"I can remember kerosene lamps and sleeping on a corn-shuck bed," he told a reporter. He also remembered "losing his virginity" to a chicken—a typically graphic and gross Larry Flynt story.

He claimed to have been a bootlegger briefly after being rejected by the Army,[39] then joined the Navy and served on the aircraft carrier *USS Enterprise*, which participated in the recovery of Astronaut John Glenn and his space capsule in 1962 while Flynt was a radar operator aboard.[40]

---

[38] "Flynt's Master Plan: Be Porn's morally Honest Man," Jonathan Key, *National Post,* Toronto, Ontario, Canada, June 4, 2011.

[39] According to some stories he was rejected because of low test scores; others said he was honorably discharged during a troop reduction.

[40] The Friendship 7 space capsule was recovered by the USS Noa, a destroyer.

In many ways, Flynt never really escaped Magoffin County. When he became wealthy enough, he had a replica of his family shack built in the basement of his homes in Columbus and Los Angeles, complete with Granny Clampett porch rockers and fake chickens in the yard.

He told a *Cincinnati Enquirer* columnist during a courtroom break that the characters in the movie *Deliverance* "are my relatives." He was not talking about Burt Reynolds. He was talking about the toothless, perverted hillbillies who kidnapped and sodomized one of the "city boys" in the woods.[41]

Flynt claimed he opened his first bar in Dayton, Ohio in 1965 and named it Hillbilly Haven. At first he said he used his own savings. Later he said he borrowed the money from his mother, who owned another bar. A very different story would eventually emerge.

Simon Leis, the IRS and the Ohio Department of Liquor Control suspected that he was bankrolled by the Mob. A 1986 investigation by the U.S. Attorney General would reveal that virtually all pornography—X-rated movies, peep shows, adult bookstores, strip clubs and Hustler-type bars with nude dancing—was controlled by organized crime.

Whatever the source of his startup capital, Larry Flynt's empire grew fast. By 1970 he had Hustler Clubs in Akron, Cleveland, Columbus, Toledo and Cincinnati.

He and his brother Jimmy started publishing pamphlets they passed out on the streets of Cincinnati, luring customers to his bar with cheesecake pictures of the dancers. The pamphlets evolved into full-color *Hustler* Magazine in 1974. *Hustler* was so obscene, some of the press workers at the Dayton printing plant refused to touch it. But within just a couple of years, the magazine was making tens of millions, with sales nationwide.

In 1971, Flynt met his fourth wife, Althea Leasure, when she applied for a job as a dancer at his Columbus club. Larry Flynt dedicated his life to proving the prosecutor's assessment that he was "the lowest of the low." Nothing illustrated it better than his treatment of Althea.

---

41 "Guilty of Bad Taste," Tom Callahan, *The Cincinnati Enquirer*, February 8, 1977.

When Althea was 7, her mother, June, left her violent, abusive husband, Robert, and took the kids to move in with her own mother and father. They were separated from Robert for three months. Then one Monday morning in 1962, while the kids were at school, Robert, 40, knocked on the door at the home of Althea's grandparents in Marietta, Ohio, near the West Virginia border.

He asked June to go with him to Florida. She said no, but he insisted and would not take no for an answer. When she still refused, he went to his car and came back with a .38 revolver. He walked in the house and shot Althea's grandfather as he sat in a chair in the kitchen; he fired another shot at her grandmother and missed as she ran; then he shot a neighbor and friend of June in the face as the woman ran for her life into the backyard. The neighbor he killed was the mother of four children.

Robert went back into the house and found June hiding in a closet. He dragged her to the front porch and shot her through the chest. She struggled free and ran about thirty feet before he shot her again, twice. Then, as he stood over the body of his dead wife, Robert Leasure shot himself in the head. He killed four people that day, including himself.

The grandmother escaped by hiding in a creek near their home. When a mailman arrived and saw two bodies in the front yard, he and the grandmother called the police.

The Leasures' five children came home from school that day to discover that almost their entire family had been murdered by their father. They were orphans. Althea and her brothers and sisters were sent to the Ohio Soldiers and Sailors Orphanage in Xenia, Ohio.[42]

But Althea escaped domestic violence only to become a victim of sexual abuse. She said later that she was sexually abused by foster parents and nuns, and ran away from the orphanage several times. She was still a teenager with severe unresolved "father issues" when she met Larry Flynt in 1971 and was hired as a stripper. She was a vulnerable, emotionally

---

42 "Four Dead in Triple Murder and Suicide," *Chillicothe Gazette,* February 27, 1962.

damaged victim of abuse and horrific violence. So Flynt immediately began to exploit his future wife for profit, first as a nude dancer, then as the first life-sized centerfold in his magazine.

They were married in 1976.

She was loyal, if not faithful. When Flynt was unable to manage his business, Althea took over and ran it for him. When she tried to create a non-pornographic magazine, he took all of the startup capital she had set aside and wasted it on his delusional campaign for president in 1984. He once bragged about giving her "the call girl of her choice in New York" as a gift.

She died of a drug overdose at age 33 by drowning in a bathtub, hopelessly addicted, with a terminal case of AIDS.

Flynt was just as toxic as a father. Asked in an interview if his 7-year-old daughter was allowed to look at porn in his *Hustler Magazine,* he said of course she was, but she "mostly" wanted to look at his picture.

In the press, Larry Flynt was a champion of the First Amendment. But most people saw what he really was. The lowest of the low.

The revered Ohio State Football Coach Woody Hayes said if he saw Flynt on the street, "I just might punch him in the nose." Woody knew a thing or two about throwing punches. He could have filled Buckeye Stadium with people who would pay to see him flatten Flynt.

In the obscenity trial, Leis called Flynt "an exploiter" of women and said *Hustler* was "printed for one reason only—the commercial exploitation of sex." In one word, he had defined Larry Flynt: exploiter.

When Leis described the magazine as "vivid, lustful and lascivious," his quote was catnip to mocking reporters. "Even Santa Claus was depicted in *Hustler* porn," Leis said. He was outraged. The press snickered.

Splashed in headlines and newsprint, his comments were easily made to sound like a tent revival preacher shaking his fist at Satan and calling down hellfire on Sodom. Leis clearly was not "with it." The theme of the '70s was, "If it feels good, do it." He was hopelessly uncool.

Dirty Book or Book Burner? a headline in *The Cincinnati Enquirer* asked. The story made the answer obvious, at least as the reporter saw it.

CHAPTER 4 • PUTTING THE SIN IN SINCINNATI

Althea Flynt leaves the courtroom with the 'slender, suave' and dapper New York defense lawyer Herald Fahringer, who was also a lawyer for the Mob. Fred Straub, *The Cincinnati Enquirer*.

Flynt's lawyers were cool, readers were told. One was "slender, suave, a well-groomed silver-haired gentleman" who was idolized by "young lawyers" at the courthouse. Another was "an old pro, slightly tousled, but cool and amiable at all times. He gives the appearance of a gentle country boy but comes in quickly and smoothly with legal objections without ever losing his cool."

But Leis, the reporter wrote, "is a rougher stone, intense, emotional, quick to anger and take offense, an outspoken foe of pornography and everything else foreign to a 'Dutch' Cincinnatian who is a devout Catholic and devoted family man." Between the lines: square, uptight, bluenose, backward Catholic West Sider.[43]

None of it was completely untrue; but all of it was only half true: the positive half for Flynt's lawyers, the negative half for the prosecution.

In *The State of Ohio vs. Larry Flynt et al.*, the "et al." included the press. Most were in Flynt's corner and seldom missed a chance to portray the battle as a threat to First Amendment rights and freedom of the press. Which was exactly how Flynt planned it. He courted reporters like one of his centerfold models, even offering at one point to help them buy *The Cincinnati Post* in a battle against management. The offer was a farce, said Assistant Prosecutor Fred Cartolano. The editor of the *Post* agreed, but the newsroom love affair with Flynt only burned hotter—mixed with an abiding loathing of Simon Leis, who represented everything

---

43 "Collision Course," *The Cincinnati Enquirer*, January 16, 1977.

that enlightened, sophisticated, anti-establishment reporters opposed.

Si Leis *was* the establishment.

Leis pointed out that *he* was not going to convict Flynt or put him out of business in Cincinnati. That was up to the jurors who represented their city. It was precisely the method of setting "community standards" that the U.S. Supreme Court prescribed for dealing with obscenity.

Cincinnati had the landmark case, but it was not alone. Many cities were frustrated and disgusted by the "sin strips" of X-rated movies, massage parlors and strip clubs that spread like Swine Flu following the Supreme Court's ruling that nude dancing was a form of artistic expression.

So when Flynt was prosecuted in Cincinnati, Indianapolis sent prosecutors and police to observe the trial and learn how they could do the same. Other cities sent representatives to a national anti-porn conference in Cleveland, where Flynt had been arrested on obscenity charges in 1976.

The Cincinnati sophisticates sang a familiar, hand-wringing chorus about "Church-innati," the backward town that would never catch up to progressive places like New York City, where Times Square was a carnival of sleaze; or Southern California, the capitol of the porno movie industry.

A parade of celebrities joined the Larry Flynt crusade: Woody Allen (later accused of molesting his adopted daughter); headline hound attorney F. Lee Baily; Harold Robbins, author of steamy potboilers; and hipster poet Rod McKuen, who summarized the pro-Flynt protests by saying, "Who am I to say what's right or wrong?"

None of that bothered Simon Leis. He was made for his role in prosecuting Flynt regardless of what the press and the intellectual elites thought. He cared about their opinions about as often as he listened to the Rolling Stones.

"What formed him was the turmoil of the 1960s," said Karl Kadon, chief of the criminal division in the U.S. Attorney's Office, who worked for Leis in the prosecutor's office. "America was changing radically and that was of great concern to him. If Si saw a problem, whatever it was, he went after it with three times the effort. He would not be defeated by any external forces or distractions. He was labeled as a moral crusader, but that's the way he prosecuted everything. That little piece of his legacy has been blown up to outsized proportions."

Flynt and Leis represented the schizoid split of the 1970s, as far apart as Beirut and Magoffin County.

The Marine

Although he always had the soul of a West Sider, Simon Leis Jr. grew up on Ludlow Avenue in Clifton, near the University of Cincinnati campus. He was the son of a tough judge.

"When I was a kid, organized crime was rampant in Youngstown, and my father was hired to go up there as a special prosecutor to break up the Mob," he recalled in 2022. "I remember he had two bodyguards who went with him everywhere. When he would go to Youngstown, leaving our mother home with six kids, she was scared to death. That was in the 1940s."

Leis attended St. Xavier Catholic High School, where Cincinnati's future political, law and business leaders are trained by Jesuits.

After high school he attended Xavier University, graduated and joined the Marine Corps. That decision "changed my life," he said. Before the Marines, he did just enough to get by. The Marines taught him discipline, toughness, pursuit of excellence and the high price that must be paid to protect freedom.

The USS Taconic, the flagship for the invasion of Beirut in 1958.
US Navy archives.

In 1958, Second Lt. Leis of the 2nd Battalion of the 2nd Marine Regiment found himself on the USS Taconic off the coast of Lebanon, climbing aboard a landing craft to hit the beach five miles south of Beirut.

The reason was more complicated than a whole box of Rubik's Cubes.

Egyptian President Gamal Nasser had nationalized the Suez Canal in 1956, igniting the Suez Crisis, which escalated into the second Arab-Israeli War. That fueled the spread of Muslim protests against the West and Soviet intrusion into Egypt and Syria.

In 1957, Ike declared the "Eisenhower Doctrine," offering to go to war for any nation in the Middle East that asked for help to stop communism in the region.

As a bloody civil war erupted in Lebanon, Muslim protesters burned a U.S. Information Service Library in Beirut, and Christian Lebanese President Camille Chamoun played the "Ike Card" to ask the U.S. for help.

On July 15, 1958, Eisenhower kept his promise: He announced Operation Blue Bat and sent in the Sixth Fleet, with more than seventy warships, including three aircraft carriers, two cruisers, two destroyer squadrons and 14,000 soldiers and Marines.

The Taconic was the flagship for the commander of Operation Blue Bat, Admiral James Holloway. It was built in 1944, near the end of World War II, and later converted into an amphibious force command ship.

The deployment was the first U.S. military action in Middle East conflicts that stretched deep into the 21st Century. Blue Bat became one of many Third World "proxy wars" against the Soviet Union during the Cold War between communism and the West after World War II.

Second Lt. Leis, 23, was not thinking about any of that as he sweated and waited to board a landing craft to assault the beach. "I was a married man for only about two months before being shipped out," he told a reporter in 2008. "And as the landing craft surged towards the beach, I thought, 'Hell, I'm too young to die.'"

The surprise that awaited Leis and 2,000 Marines when they waded ashore was not grenades, mortar rounds and machineguns. As carrier

CHAPTER 4 • PUTTING THE SIN IN SINCINNATI

U.S. Marines wade ashore on the beaches of Beirut in Operation Blue Bat on July 15, 1958.

planes roared overhead, the Marines in camo were shocked to see the beach crowded with girls in bikinis and sunbathers spread out on towels. Young men in swim trunks rushed to help the Marines drag their equipment through the surf, while vendors gathered around them to offer cigarettes, soft drinks and candy.

"We were told we were going into combat," Leis said, "so that's what we expected."[44]

His mission was to secure the airport in Beirut. A second wave would secure the Port of Beirut. So he and his men, each loaded with nearly 100 pounds of gear, set off in the 90-degree heat for the airport. Although well-armed Arab militants had killed hundreds in the city, the Marines' overwhelming show of force encountered no resistance.

Operation Blue Bat stayed three months, then pulled out on October 25. The message had been delivered to the Arab and Muslim militants and to the Soviets. The region was torn by turmoil in the following years with military coups, rebellions, religious civil wars and bloody battles between Arabs and Muslims vs. Jews and Christians. But after Blue Bat, a troubled peace prevailed until the Six Day War in 1967, when Israel defeated Jordan, Egypt and Syria.

---

44 "D-Day With Bikinis," Alasdair Soussi, *The National*, July 18, 2008.

Simon Leis Jr. was sworn in as an assistant U.S. Attorney by his father, Judge Simon Leis Sr. on November 24, 1969. The son was appointed and sworn in as Hamilton County Prosecutor in 1971, on the same day his father retired. The Cincinnati Enquirer.

Leis finished his four-year enlistment and returned to Cincinnati. He went to night school at Salmon P. Chase Law School in Northern Kentucky, and earned his law degree. He worked as a prosecutor for the City of Cincinnati, then as an assistant U.S. Attorney. In 1971 he was appointed as Hamilton County Prosecutor to fill a vacancy, the same month his father, Hamilton County Common Pleas Judge Simon Leis, retired.

Simon Leis Jr. replaced Prosecutor Melvin Rueger, who was appointed to replace Judge Simon Leis Sr. – a typical move in the grand musical chairs tradition of the local Republican Party.

In spite of all the protests and snarking by the press—or perhaps because of it—Leis was re-elected as prosecutor three times. The popularity of movie vigilantes such as *Dirty Harry* and Charles Bronson's *Death Wish* series was a reflection of the public disgust with permissive courts and rising crime chaos. Law and order was the ticket to the White House for Richard Nixon in 1968 and 1972, and it was just as effective in Cincinnati for Simon Leis.

Leis served briefly as a Hamilton County Common Pleas Judge, but hated it. "I was bored stiff. I like to be in the game, not on the sidelines or as a referee."

So in 1988 he ran for sheriff and won—again and again and again. He was re-elected five times and became the county's longest serving sheriff.

Between 1988 and his retirement in 2012, he was a favorite lightning rod for the left. It was almost impossible for reporters to mention his name without an eye-roll of scorn. But the voters backed him overwhelmingly. Each re-election was another bucket of cold-water to remind the newsroom that it was not in the same Zip Code with most of its community. And that was yet another reason for progressive journalists to dislike the hardheaded conservative Marine who was prosecutor and sheriff.

NOT IN OUR TOWN · PETER BRONSON

Walk on the Wild Side

5
'Do You Take Checks for That?'

About the only thing Simon Leis and Larry Flynt had in common was that both were veterans. But even their military service had starkly different results.

Leis came home from the Marine Corps as a red-white-and-blue patriot who loved his country and continued to serve it in the Marine Corps Reserves and through law enforcement. He never hesitated to defend traditional American values just as he had waded ashore in Beirut, ready for battle.

Flynt, however, left the Navy hating America. He desecrated the flag, opposed the war in Vietnam, dishonored the young men who fought and died for their country and used his magazine to undermine traditional American morality and virtues. He also exposed the hypocrisy and immorality of the nation's most powerful leaders—low-hanging fruit and easy targets.

Flynt and Leis were born to be enemies like Goldfinger and Bond. And the press loved it.

During the Watergate scandal that forced the resignation of President Richard Nixon in 1974, enrollment in journalism schools hit an all-time peak, flooded with idealistic students who wanted to be Bob Woodward and Carl Bernstein, the *Washington Post* reporters who were sanctified in *All the President's Men* because they "brought down a president"—at least in the movie version of reality. Newsrooms were flooded with eager job applicants who were in a hurry to change the world. Supply far exceeded demand, but those who did get jobs in the media tipped the balance of power.

Traditional standards of accuracy, fairness and objectivity were scorned; the "new journalism" taught on campuses was more like a

Jerry Springer, the rising star and 'free spirit' at City Hall in the 1970s.
The Cincinnati Post, Kenton County Library archive.

political campaign or a religious crusade. The ideal of the "invisible" reporter who left no personal fingerprints on a story was old fashioned. Reporters became the star of every story, with an attitude and an opinion baked in. Inspired by two longhaired movie heroes, rookie reporters used their note-taking ballpoints like switchblades to stick a knife in the ribs of "the establishment."

They saw corruption (and Page One bylines) under every bed—as long as it was in a Republican or conservative household.

By no coincidence, 1974 was also the year the press decided it really did not like Prosecutor Simon Leis.

Before Flynt went to trial, even before Leis prosecuted the police chief and exposed corruption, he had committed a cardinal sin: He was blamed for the resignation of every newsroom's favorite anti-establishment Democrat, Gerald Springer.

"Jerry" Springer was described as Cincinnati's "brightest ascending star" in the Democratic Party, about to become the city's youngest

CHAPTER 5 • 'DO YOU TAKE CHECKS FOR THAT?'

Jerry Springer was an early postmodern politician, getting attention with self-mocking, trivial stunts. As a councilman, he wrestled a bear. *The Cincinnati Enquirer.*

mayor at 30, just three years after being elected to council in 1971. "Don't trust anyone over 30," the hippie slogan said. But as in many things, an exception was made for Jerry Springer.

The son of German-Jewish immigrants from London, England, Springer grew up in the Queens neighborhood of New York City and became an acolyte of the martyred JFK. He was anti-war, anti-establishment and anti-everything that represented uptight, conservative Cincinnati. He wore long hair, wire-framed glasses and casual clothes—more likely to walk into city hall in Earth Shoes than wingtips. He was "brash," "energetic" and "unconventional," the newspapers said approvingly. He even *sounded* like JFK, cultivating his broad-vowel, East Coast accent; and he had a Kennedy pedigree as an organizer for Bobby Kennedy's campaign, as well as a stint on Governor John Gilligan's Task Force on Youth.

His new wife was headlined as "Cincinnati's First-Lady Elect" even before the election. It would prove to be a premature headline. But the script was already being written: Becoming mayor would be only a brief layover on Springer's first-class flight to Congress, governor and beyond.[45] Hypocritocles, the two-faced god of politics, beckoned.

Springer had a charming, off-beat, ad-lib sense of humor. When asked what he would wear to a costume party, he joked, "I might dress

---

45   "Miki Springer, First Lady-Elect," *The Cincinnati Enquirer,* July 4, 1974.

up as a mayor." When new buses were displayed in front of city hall, he jumped aboard one of them and drove it away as the press and council members looked on in astonishment. He spent the night in jail posing as a vagrant. He did editorials on hard-rock stoners' station WEBN, called "The Springer Memorandum."

His chief of staff said, "Anyone who doesn't know that Jerry is a free spirit is a dead person."[46]

In short, Jerry Springer was everything reporters loved. He was a pioneer of postmodern politics: It doesn't matter what you do or even if you accomplish nothing; just *say* the right things.

Then one Monday morning at the end of April 1974, without any warning, he mysteriously resigned from City Council. Cincinnati's "brightest star" had fallen.

Reporters and local pundits scrambled to figure out why. Council members begged him to reconsider. Then on Wednesday, Springer appeared at a news conference, "red-eyed and shaken," and read a statement:

"On two occasions I have been a customer of a health club in Northern Kentucky and engaged in activities which, at least to me, are questionable," he explained. He said he was voluntarily cooperating with an FBI investigation, but insisted, "I have visited health clubs in Cincinnati on a number of occasions. These were solely for legitimate purposes. To the best of my knowledge, no club in Cincinnati I visited was engaged in any improper or illegal activities."[47]

Then he dropped the punchline: He had paid for both visits with personal checks.

"How much?" someone asked.

"I forgot," he said.

As if.

It was a carefully massaged, kissing-cousin of the truth. The "health club" was in fact a rundown motel, the President Motor Inn in Fort

---

[46] "V-Neck Mayor," *The Cincinnati Post*, November 19, 1974.

[47] "Activity Questionable, Says Springer," *The Cincinnati Enquirer*, May 1, 1974.

Wright, Kentucky, next door to mobbed-up Newport. The FBI investigation had caught three Cincinnati men providing prostitutes at the motel. That was definitely illegal and improper. Jerry Springer had paid a hooker with a check, and that was not just "questionable" in his own eyes, it was criminally stupid.

Former Cincinnati Police vice detective and private investigator Jimmy Simon said, "I talked to one of the girls. She said it wasn't just one or two checks. He was a regular."

The irony was thicker than a Magic Fingers motel mattress: *Vice-Mayor Jerry Springer* had been the crusader for a new ethics code for city hall to capitalize on Watergate with "that favorite liberal cause, morality in government," *Enquirer* politics reporter Graydon DeCamp wrote.

Yet even after Springer's red-eyed, nuanced confession, Mayor Ted Berry and council's Democrat-Charterite majority coalition tried to refuse to accept his resignation. Charterites, the genteel tea-and-bowties party founded to protect clean government, were willing to look the other way for their naughty boy Jerry. Councilman David Mann, who was reluctantly appointed by council members because Springer demanded it, repaid the favor by claiming his friend Jerry was the victim of a dark conspiracy by the prosecutor and Republicans.

Springer insisted his "conscience" prompted him to turn himself in to help an investigation by the FBI. When reporters wondered how he knew about the FBI investigation, he was vague. "I hear things," he said.

"Politicians are often more reluctant to forgive political transgressions than they are to forgive personal or moral ones," DeCamp wrote. That could have been Nostradamus predicting the Clinton scandals.[48]

The prosecutor, Si Leis, had a different version of events.

"One of our assistant prosecutors had a private practice before joining my office, and one of his clients had told him that Jerry Springer was going to whorehouses in Northern Kentucky and had paid with a check.

"I thought, 'My God, our next mayor is running across the river to whorehouses? We don't need that kind of leadership.' So we went to

---

48 "Political Breaks Sometimes Happen With Breathtaking Suddenness," Graydon DeCamp, *The Cincinnati Enquirer*, May 5, 1974.

Socco Wiethe, the chairman of the Democratic Party. And he agreed we should ask Springer to resign and get out of town."

After a long private meeting, "Springer finally agreed," Leis said, "and we didn't file charges. I never did bring charges against him. He resigned, but he did not leave town."

Leis and Wiethe were double-crossed. In fact, by the end of the week, Springer even announced that he had changed his mind. His resignation would be finessed so he could stay on council, with the support of the Democrat-Charterite coalition.

Phone lines at city hall lit up with angry calls. Many wanted to know how the same Democrats who demanded the removal of President Nixon could give Springer a "Get Out of Jail Free" card.

Others defended the hipster vice-mayor. A letter to the editor said, "If we are ever to climb out of the quagmire of political mistrust and corruption ... we need men of his caliber desperately—and I am thinking of much higher offices than City Council. The Cincinnati public should stand and give Jerry Springer a rousing ovation, not only for his high standards ... but for his shining courage and honesty in admitting he that he had faltered, on occasion."

It was not postmodern Seinfeld satire. It was serious. Jerry Springer was *that* popular among some voters who could not get enough of the Springer Kool-Aid.

But not everywhere. A letter the same day wondered why Councilman David Mann accused the prosecutor of misusing his office. "Why? Because Mr. Leis had the temerity to uphold the law, even where politicians were involved? ... Is he suggesting that Leis should keep hands off politicians?"

A black political group protested that council members were looking the other way for "the white boy," while black Democrat William Chenault, next in line behind Springer for mayor, was getting stiff-armed. Chenault said the other councilmembers were "in effect, condoning what he did."

Springer dropped his bid for mayor. Then eleven days after he resigned, he gave up on returning to council. Pale and shaky, Springer

CHAPTER 5 • 'DO YOU TAKE CHECKS FOR THAT?'

Jerry Springer shakes hands with Councilman Ken Blackwell after his triumphant return to City Council. Springer was elected mayor in 1977.
Gerry Wolter, *The Cincinnati Enquirer*.

made it sound like he was nobly stepping aside to avoid distractions from "the issues."

But *he was* the issue. Council members had put their fingers in the wind and felt a tornado coming. They ran for the storm cellar and refused to go on record to support him. He had no choice. He was burned toast.

"The only things I've got now are my wife and the fact that I told the truth," he said—which was half true. He still had his wife.

But that was not the end of the Jerry Springer story.

Comeback is Complete, a big headline said after the 1975 city election. Jerry Springer was re-elected to city council and would become mayor after all in 1977. Stories now referred to him as a "participant" in a "questionable incident"—almost an innocent bystander.

"It's been a rough year and a half in exile," he told the gathered reporters as he celebrated his victory. "Exile." As if he had nothing to do with his "timeout" from politics.

It was a rougher year for the prostitutes who were forced to testify with immunity, and rougher still for the men who went to prison for pimping the hookers to Jerry Springer.

If asked at all about the "Kentucky incident" that briefly derailed his train to glory, Springer was terse. "Hey, I was a kid then," he said. "Everybody makes mistakes. The people spoke."

Leis wondered, "When did people stop caring about morality?"

Reporters loved Springer's liberal activism. Ohio voters said "No thanks" when he ran for governor. Michael Keating, The Cincinnati Enquirer.

Springer ran for governor of Ohio in 1982, and even tried to inoculate himself with campaign ads that mentioned the infamous sex checks before his opponents could. Ohio said no.

Eventually, he was hired to do political reporting and commentary by Cincinnati's third-place TV station, WLWT. He rose to anchorman and managing editor, with a signature line like a Hallmark card for Any Occasion: "Take care of yourself and each other."

He became the top anchorman in the city, paired with Norma Rashid, winning Emmy Awards for his editorials. A similar gig in Chicago flopped, but by then he had launched *The Jerry Springer Show,* which started as a political forum and degenerated into a schlocky *Hustler Magazine* to Phil Donahue's classier *Playboy* talk show. Shouting, insults, cursing and chair-tossing TV brawls ensued. Ratings were good. When a woman was killed by her husband after they were guests on the show, her family accused Springer of inciting murder.

Springer went on to acting and TV projects, including appearances on *The Simpsons, Married... with Children, Austin Powers: The Spy Who Shagged Me* and *Ringmaster,* about the host of a wild and raunchy talk show, named Jerry Farrelly. Art imitated life.

Springer would have been a natural for a role in *The People vs. Larry Flynt*—perhaps as one of Flynt's sharp-dressed lawyers or a customer who tries to tip a stripper by tucking a personal check in her G-string. Flynt and Springer both dominated local news with R-rated headlines, and both were brought down by Prosecutor Si Leis.

CHAPTER 5 • 'DO YOU TAKE CHECKS FOR THAT?'

At the end of 1977, the readers of *The Cincinnati Enquirer* ranked Jerry Springer's comeback as the eleventh most important story of the year, far behind (1.) the Beverly Hills Supper Club Fire; (2.) Larry Flynt; and (3.) the record cold winter that froze the Ohio River. Newsroom staffers were more enthusiastic about the Second Coming of Springer. They ranked his triumphant return twice as high.[49]

The only thing colder than the winter of 1977 was the press relationship with Simon Leis after he busted Jerry Springer in 1974.

---

[49] "Top Stories of 1977," *The Cincinnati Enquirer*, January 1, 1978. The ruling overturning charges against Police Chief Carl Goodin made the top ten on both lists.

I Walk the Line

6
'Boot the hogs'

"I won that case with a piece of chalk," the prosecutor said.

In his final argument for the prosecution of Larry Flynt for obscenity and organized crime, Si Leis approached the jury box and held up a stick of yellow chalk. He had their full attention. Even the judge leaned forward to see what he was doing.

"There's no such thing as moral neutrality," Leis told the jury. "You've got to take a position. You've got to protect our community and protect our offspring."

Then he bent down and used the chalk to draw a long mark on the courtroom floor in front of the jury. He pointed to it and said, "You've got to draw that line."

Sitting a few feet away at the defendant's table, Flynt looked at the prosecutor's spit-shined Marine Corps combat boots he wore during a heavy snowfall and blurted, "My God, I'm being prosecuted by a storm trooper." Leis thought that was hilarious.

Flynt was already facing a sentence for perjury and bribery in a conviction the month before. Now, he could be sentenced to twenty-five years in prison. He insisted he was only guilty of "bad taste." His *Hustler Magazine* was "nothing more than a mirror" to show everyone that they were just like him. People who thought the magazine was criminally obscene "don't know what they're talking about or don't know what they're missing," he told the press.

Flynt's lawyers closed the defense case by telling the jury, "You don't have the right to tell the people of Cincinnati they can't read it."

Leis had the last word. "Sex is a beautiful thing, a God-given characteristic, a God-given sense of pleasure—provided it's used in the proper

Prosecutor Simon Leis on his way to the courtroom for the Larry Flynt trial, with first assistant prosecutor Fred Cartolano in 1976. Tom Hubbard, *The Cincinnati Enquirer.*

environment. But alas, what have these defendants done to it? Put sex on the level of an animal. That is what the law calls obscene."

He told the jury Flynt's New York lawyer was wrong. The law and the Supreme Court gave the jury the authority to set local standards for what could be sold in Cincinnati. "If it's sick or morbid to *you*, it's obscene."

When both sides finished at last, Judge William Morrissey gave his instructions to the jury. "'Patently offensive' must be interpreted to mean beyond the customary limits of candor, grossly obscene or bizarre," he said. "Contemporary community standards are those of the average person, not the most permissive and liberal or the most restrictive or conservative."

Next, the judge defined organized crime: five or more people who "cooperate on a continuing basis to promote or engage in pandering obscenity for financial gain."

The jury retired to their deliberations room and got to work. It took them eighteen hours over four days to finally thrash out a unanimous verdict: Guilty on both counts. The chalk won. They drew the line.

CHAPTER 6 • 'BOOT THE HOGS'

The U.S. Supreme Court's "community standards" ruling that the jury followed was first adopted in 1957, when the court dialed back more restrictive laws that could be stretched to ban materials about birth control and abortion as well as pornography. In 1973, the court clarified its definition of obscenity as anything that "lacks literary, artistic, political or scientific value."

In a 1964 case, Justice Potter Stewart, a Midwesterner who grew up in Michigan and served on the U.S. Sixth Circuit Court of Appeals in Cincinnati before joining the Supreme Court, famously said of pornography, "I know it when I see it." It was a famous dodge that let the court wiggle off the hook and avoid giving communities a definition of obscenity.

But the jury in the Flynt case knew it when they saw it, too.

In coming years, the Supreme Court would cut holes in the fence around obscenity with a ruling that nude dancing was "artistic expression," permitting a new proliferation of strip clubs, X-rated theaters and massage parlors. But on February 8, 1977, jurors decided Flynt's magazine had no redeeming value and was too obscene for Cincinnati's community standards.

After the verdict, Flynt demanded to be sentenced immediately and insulted Judge Morrissey. "You haven't made any intelligent decision through the course of this trial," he ranted. "I don't expect one now." With his typical flair for histrionics, he compared himself to a ruthless killer who had recently chosen to be executed by a firing squad in Utah: "I want the same thing as Gary Gilmore.[50] Let's do it."[51]

The judge was glad to grant his request, but reluctantly decided against the firing squad.

He sent Flynt directly to jail: six months and a $1,000 fine for pandering obscenity; the maximum 7 to 25 years and a $10,000 fine

---

50 Gilmore got his wish. After a 10-year pause in executions following a 1972 Supreme Court ruling that they were "cruel and unusual," the court issued new guidelines and Gilmore, murderer of two victims, was the first inmate executed in America. He was killed by a firing squad in Utah on January 17, 1977.

51 "Flynt Found Guilty, Cuffed, Led Away," Peggy Lane, *The Cincinnati Enquirer*, February 9, 1977.

Larry Flynt in handcuffs, left, surrounded by a posse of reporters on his way to jail after being sentenced for obscenity and organized crime on February 8, 1977.
The Cincinnati Enquirer.

for engaging in organized crime; and an $11,000 fine against Hustler Magazine Inc.

Flynt's wife, Althea, his brother Jimmy Flynt and the production manager of the magazine, Al Schenk, were acquitted.

Leis and Cartolano were "elated" with the verdict.

It would not stop all the obscene "trash," Cartolano told The *Cincinnati Post,* "but it's going to cause the others to draw back a little and think. And if they think, they'll tone it down a little. If Hustler is not around, they won't have to compete with it" by stretching the boundaries of obscenity. *Playboy,* for example, "let Hustler drag them down to its level," he said.

Leis and Cartolano wasted no time to announce another round of twelve fresh indictments for disseminating material harmful to juveniles. On November 29, just days before his trial was supposed to begin, Flynt had mailed pamphlets to 400,000 Hamilton County residents that showed explicit, horrifyingly maimed bodies of soldiers in Vietnam.

What Flynt hoped to achieve by that was anyone's guess. He said he wanted people to see the real pornography, meaning the war.

CHAPTER 6 • 'BOOT THE HOGS'

The bad news snowballed for Flynt that cold winter. A week later, the IRS came after Flynt in federal court for $20,000 in unpaid taxes. And a Columbus, Ohio prosecutor, who was in the packed courtroom for the Cincinnati trial, said he was considering civil or criminal prosecution of Flynt's Hustler Inc. headquarters in Columbus.

Flynt wore a defiant grin as he was cuffed and led to jail, surrounded by a jostling throng of lawyers and reporters. He boasted that he would continue to sell *Hustler* in Hamilton County even though his own lawyer said that would be foolish. But then, after a few days behind bars, his tough-guy bravado evaporated like smoke.[52]

In an emotional jailhouse interview, he lamented the lack of support for his cause and said his first priority was no longer money, but getting out of jail. "When you hear those steel doors close behind you, you have a good cry," he said. "I have a right to be free (and) express my thoughts without censorship from others."

The Supreme Court may have flinched from defining obscenity, but it always made one thing very clear: Raw obscenity was not protected by the First Amendment and never had been. Flynt's "thoughts" were not on trial. His pictures were. But the press and a cast of celebrities would not be confused by the facts. They rallied for "freedom of the press" and Flynt's "free speech."

A few weeks after Flynt was sent to jail, a full-page ad ran in the *Washington Post* and the *New York Times*. "Larry Flynt: American Dissident," it said, comparing the porn peddler to Alexander Solzhenitsyn and other writers and artists who were sent to gulag prisons in the Soviet Union. The ad was signed by ninety members of "Americans For a Free Press," including Woody Allen, Vincent Canby, Ramsey Clark, Judith Crist, John Dean, Daniel Ellsberg, David Halberstam, Hugh Hefner (of course), Joseph Heller, Norman Mailer and Gay Talese—the liberal literati of 1977.

In an editorial, *the Wall Street Journal* called BS, saying it was "a monstrosity to compare Mr. Flynt, who made millions from his seamy

---

52   "Flynt Facing More Trouble, Jail a Reality," Peggy Lane, *The Cincinnati Enquirer,* February 12, 1977.

activities, with Soviet dissidents, who are tossed in labor camps and insane asylums."

Conflating real political expression with obscenity in the "American Dissident" ad was too much, even for members of the New York elites. One unnamed artist/intellectual demanded to have his name removed after he bought and opened a copy of *Hustler Magazine* to see the "free speech" he was defending: "photos of crotches and barnyard cartoons," the *Wall Steet Journal* editorial said. "Even in literary salons, it seems, it's not quite possible to suppress entirely the forbidden thought that there may after all be such a thing as obscenity."

The editorial could not resist the mandatory New York swipe at Cincinnati as a boondocks backwater of ignorance: "Now this particular prosecution in Cincinnati may in fact be flawed. Reports suggest that the populace there is in a frenzy against pornography, that the prosecutor was vindictive, that the judge was biased."

But it acknowledged that local communities were helpless against "the powerful elite in this society that denies the majority's right to censor even the most blatantly offensive sexual publications. ... For our part it is hard to avoid some sympathy with the citizens of Cincinnati in their desire for a cleaner environment."

That "powerful elite" included the Mafia and its New York lawyers—and most of the press that sided with Flynt to pretend "photos of crotches" were sacred freedom of speech.

The editorial board of *the Wall Street Journal* also scoffed that, "Mr. Flynt's only connection with organized crime comes through the technicalities of Ohio law." They were wrong.

But they had at least dared to reveal a "forbidden thought": There could be such a thing as obscenity and some publications so toxic they are "not to be defended."

That thought did not even occur to most of the press. They made Leis their target and blamed him personally for the "censorship" of *Hustler*. Some claimed he "despised" Flynt.

Leis always insisted it was not personal. He was only responding to community demands to make Cincinnati "porn-free." Years later,

CHAPTER 6 • 'BOOT THE HOGS'

he explained how the charges against Flynt and *Hustler* originated at about the same time some Cincinnati cops shot up the windows at adult bookstores:

"In the mid-1970s, a group of concerned citizens came to me and wanted to know what could be done about the dirty bookstores and peep shows. Based on their request, I went into one of the bookstores where they had these peep shows in back where you could watch porn. As soon as I walked in, I could smell the stink of these guys in there and what they were doing. It was absolutely disgusting.

"So we started closing these stores down. And then someone wanted to know, what about *Hustler*? Compared to the stuff in the stores that were being successfully prosecuted, *Hustler* was just as bad or worse. We realized they were right."

The citizens who demanded action were part of a strong and growing anti-porn crusade at the time, founded as Citizens for Decent Literature (CDL) in 1956. By 1977, CDL stood for Citizens for Decency Through Law. A CDL leader replied to the press and celebrities who held rallies for Flynt in a letter to *The Cincinnati Enquirer* on February 28, 1977.

> We must point out that the obscenity convictions are consistent with every other community where *Hustler* has been brought to trial. Flynt knew the magazine was obscene. Yet he continued to put himself above the law and operate his syndicate for the purpose of profiting from a crime. This, by definition, is organized crime.
>
> So often prosecutors are told not to pick on the "little guy" selling obscenity, but to go after the organizer. Well, Cincinnati can be proud that Si Leis had the dedication to develop the case against the publisher....
>
> It is unfortunate that so many newspapers have been "hustled" by Flynt's song and dance about the First Amendment. We repeat, for the hundredth time, obscenity is not protected by the First Amendment. Laws against it have existed and have been enforced since the amendment was written. Those predicting censorship of genuine press are chasing windmills.... Not one serious work of art has ever been successfully prosecuted. Not one, ever.

> The alternative to all this is a world of Flynts. A world selling degeneracy instead of devotion, abusing instead of caring, promoting lust instead of love. Our Constitution has evolved for the purpose of protecting human dignity. Pornographers like Flynt stand in direct conflict to that goal.
>
> Congratulations, Si Leis and the people of Cincinnati! You have begun the long road back to moral sanity.

It was signed by Edward F. Kondrat, Vice President, Citizens for Decency Through Law, Cleveland.

But there was no doubt that it expressed the opinion of CDL's leader and founder, Charles H. Keating, who was a powerful ally of the prosecutor.

About a month after the trial, Keating was the key speaker at an anti-porn rally in Columbus. As Larry Flynt's brother and wife and a handful of *Hustler* employees booed and heckled him, Keating told the crowd of more than 300, "If the people of this country did not want curbs on pornography or pornographers in jail, these laws would be quickly repealed. All you need to put the pornographer in jail is a good prosecutor and a willing court."

Keating spoke for many of his CDL supporters when he said that contrary to the media, being against pornography did not make someone a frenzied, backward illiterate. "Pornography is sold by the hogs and pigs of our society," he said. "I'm willing to put the boot to the hogs."

Everybody Wants to Change the World

7
Busted Heads and Breaking News

THE CINCINNATI ENQUIRER, 1972—Jim was on the phone, probably talking to "the man upstairs." So Jake avoided the hotseat and sat on the edge of an empty battleship-gray desk in the U-shaped "rim," where copyeditors worked, taking stories handed out by Punch, whose desk was in the "slot" at the open end of the U.

Copyeditors were a weird bunch, Jake thought. They were the language engineers of the news business; people who knew the AP Stylebook the way Martin Luther memorized the Book of Romans. They were as precise as mathematicians, working chalk-board quantum physics equations in participles, quotes and commas. Reporters who were incapable of learning the proper use of "that" vs. "who" or "its" vs. "it's" drove them bughouse nuts.

"Who is Mr. Somesay?" Punch wrote in the margins in angry red pencil, circling a sentence that began, "Some say the governor…" — an old trick to slip in the reporter's opinion. "We don't quote your imaginary friends," he added. "Find a real source." Then he pushed the story back to the City Desk, where Jim might send it back for rewrite or summon the reporter to the hotseat for a one-way conversation about the invisible Berlin Wall that separated news and opinion.

Punch was king of the Copydesk, and Judy was the queen. "Pro-choice quotes are attributed as 'said,' but pro-life quotes are attributed as 'claimed,' insinuating they are dishonest or untrustworthy," Judy wrote on a story about an anti-abortion protest. "Rebuttal quotes from Right to Life are pushed to the end of the story, which will be buried on a jump page."

She passed it to Punch, saying, "Gee, I wonder what side our reporter is on." Punch took a quick look, shook his head and wrote "REWRITE" across the top, then pushed the story onto a vertical steel icepick on a wooden stand. "Spiked."

"Did you see that one about the 'pubic comments' at the school board meeting?" Judy asked with a chuckle, making quote marks with her fingers around the word "pubic."

Punch chuckled, blushed and shook his head. "No, but I did find out we have an 'electrical college.' Did you know presidents are now chosen by a vocational training school for electricians, according to our esteemed political reporter?"

"Idiocy is contagious," Judy replied. "Spend too much time around politicians and your IQ drops forty points. And that puts most of the newsroom below zero."

Compared to copyeditors, reporters were not complicated. They shared the same hobbies: drinking, talking about their stories, and talking about their stories while drinking. They all wanted pretty much the same thing: Page One bylines and meaningless contest awards that would help them get promoted from their low-paying job to another low-paying job with more work. Give a reporter an award that was worth less than a "free prize" from a box of Frosted Flakes and they would be deliriously, champagne happy.

Never mind that the prizes were never from readers, who actually mattered. The winners were always chosen by other journalists, to make sure the most politically correct stories were held up as examples of "excellence." Contests were carrots and sticks for conformity. Reporters were easy to steer.

Copyeditors were wired differently. They were the kind of people who played chess matches by mail that lasted for months, with opponents in Madrid or Moscow—or Moscow *and* Madrid at the same time on two chessboards. They worked the *New York Times* Crossword Puzzle in ink and complained at the lack of originality in the clues: "Woodwind, four letters?" one would ask with a smirk? "Oboe," another would reply. "Always. And look here: Nine Down: 'Capital' is 'Ulan Bator' again."

They even had their own dress code that made "casual Friday" look like hangover Monday. The theory was that copyeditors did not meet the public. But there were plenty of guests whose illusions of newsroom glamor were shattered by men and women dressed for mowing the lawn and cleaning the oven.

Whereas reporters knew just enough about their beat to be dangerous, and most editors had done tours of duty through enough beats to know a little bit about everything, copyeditors really did know a lot about everything, and some knew a whole lot about certain specialties. The Copydesk was the newsroom junk drawers of trivia—you never knew what you would find in there. The rim had an opera buff who could name the Italian composer of a 1904 opera based on a French novel about an American Sailor in who falls in love in Japan: Puccini's *Madame Butterfly*, of course. There was a copyeditor who had never worked in the sports department but knew the batting averages and stats for every Cincinnati Redstockings player since 1881. "Mike the Mechanic" could turn plodding, cement-shoes prose into newsprint poetry. He could also adjust the timing and fuel mix on your Chevy if you took him a six-pack on the weekend. A copyeditor named Mathews became "Math-matic" because he was like the one-eyed man in the kingdom of the blind: He knew enough arithmetic to rescue reporters from their math illiteracy, such as polling results that added up to more than 130 percent.

Copyeditors were the know-it-alls who ran the board when they played Scrabble. They knew the TV gameshow answers before the host finished asking the questions. They knew the important distinction between "flout" and "flaunt," or "founder" and "flounder," and they would gladly tell it to you even if you did not ask and really, really did not want to know.

But when it came to crime, the acknowledged newsroom encyclopedia about cops and local criminal history was City Editor Jim Gardner. His sources were manifold and mysterious. There was hardly a cop on either side of the Ohio River who did not know him and respect his coverage of their tough, thankless, dangerous work.

As Jake waited for Jim to get off the phone, he noted that Judy sat at the right hand of Punch, as always. To her friends and family outside the newsroom she was "Judith." But at work she was Judy because "Punch and Judy" just naturally fit the entertainment they provided to the rim editors.

They brought to mind Abbot and Costello or Mutt and Jeff. Judy wore print dresses and was as round and overstuffed as a davenport pillow. Punch was a human coat hanger, six foot six and so thin he complained that he had to run around in the shower to get wet.

With her graying hair, wire-rim glasses on a string around her neck and comfortable housedresses, Judy looked like a gentle granny. But she could curse like a lumberjack with a crushed thumb. Her wit was as sharp as a straight razor, and could cut a reporter's story apart like open heart surgery. If they heard what she said about the copy they turned in, most reporters would probably give up and find a job selling insurance.

Punch, though, was suspected of being a closet Christian. He blushed like a stoplight when Judy got going. The ancient brown Arnold Palmer button-front cardigan that hung on the back of his chair was so spattered with the remains of lunches and cigarette burns, it looked like a torniquet from a World War I field hospital. His speech was as conscientiously clean as a church potluck prayer. "Now, Judy," he would occasionally protest.

Where Judy could carve out a reporter's spleen without leaving a scar, Punch was kind. "Remember, the principal is your pal," he would say to teach the difference between "principle" and "principal." Punch was patient. Except for the infamous "dashes" incident—which could still make him hot enough to light a kitchen match with his glare.

It started when the Republican chairman of the county commission lost his temper and cursed at one of the commissioners—a Democrat—during a heated argument over the county prosecutor's battle to close adult bookstores. When the Democrat insisted pornography was a "victimless" crime, the Republican replied with a two-syllable obscenity that could also be described as an indispensable agricultural commodity.

The newsroom split into two factions. The younger crowd, including most reporters, wanted to spell it all out, to show the intensity of the argument and because it would embarrass the Republican, a devout Catholic and opponent of "filth."

The older editors argued for using only the initials, familiar to everyone: "BS."

Punch wanted neither of the above in a family newspaper, but soon realized he would lose that argument. So he came up with a compromise: "Let's just use four dashes," he said. Both sides could go with that. The final version went to the presses at the last minute.

The next morning, readers laughed so hard they choked on their coffee. The newsroom phones lit up. The printed story used dashes—for only the *first* four letters that were harmless. "Bull" became "----." The second four were spelled out.

"I thought I learned a lot of profanities in the Army," one caller said. "What the heck was so bad you could not spell it compared to that?"

Punch always wondered if Judy had something do to with it. And she still enjoyed bringing it up from time to time to rankle him. "Well, dash-dash (bleep)," she would say if she spilled her tea. Punch would pretend he didn't hear it as the color climbed up out of his collar.

The Copydesk spared nobody, Jake thought—including the Copydesk. There was a bulletin board in the breakroom reserved for "Busted Heads"—unintentionally comical and embarrassing headlines that somehow snuck past all the copyediting guards and barbed wire to make an Alcatraz escape into the morning paper.

Mayor Wants to Cut Poor People in Half

KIDS COOK AND SERVE GRANDPARENTS

Astronomer Wants to Probe Uranus

GRANDFATHER DELIGHTED WITH NEW UPRIGHT ORGAN

Judy had an especially sharp eye for the more risqué examples. She had chosen an "unfortunate juxtaposition" that showed a picture of a man bending over the back of a sheep, directly under an unrelated headline about federal subsidies: **New Source of Relief for Frustrated Farmers**.

A special "Hall of Shame" corner was reserved for embarrassing corrections.

"Correction: Saturday's story said 'Ringo Starr was performing on drugs.' Ringo Starr was performing on drums."

Corrections were treated like having a rotten tooth pulled: Avoid it as long as possible. If it absolutely has to be done, make it as short and painless as possible, then keep your mouth shut, hoping nobody will notice.

"Correction: In Wednesday's edition, Mr. and Mrs. Bridges were listed under recent divorces. They were recently married, not divorced."

"Hey, Jake," Judy said, "is that a shirt you're wearing or wrapping paper left over from Christmas? Does it have a volume button?"

"Compared to the other ones I saw at Shillito's, this one is subtle," Jake said.

"Subtle like an ax murder," Judy said. "Next time give me a warning so I can wear sunglasses."

Jake was about reply when he heard cursing through the phone that Jim was holding about four inches away from his ear. Then Jim said, "Yes, sir," and hung up the phone. Jake gave him time to light a smoke, then sat in the hotseat across from Jim's desk.

"What's up, Jake," Jim asked, looking a bit stressed, or at least as stressed as a guy could be over a 15-cent newspaper after he had survived the Battle of the Chosin Reservoir against a million Chinese in frozen North Korea.

"That wasn't the man upstairs, was it?" Jake asked.

"No, Mr. Lindner is a gentleman. I've never heard him raise his voice, much less yell and curse. And he pretty much leaves us alone to run the asylum unless the inmates take control. Guess again."

"Charlie Keating?"

"No, contrary to newsroom mythology, that doesn't happen. Sometimes I wish some of the alleged reporters around here would spend as much time writing stories as they spend making them up."

"I give up."

"Old Yeller."

Old Yeller was the newsroom name for a notoriously short-tempered city councilman voters had promoted to Congress, where he was now

CHAPTER 7 • BUSTED HEADS AND BREAKING NEWS

terrorizing staffers on Capitol Hill—much to the relief of everyone at city hall.

Jake said, "Ah, of course. Last time he called me I finally had to lay down the phone on my desk, and you could still hear him cursing me from here to Fountain Square. Even Murray the atheist was shocked." Murray was the religion reporter who had finagled the easy beat by pointing out that he was scrupulously non-denominational and religiously impartial because he didn't believe in anything.

Jim laughed. "Something the congressman read disagreed with him and his buddy Jim Beam this morning. I think I heard him throw something in his office. But next time I see him it will be handshakes and smiles warm enough to melt an igloo. He's a professional politician with an advanced degree in fertilizers. So, you were saying..." he prompted.

"I got an interesting call I wanted to tell you about."

"From who?"

Judy frowned, shook a finger at Jim and snapped, "*Whom!*"

Jake smiled at Judy and told Jim, "I promised not to share *whom's* name with anybody but you, and only then if you torture me."

"That can be arranged," Jim said with one of those unreadable smiles. "But for now, just tell me what's so interesting."

"Apparently, this guy has spent enough time in the Hustler Club to qualify for a PhD in anatomy."

"Why do we care about a barfly who window-shops in a strip club and thinks he's a double-ought secret agent?"

"It's a dirty job," Jake joked, "but someone has to do it."

Jim laughed. "There's your headline," he said, "but what's the story?"

"He was paid to be there," Jake said. "He was hired to watch go-go girls in skimpy two-piece swimsuits bump and grind as he drank rum-and-Coke highballs. There were four of these undercover guys, working in shifts. Two from the IRS, one from the DOJ and this guy who called me, hired by the Ohio Department of Taxation."

Jim looked interested. "And here I thought those tax men only lusted after my money. Tell me more."

"He said when he was recruited for the job he couldn't believe it. He thought it was a gag for that TV show *Candid Camera*. But it was no joke. They hired him to sit there for four hours at a time and count drinks."

"An audit," Jim said, nodding.

"Correct. They posed as local businessmen, salesmen, neglected husbands. He was afraid to let us use his name because of what they found and where their investigation went."

"Let me guess," Jim said. "If state and federal tax auditors are involved with the DOJ, that sounds like money laundering."

"That's what he said. The bar was buying enough liquor from the State of Ohio to sell about $500 worth of drinks a day, but they were reporting sales of $2,000 a day on their taxes."

"That means lots of dirty money is coming from somewhere."

"Their counts confirmed it. He said state and federal officials believe Flynt's bar is laundering money from organized crime."

"That means Newport," Jim said. "Casinos, strip clubs, prostitution and numbers rackets, right across the river. I've often wondered what they do with all that cash."

"It makes sense," Jake said. "Screw Andrews was making $2 million a year off the numbers racket alone when they raided his Sportsmen's Club in 1961. That's just one guy, one club. Where's all that money going to get washed?"

"I can see why your guy is nervous," Jim said. "How long has this Maxwell Smart investigation been going on?"

"He told me it began in early 1968, then ramped up in 1969 when *Life Magazine* published that investigative story about Mafia ties to Governor Rhodes."[53]

"I remember the story. It died faster than a wet match in a monsoon. So they might think there's some connection to Jim Rhodes. And the Mob. And the Hustler Club and Larry Flynt. Assuming this guy is not some crank."

---

[53] "The Governor and the Mobster," Denny Walsh, *Life Magazine,* May 2, 1969.

"He sounds legit," Jake said. "But it's just one guy. And the tax people don't have to tell us anything. They hide behind confidentiality. What do you think?"

Jim crushed his cigarette and leaned back, thinking. "If this guy's story checks out and indicates that Flynt is linked to the Mafia, I will need to know *whom him* is," he said, shooting a glance at Judy to underline his fractured grammar. "This might be pretty good."

Jim did not believe in superlatives. There were not enough in the world to describe what he saw in Korea. So for him, "pretty good" was about as good as it got.

NOT IN OUR TOWN · PETER BRONSON

8
The Other Charlie Keating

Among faithful subscribers, *The Cincinnati Enquirer* was known as "The Grand Old Lady of Vine Street"—the personification of a dignified dowager. And no place at the Enquirer Building on Vine was more dignified than the publisher's office on the fifth floor.

It was paneled in polished cherry wood, with tasteful carpets and muted, matching drapes. Museum-worthy paintings of the city by local artists adorned the walls. In two of them, editions of *The Cincinnati Enquirer* were strategically placed in still-life paintings from the late 1800s.

A secret button on the publisher's desk could magically open and close the office door for private meetings when business leaders, congressmen, U.S. Senators, governors and even presidents visited to seek endorsements or drop by for a chat on current events with "the man upstairs."

Charlie Keating, left, and his brother Bill were law partners at Keating, Meuthing & Klekamp. Bill went into politics and became publisher of *The Cincinnati Enquirer*; Charlie chose business and became the biggest homebuilder in the Southwest. The Keating family.

Among all his many careers, including judge, councilman, Congressman and corporate executive for Gannett Corp., Bill Keating's favorite was being publisher and president of *The Cincinnati Enquirer*. Courtesy of the Keating family.

The fifth floor was insulated from the shouts and ringing phones in the newsroom below, or the rumbling V8-powered presses in the basement. It was cloaked in quiet like a library, draped in a respectful funeral-home hush.

Then one morning the Grand Old Lady's prim repose was shattered by the ear-splitting pop and chainsaw chatter of a motorbike revving down the hall.

Riding it like a six-foot-five stork on a roller skate was Charlie Keating, showing his teeth with a devilish grin, roaring off the elevator and straight for the holiest newspaper temple, the publisher's office.

His younger brother, Bill, president of *The Enquirer*, was so well mannered he could hardly be imagined without his suit jacket on, even when seated at his antique, hand-carved desk behind those push-button doors.

Bill was shocked, then mortified. But what could he say? His brother got him the job by persuading the owner of the paper, Carl Lindner Jr., to put Bill in the publisher's office.

The legend of the motorbike in the publisher's office lived on in Cincinnati for years, along with another one about the time Charlie

CHAPTER 8 • THE OTHER CHARLIE KEATING

turned rabbits loose in Lindner's immaculate, white-plush office.

That was Charlie Keating. Brash. Flamboyant. Magnetic. Charming. Abrasive. Wild. Arrogant. Reckless. Nothing at all like the humorless, uptight prude painted by his enemies. He was known to his most devoted staffers as "the Pied Piper." They would follow him anywhere and work tirelessly, pouring themselves into his cases, causes and crusades.

Later, he became known to most of America as the two-dimensional stick figure the media draws when it needs a bad guy: "Crook."

But he was much more complex and interesting than that. Charlie Keating was the kind of story America loves.

He was tall, rich and handsome, a man who had everything: a lovely wife and a beautiful family of five pretty blond daughters and a son, Charles Keating III.[54] At the peak of his career, he had a sprawling estate in sun-splashed Phoenix and led the biggest home-building company in the booming Southwest, as he filled in empty maps of sand and cactus with whole Zip Codes of new homes, schools, shopping centers, churches and families.

He could pick up a phone and command the attention of the most powerful men in Washington, all the way to the White House. He had his own plane and flew it himself to his Caribbean getaway. His career history was the stuff of comic-book heroes: former Navy fighter pilot, all-American swimmer, legal counsel and adviser to one of the wealthiest men in the world, founder of a world class youth swimming program, principal in a successful law firm and leader of a national crusade against obscenity.

On the day he showed up with the motorbike he was already one of the most powerful men in Cincinnati. Then in 1976 he bought American Continental Homes from Lindner for $300,000 and soon moved his family to Phoenix. In ten years, American Continental Corporation

---

54 Charles H. Keating III was another outstanding swimmer and represented the USA in the 1976 Summer Olympics. His son, Charles H. Keating IV was a Navy SEAL and became one of the earliest casualties in the Iraq War, killed in March 2016 during a mission to rescue American advisors. He was awarded the Silver Star and the Navy Cross.

was worth more than $1 billion—an empire of housing, banks and insurance, helicopters, airplanes, yachts and exotic sportscars.

And then it all came crashing down in the late 1980s. When his California bank, Lincoln Savings & Loan, was investigated, it became Washington's textbook example of the 1990 "S&L Crisis."[55] The albatross of the whole nationwide meltdown was hung around his neck.

The big story in Washington that year was "The Keating Five": Senators John Glenn, Dennis DeConcini, John McCain (the only Republican), Don Riegel and Alan Cranston, who were accused of pressuring federal regulators to back off after Keating asked them to intervene to defend American Continental.

Asked if he expected his contributions to influence the ethically fungible senators, Keating answered, "I want to say in the most forceful way I can: I certainly hope so."

Wealth has oiled the gears of politics since ancient Rome. Senators doing favors for wealthy donors was always routine, and questioning bureaucrats who might cripple the biggest developer in the West made sense to protect jobs and Arizona's economy. But Washington needed someone to blame for the mess created by the deregulation of savings and loans, and Congress was not about to blame itself when 747 banks collapsed at a cost of $160 billion.

Keating was convicted for improperly using deposits from Lincoln Savings & Loan to fund housing and hotels he was building. Keating insisted he was innocent and that depositors would have recovered their savings if regulators had not seized his assets and paralyzed his projects.

He was parked in a federal prison in Tucson for four and a half years, then finally released when his convictions were overturned—long after anyone cared or bothered to correct the record.[56] He joked to friends

---

[55] Between 1986 and 1995, one third of the Savings and Loan associations failed at a cost of $160 billion. The taxpayer bailout cost $132 billion. One of the main causes was sloppy deregulation by Congress that encouraged reckless lending.

[56] The judge in the case was Lance Ito, made famous by the O.J. Simpson trial.

CHAPTER 8 • THE OTHER CHARLIE KEATING

Charlie Keating and his wife Mary Elaine at home for a poolside fundraiser that featured entertainer Bob Hope. Courtesy of the Keating Family.

that prison was "exactly like" *The Shawshank Redemption:* "Everyone has nicknames."

Put on trial again, he pleaded guilty and was sentenced to time served. As part of the deal, the federal government agreed to drop charges against his son, who was used for leverage against his father.

Charlie Keating admitted that his brazen belligerence made him an easy target. He regretted that he had provoked federal regulators by insulting them as hack bureaucrats who never had a job in the real world. True, perhaps, but recklessly foolish.

And the press added two more indictments: his wealth and his work as the leader of a national campaign for "decency."

News stories insinuated that his houses, airplanes and luxury lifestyle were financed by depositors in his bank. That was untrue. They also crowed about his leadership of Citizens for Decency Through Law, as if to say, "See, conservative moralists are all crooks."

What most Americans did not know about Keating is that he started with nothing. Keating was raised in the Clifton neighborhood in Cincinnati, near the University of Cincinnati campus. He and his younger brother Bill had to grow up fast. When they were boys, their father was disabled by a disease similar to Parkinson's, then was severely injured in a gun accident. He lost his job at the dairy and the family had to get by on his disability income.

They moved out of the home their father had built himself, near Xavier University, and both boys went to work, doing whatever they could to help pay the bills. Bill delivered newspapers. Charlie cleaned septic tanks for a while. Both became outstanding swimmers at St. Xavier High School. Charlie Keating became the first all-American athlete at the University of Cincinnati. Bill won nearly as many swimming titles. Both earned law degrees.

And they both became remarkably successful. Bill rose from city councilman to judge, congressman, president of *The Cincinnati Enquirer*, Gannett Company legal counsel and vice president in charge of news, and board chairman and president of The Associated Press.

Charlie became a trusted attorney and adviser to Carl Lindner Jr., an international financier and businessman who started with an ice cream store, then owned supermarkets, banks and corporations. Over the years, Lindner owned a dizzying list of properties, including United Dairy Farmers, Thriftway, United Fruit (Chiquita), Savings & Loans, Provident Bank, amusement parks, Penn Central and National General, a conglomerate that published books, produced movies and sold insurance. At various times, Lindner owned both amusement parks in Cincinnati—Kings Island and Coney Island—and the Cincinnati Reds. By the time he passed the empire on to his sons, his American Financial Group and Great American Insurance Group were a Fortune 500 company with an investment portfolio that reached $14 billion in 2021.

And Charlie Keating was a big part of that tremendous growth in the early days.

One day in 1971, Lindner and his inner circle of top executives were talking business at one of their regular meetings of "the lunch bunch,"

CHAPTER 8 • THE OTHER CHARLIE KEATING

when the topic of the local morning paper came up. Scripps-Howard was being forced to sell *The Cincinnati Enquirer* because it already owned the afternoon paper, *The Cincinnati Post*.

An employee purchase had been proposed, but the deal, if accepted by Scripps, would be a bargain-basement discount, Lindner said.

"Give me a blank check and I will go buy it," Charlie spoke up.

By the end of the day, he had bought *The Cincinnati Enquirer* for Lindner with a $1 million deposit. And when it came time to appoint a president and publisher, Charlie insisted on his brother, Bill, who was then in Congress, considering a run for the Senate.

Bill jumped at the chance to return to Cincinnati and help his wife, Nancy, raise their seven children. The boy who had delivered *The Enquirer* was now running it. As publisher he became known as "Mr. Cincinnati," the quiet, polished, selfless power broker who was behind the scenes in most of the city's growth and success stories for the next decade. In the arts, sports, growth and government, Bill was there making it happen, without taking credit.

Bill and his brother were night and day opposites. Bill was reserved, Charlie was brash; Bill was admired, Charlie made enemies; Bill gave credit to others, Charlie sucked the air out of a room.

"Charlie was a character," a close coworker said. "He was always the center of attention. He would take these amazing risks, but they always seemed to pay off for him. When he walked into a room it was as if nobody else mattered."

Nobody loved a practical joke more than Charlie Keating. But when he was serious, nobody was more focused. When he set his mind on something, almost nothing could stop him. And he had made up his mind to stop one of the biggest cash machines for organized crime: pornography.

You Can't Always Get What You Want

9
Rotten in Denmark

The 1950s was a schizophrenic decade in TV Land. American life was divided into cheerful sitcom suburbs as fake as margarine, or gritty inner-city punks who fought with switchblades in the *Blackboard Jungle*. But far from Hollywood, in the heartland where ordinary people lived and worked and raised their families, there were serious men who cared about serious things.

In 1956, a group of those men gathered at the Milford Retreat House northeast of Cincinnati for a meeting led by Father Nicholas Gelin.[57] The Jesuit priest had come to Cincinnati in 1948 and would be transferred back to Cleveland in 1957. But during his brief tour of duty in Cincinnati he had a profound impact.

As word got around, attendance at his Men of Milford Jesuit Retreat League meetings grew to more than 3,000 a year. Men flocked to hear him call them to battle in the early skirmishes of the culture wars. And one of the men in the crowd would leave with a new mission—a rebel *with* a cause that would change the world in a small but significant way. As he listened to Fr. Gelin describe a poison that was killing innocence, exploiting women, crippling men and corrupting America, Charlie Keating made up his mind to do something about it.

"He 'volunteered' me," Keating would say about Fr. Gelin years later.[58]

The snake in the garden was hard-core pornography.

Whatever the priest said, it was absorbed by the young lawyer like a communion wafer. While others just complained, Keating would make

---

[57] "Father Gelin Moving to Post In Cleveland," *The Cincinnati Enquirer*, December 18, 1956.
[58] "CDL President Offers View, Insight Into Finances, Problems of Group," *The Cincinnati Enquirer*, August 31, 1974.

it his personal crusade to take action. He vowed to attack the problem with all the weapons of the legal system and the growing, successful law firm he had founded on the eighteenth floor of the Provident Bank Building, Keating, Muething and Klekamp.

Soon Keating was traveling around the city to speak to students at Catholic schools. That led to invitations from other cities in Ohio, and then a national speaking tour. That grew into a nationwide organization with 300 chapters in dozens of states, offices in Los Angeles and Cleveland, and highly trained teams of attorneys who traveled around the country to help local police and prosecutors win obscenity cases against the deep-pocket porn producers who worked for the Mob.

The same year of the retreat, 1956, Keating founded Citizens for Decent Literature, which became Citizens for Decency Through Law (CDL). It started in churches and schools and spread like a prairie fire in a high wind.

"In our nation, the only way to fight a criminal is through established laws," he said, "and pornography is a crime."

As he would quickly learn, it was more than that. It was organized crime. He would soon be the No. 1 enemy of *Playboy Magazine* publisher Hugh Hefner, *Hustler* publisher Larry Flynt and the shadowy organized crime families who ran adult bookstores, X-rated theaters, topless bars and sin strips in most of the cities in America.

His battle was supported by 200 letters and dozens of speaking invitations each week. The letterhead for CDL listed 126 names of governors, members of Congress, church leaders and school officials all over the nation. "I don't receive any money from CDL at all," he said in 1970. "In fact, I contribute. The CDL expenses have cost me as much as $25,000 a year out of my own pocket."[59]

In 1971, while Larry Flynt was providing hookers for VIP sex parties, Keating had already had his first big court victory over obscenity. It began in 1969, when two Cincinnati Police detectives went to a rundown movie house on McMillan Street in Cincinnati, and bought tickets to

---

59   About $186,000 in 2022 dollars.

watch a showing of the Russ Meyers movie *Vixen*. When it was over, they had seen enough. They confiscated the film and brought charges of obscenity against the theater owner and the Los Angeles owner and distributor of the movie.

The case became known as *Keating Vs. Vixen*. Under local ordinances, Keating was able to make a citizen's complaint that the movie was a nuisance. When he did, the theater owner and movie producer sued him in federal court.

When Keating's complaint went to court, Common Pleas Judge Simon Leis Sr., father of the future prosecutor, watched the movie and declared it obscene.[60]

By the standards of the times, *Vixen* was hard-core. But as the movie poster advertised, critics were eager to demonstrate how enlightened they were. "A fun drama about a singing lady," said *New York Times* critic Judith Crist.

An appeal by the producers was rejected by the Ohio Court of Appeals, but the case was far from over. It went to the Ohio Supreme Court, which also finally affirmed the ruling by Judge Leis in 1973. Keating had won. *Vixen,* shown in seventy theaters around the country, was banned in Cincinnati, and the theater owner pleaded guilty to obscenity charges.

Along the way, Keating was tangled in litigation and constant court appearances, but learned a major lesson—at significant personal expense. "This kind of legal complication is more than most people can walk into," he said. "The (pornographers) can deposition me, hold me in a courtroom. I think they're bullies trying to scare away the opposition. While it isn't any fun, I am not scared. But most laymen wouldn't understand."[61]

He was right. The porn industry and its expensive lawyers would crush anyone who did not have the power, backing and resources that Charlie Keating had. He saw that the porn industry's enormous profits could be used to hire teams of the best lawyers money could buy; cases

---

60 "Vixen Obscene, Judge Leis Rules," *The Cincinnati Enquirer,* November 18, 1969.

61 "Who Charlie Keating Thinks He Is," *The Cincinnati Enquirer,* October 25, 1970.

could be dragged out for years of appeals, to overwhelm the expertise and resources of local prosecutors.

So Keating and CDL created their own strike-team of expert attorneys.

Bruce Taylor, as general counsel for CDL, was one of the best. He traveled the nation while prosecuting more obscenity cases than anyone in the country. Among his first targets were Larry Flynt, Flynt's wife, Althea, and his brother Jimmy Flynt, while Taylor worked as a prosecutor for the City of Cleveland.

After he joined Keating's CDL team, he helped to prosecute one of the biggest porn cases in the country, the FBI Miporn investigation in Miami, Florida in 1980. As he arrived in the courtroom for the Miporn case one day, he was surprised to see the slick, well-dressed, GQ-handsome New York lawyer for Larry Flynt, Herald Fahringer, defending mobsters in Miami. He was impressed with Fahringer's style, fame, bespoke loafers and polished skill in court. But he was not surprised at the connection of porn to the Mob. That was already well known by the FBI, local police and the CDL.

As early as 1970, the FBI said unequivocally that organized crime families controlled nearly all of the pornography in the country.

By then, Keating was making national headlines. During the *Vixen* battle, local reporters and letters to the editor called him a "prude" who was waging a "holy war" of "deplorable censorship." In addition to covering startup costs for CDL from his own pockets, Keating was also paying a personal price. But his single-minded perseverance made him almost invulnerable to criticism.

"We're not the ones who make sex dirty," he said. "That's the pornographers."

He soon attracted the attention of the White House, and was appointed to the President's Commission on Obscenity and Pornography. It was the start of a long and dangerous battle in the trenches where porn met the second oldest profession, politics.

The commission was formed by President Lyndon Johnson in 1968, in response to congressional concerns about recent Supreme Court rulings that liberalized obscenity laws and spread pornography. Peep

CHAPTER 9 • ROTTEN IN DENMARK

In March 1968, President Johnson addressed the nation to announce that he would not seek re-election.
Yoichi Okamoto, National Archives, LBJ Library.

Richard Nixon's campaign button from 1960 foreshadowed his winning 1972 campaign on "law and order."

shows, strip clubs, topless and bottomless bars, nude dancing and even live sex shows were popping up in cities all over the country.

But then as soon as his commission was appointed, President Johnson announced he would not run for re-election because of his unpopularity over the war in Vietnam. His vice president, Hubert Humphrey, lost to Republican Richard Nixon, who was elected on his promise to restore "law and order." Voters were fed up with permissiveness, rising crime and a quagmire war that was tearing the country apart on generational fault lines.

So when a vacancy came open among the 18-members chosen by President Johnson, the new Republican President appointed Charles Keating to the President's Commission. It was like throwing a mongoose into the reptile house. The fight was on.

Johnson's handpicked committee was composed mostly of college professors and ACLU lawyers. Keating brought a different perspective: Catholic, conservative businessman from the heartland. It was not welcome. When he asked questions, he was stonewalled by the staff. The president of the commission, William Lockhardt, dean of the University of Minnesota Law School, was a member of the ACLU and an adamant defender of "the Danish approach."

At the time, Denmark was widely admired by sophisticates for its progressive "anything goes" legal pornography.[62] Lockhardt, whose daughter lived in Denmark, was one of the admirers of the "Danish Model." But he greatly overestimated the appeal of the Danish approach in America.

When the commission's report came out in 1970, shock waves in Congress could be felt as far as Los Angeles. What started as the Johnson Report was now disingenuously known in the press as the Nixon Report, although only one member on the commission was Nixon's choice. A more honest name would have been the "LBJ-Lockhardt Report," or the "Denmark Report."

Among their findings:[63]

- "The commission recommends that Federal, state and local legislation prohibiting the sale, exhibition or distribution of sexual materials to consenting adults should be repealed." (Translated: Legalize pornography.)
- "The commission believes that there is no warrant for continued governmental interference with the full freedom of adults to read, obtain or view whatever such material they wish." (Translated: Anything goes.)
- "Massive sex education" should be launched to promote an "acceptance of sex as a normal and natural part of life and of oneself as a sexual being. It should not aim for orthodoxy; rather, it should be designed to allow for a pluralism of values." (Translated: Indoctrinate the public to accept porn as normal and healthy.)
- "Extensive empirical investigation, both by the commission and by others, provides no evidence that exposure to or use of explicit sexual

---

62 By 1984, Denmark and The Netherlands were exporting "90 percent of the child pornography entering the U.S." Testimony in U.S. Senate Hearings on Child Pornography and Pedophilia, Feb. 21, 1985.

63 *Report of the Commission on Obscenity and Pornography* by Commission on Obscenity and Pornography, Bantam Books, 1970.

CHAPTER 9 • ROTTEN IN DENMARK

Charlie Keating at his desk in 1971. He was more than a match for the 15 members of the President's Commission on Obscenity who wanted to legalize porn. Allan Kain, *The Cincinnati Enquirer.*

materials play a significant role in the causation of social or individual harms such as crime, delinquency, sexual or nonsexual deviancy or severe emotional disturbances." (Translated: Porn is harmless.)

- "It seems to us wholly inappropriate to adjust the level of adult communication to that considered suitable for children. Insufficient research is presently available on the fact of the exposure of children to sexually explicit materials to enable us to reach conclusions." (Translated: Rules to protect children only get in the way of our adults-only fun.)

Keating and two other conservative members were denied a chance to write a minority report rebutting the findings, so Keating got a court injunction against publication of the majority report until the minority could respond. The minority reports were blistering. Highlights of the Keating rebuttal:

- He said the majority report was rigged by pro-porn/ACLU-member Lockhardt, who hijacked the commission and allowed his handpicked staff to write the conclusions. "The commission majority report can only be described as a travesty, preordained by the bias and prejudice of its chairman, closely followed by his staff, who has long advocated relaxation of restraints for the dealers in pornography."
- Keating said Lockhardt rejected his demands for more frequent meetings and public hearings to make the commissioners do their jobs. He said it was "astonishing" that no press were allowed and members had to take "a vow of silence" by promising they would not speak publicly about the commission's work.
- He wanted Lockhart to be investigated for concealing $2 million in spending and refusing to divulge the approval of contracts. One of the contractors was Danish Professor Berl Kutschinsky, whose research for the committee claimed that legalization of porn in Denmark *reduced* sex crimes. Critics said the Kutschinsky study was flawed and sloppy. Keating had CDL contact Copenhagen's police chief, who said violent sex crimes had *not* decreased as Kutschinsky claimed. Yet the bulk of the commission's budget had been spent on the Kutchinksy study from Denmark.
- Keating wrote, "Credit the American public with enough common sense to know that one who wallows in filth is going to get dirty. This is intuitive knowledge. Those who will spend millions of dollars to tell us otherwise must be malicious or misguided, or both."
- And, "Unfortunately, what was intended to provide to our legislators a blueprint for coping with a problem, has been turned 180 degrees into a blank check for the pornographers to flood our country with every variety of filth and perversion."
- Keating's allies on the commission, The Reverend Morton Hill, a Catholic priest, and The Reverend W.C. Link, a Protestant pastor, said:

- "The commission's majority report is a magna carta for the pornographer. ... It is slanted and biased in favor of protecting the business of obscenity and pornography, which the commission was mandated by the Congress to regulate."
- "The leadership and majority recommend that most existing legal barriers between society and pornography be pulled down. In doing so, the commission goes far beyond its mandate and assumes the role of counsel for the filth merchant—a role not assigned by the Congress of the United States."
- "We submit that the purpose of the commission's report is to legalize pornography."[64]

The Senate responded to the LBJ-Lockhardt recommendations to legalize pornography with outrage and scorn. Only five senators voted to accept it. It was overwhelmingly rejected. A Gallup poll found 85 percent of Americans wanted tougher laws against porn—not legalization.[65]

President Nixon said, "So long as I am in the White House, there will be no relaxation of the national effort to control and eliminate smut from our national life." He concluded, "The Commission on Pornography and Obscenity has performed a disservice, and I totally reject its report."[66]

The porn commission was a disaster. Although outnumbered 15-3, Keating had won. Or had he?

Popular culture had the last word. The advocates of legalized porn, such as Hefner's "Playboy Philosophy" editorials and many in the media, embraced Kutchinsky's flawed "proof" and phony "empirical evidence" that porn was harmless and healthy. The press took away only the discredited conclusion and ignored criticism, protests and evidence to the contrary.

---

[64] The Hill-Link Minority Report of the Presidential Commission on Obscenity and Pornography, 1970.

[65] "Pornography: Right or Ruin?," Bob Fresco, *The Cincinnati Enquirer,* November 26, 1970.

[66] Statement About the Report of the Commission on Obscenity and Pornography, President Richard Nixon, the White House, October 24, 1970.

The media "narrative" was like a stubborn stain that could not be washed away. Even fifteen years after the Denmark Report was issued, Reverend Hill still had to remind the press that it had been overwhelmingly ridiculed and rejected. A typical news story had reported that the 1970 commission concluded "there was no evidence linking sexual material to delinquency or criminal behavior"—with no mention of the minority rebuttal that proved the opposite, or the almost unanimous rejection by Congress.

That was exactly what Hefner, Flynt and the organized crime families who ran the porn industry wanted.

Keating and his allies believed that the commission was rigged. They said the report looked "as if the pornographers wrote it," and was stacked with members who were "in favor of the industries to be affected."

Keating blamed two top advisers to President Johnson for loading the lopsided commission: Abe Fortas and Jack Valenti. Fortas worked for a law firm that defended obscenity, and was forced to resign from the Supreme Court in 1969 for taking a bribe, after CDL sought his removal. Valenti was a "trusted aide" of President Johnson with no clear job title, who joined the administration on the day JFK was assassinated. Valenti's heavily redacted FBI file suggests he was probably a CIA asset, and was an associate of a "top hoodlum" in his hometown of Houston. The CIA worked closely with the Mob in the 1960s.[67]

Was the "fix" in for the LBJ commission? At the time, the Mafia had reached deep into politics with bribery and extortion. It owned FBI Director J. Edgar Hoover, who bet on the horses with inside tips from his Mob friends, and was vulnerable to extortion as a closet homosexual. Hoover was appointed "director for life" by President Johnson after President Kennedy was killed. Hoover had extensive blackmail files on Johnson and most of the nation's leaders.[68]

---

67 Valenti was the father of the Motion Picture Ratings system that replaced a more restrictive Hays Code that said, "No picture should lower the moral standards of those who see it." The new Valenti ratings became a marketing tool to sell "Restricted" and X-rated movies.

68 Johnson was vulnerable to blackmail by Hoover and others: He was a philanderer; he stole an election in Texas; and it was reported that Johnson helped New Orleans Mob boss Carlos Marcello avoid deportation.

CHAPTER 9 • ROTTEN IN DENMARK

If the Mob could reach out and compromise the director of the FBI, it could reach anywhere in government.

For example: Ronald Goldfarb, a top U.S. attorney under Attorney General Bobby Kennedy, who helped clean the Mob out of Newport, Kentucky, was convinced that the underworld bosses killed JFK to stop Bobby's war on organized crime. Goldfarb was part of that battle, and saw first-hand what the Mob could do when threatened. The evidence is compelling, including words from the crime bosses themselves.[69]

- Chicago crime boss Sam Giancana: "We took care of Kennedy. The hit in Dallas was just like any other operation we'd worked on in the past."[70]
- Florida Mafia boss Santo Trafficante: "We shouldn't have killed Jack; we should have killed Bobby."
- New Orleans boss Carlos Marcello: "Someone should kill that SOB Kennedy."
- Teamsters President and Kennedy hater Jimmy Hoffa: "I told you they could do it. I'll never forget what Carlos and Santo did for me." Marcello was approved for a huge "loan" from the Teamsters Pension Fund immediately after the assassination.

If the Mafia did conspire to assassinate a U.S. President, it easily had the means, motive and the opportunity to manipulate the composition and direction of LBJ's 1970 porn commission. The commissioners, who were handpicked for their progressive "anything goes" morality, may have remained blissfully unaware that they were being played.

As Keating demonstrated, the LBJ commission had an infection of "Newport Eye." No hearings. No press. No comments. No reports on spending. It was manipulated by staffers and "experts" who were

---

69　*The Last Investigation,* Gaeton Fonzi, Thunder's Mouth Press, 1993; *Forbidden Fruit: Sin City's Underworld and the Supper Club Inferno,* Peter Bronson, Chilidog Press, 2020. FBI records and report of the 1979 House Select Committee on Assassinations.

70　Mob boss Sam Giancana shared a girlfriend with Frank Sinatra and JFK, Judith Campbell Exner. She said Giancana told her he had delivered the election to JFK with Mob voter fraud in Chicago. ibid

carefully selected to support reduced enforcement of pornography laws—conclusions that were certain to be scorned and rejected, but just as certain to give the porn industry the credibility and "expert research" detergent it needed to launder "dirty pictures" into "healthy sexuality."

Whether it was a "fix," blind embrace of the Danish model or just stupidity, the 1970 commission report delivered what the Mob bosses could only hope for: enduring mythology that porn was harmless, and "studies proved it."

The 1970 President's Commission on Obscenity and Pornography was not without humor and irony. Two men were sent to prison for publishing an "illustrated" version of the report. They were prosecuted using the same laws the report said were "extremely unsatisfactory" and unenforceable: obscenity.

Fifty years later, the illustrated version sold for $393 on Amazon. The version without pictures could hardly be found.

What's Goin' On?

10

Getting Wise to the Wiseguys

It was about noon on April 12, 1977 when a man with shoulder-length hair and a star tattoo on his right forearm quietly walked up behind a young woman who had just parked her car on the University of Cincinnati campus. He grabbed her from behind and stuck an "unknown object in her back," the police report said. She was dragged into nearby Burnet Woods and raped.[71]

In a speech a month later to the national convention of Citizens for Decency Through Literature, Charlie Keating told the rest of the story: "Weeks before the assault, a well-known pornographer—speaking at the Signal Alpha Epsilon fraternity house on UC's campus—referred to the girl by name, saying he would pay money to embarrass her."

Keating said the victim was doing well and had agreed with her mother to rule out an abortion if she became pregnant. Then he dropped the bomb that made his audience gasp: "I can't tell you how proud I am of my wife and daughter for their faith and courage."

The victim was his daughter.

The well-known pornographer was Larry Flynt, who had offered a bounty for the rape of Keating's daughter.

The abduction took place just weeks after Keating had encouraged the successful prosecution that sent Flynt to jail. The war on porn was getting dangerous for Keating and his family.

Bob Hubbard, who was dating another of Keating's daughters at the time, said, "I remember a lot of security, police outside the house. I didn't know the specifics, but there was tension around that."

---

[71] "Pornographer Allegedly Incited Abduction, Rape Case In City," *The Cincinnati Enquirer,* May 24, 1977.

Hubbard, who married the Keating girl he was dating, later went to work for CDL and Keating. There was never any question in his mind or Keating's that Flynt was connected to organized crime figures across the river in Newport, who had already done much worse than rape for hire.

The Keatings soon moved to Phoenix, but Charlie did not back down in his battle against pornography. He turned up the heat like the Arizona sun. And that made him a threat to the porn industry and the Mob bosses who ran it.

At a 1982 convention of the Adult Film Association of America in New York, Keating and CDL were named as the top threat to the porn industry, and contributions were raised for a "war chest" to fight CDL. Some of the most famous First Amendment lawyers in the nation served as AFAA legal advisers—hired guns for the porn industry.

As they listened over lunch, a top porn industry lawyer spoke: "Five years ago, you could still depend on the ignorance and inexperience of local prosecutors to win you cases."[72] No more, he complained. CDL lawyers, carrying briefcases packed with evidence and legal precedents, met them in every town and slugged it out. The smut sellers were getting their clocks cleaned.

The CDL anti-obscenity SWAT teams knew who they were up against. Their opponents in court were the well-dressed, cleaned up, respectable new face of the Mafia. But behind the polished defense lawyers in their tailored suits were the same grubby gangsters who ran all the old rackets: illegal casinos, numbers games, bootleg booze, prostitution, heroin, "protection," cocaine, extortion, corruption of police and public officials, hijacking, black markets, loan sharking, sex trafficking, beatings, arson and murder.

The Supreme Court's landmark *Miller* decision on obscenity in 1973 had forced cities to set their own standards. Cincinnati no longer had to allow what Las Vegas or Times Square tolerated. But it was difficult and costly to draw the line on "community standards." The big-name lawyers for the porn industry, often treated as celebrities in the press,

---

72 AFAA Targets CDL, The National Decency Reporter, September-October, 1982.

made it difficult, costly and politically risky for local leaders to take a stand for decency. Politicians, afraid of being called "book burners" in local headlines, usually surrendered and did nothing.

"You can't legislate morality," was the anthem of the times. "It's a victimless crime," was its chorus. "Experts say porn is harmless and healthy," the headlines sang along. By putting the burden on local government to set standards, the *Miller* decision opened the floodgates to porn, and the Mob moved in. Sin strips spread to nearly every city and town like a sexually transmitted disease.

In response, Chicago, New York, Minnesota, Pennsylvania, Los Angeles and other cities and states launched special investigations of organized crime and pornography, attacking the growing decay not as a crusade for decency but as a battle against underworld crime and community blight. They all confirmed that pornography was a Mob racket.[73]

- In 1975, Los Angeles Police Chief Daryl Gates said that 95 percent of the hard-core porn and X-rated movies in America came from his city, and 90 percent of it was controlled by the Mob.[74]

- In 1978, the Washington DC Metropolitan Police Department issued a report finding "traditional organized crime ... did essentially control much of the major pornography distribution in the United States during the years 1977 and 1978." It concluded that the "large amounts of money involved, the incredibly low priority obscenity enforcement had within police departments and prosecutors' offices ... and the imposition of minimal fines and no jail time upon random convictions resulted in a low risk and high profit endeavor for organized crime figures."[75]

---

[73] Report of the Attorney General's Working Group on the Regulation of Sexually Oriented Businesses, June 6, 1989.

[74] *Final Report of the Attorney General's Commission on Pornography,* Rutledge Hill Press, 1986; Los Angeles Hearings.

[75] The lead detective for the investigation and report was Carl Shoffler, who had arrested the Watergate Hotel burglars in 1972.

- Also in 1978, the FBI reported that pornography was a major income source for organized crime, third behind gambling and drugs. By 1981, the Mob's porn profits were $8 billion a year.[76]
- In a Chicago courtroom, Los Angeles Mafia hit man Jimmy Fratiano testified that "large profits have kept organized crime heavily involved in the obscenity industry." He said, "Ninety-five percent of the families are involved in one way or another in pornography. ... It's too big. They just won't let it go."[77]
- Thomas Bohling of the Chicago Police Department Organized Crime Division, Vice Control Section, told the Pornography Commission that "it is the belief of state, federal and local law enforcement that the pornography industry is controlled by organized crime families. If they do not own the business outright, they most certainly extract a street tax from independent smut peddlers."
- In 1979, Phoenix found a new side effect of porn blight: the collateral damage of community decay. A city investigation reported that crime in "sin strips" was 500 percent higher, and sex crimes were ten times higher. So much for that glamorous Danish model.
- Indianapolis also noted alarming side-effects of sin strips: sex-related crime "including rape, indecent exposure and child molestation, was found to be 77 percent higher in those areas." Cincinnati Vice Squad Detective Thomas Streicher was right: "The perverts who are drawn to those places hurt children."
- A 1984 City of Los Angeles report said that Hollywood had eleven "adult" businesses in 1969; by 1975, there were eighty-eight. The police chief said, "Organized crime families from Chicago, New York, New Jersey and Florida are openly controlling and directing the major pornography operations in Los Angeles."

---

76   $25 billion in 2022.

77   Also known as "Jimmy the Weasel," he admitted killing at least five people, and became an informant after he was arrested for the 1977 Mafia bombing of Danny "the Irishman" Greene in Cleveland, a hit ordered by "Jack White" Licavoli of the Licavoli crime family that was linked to Ohio Governor James Rhodes by *Life Magazine* in 1969.

CHAPTER 10 • GETTING WISE TO THE WISEGUYS

Cities across America found shocking spikes in crime around "sin strip" blight. An example was Newport, Kentucky, where strip clubs and adult bookstores and theaters moved in after the Mob's gambling clubs were driven out. *The Cincinnati Post*, Kenton County Library

City after city and state after state reported the same symptoms: declining neighborhoods, falling property values and rising crime—a direct contradiction of the 1970 report that legal porn was "harmless" and even reduced crime.

The nation was finally getting wise to the "wiseguys" behind hard-core porn.

Crimes that came with the porn racket were right off the Mafia á la carte menu: murder, beatings, arson, extortion, prostitution, sex trafficking, sexual abuse, narcotics distribution, money laundering, tax violations, copyright violations (pirating) and fraud.

"Vice breeds vice," a Minnesota investigation by police, prosecutors and politicians concluded. Sin strips had turned middle-class neighborhoods into "war zones."

One name kept popping up wherever investigators followed the money: Reuben Sturman of Cleveland. The "Porn King" controlled half of all the sales of hard-core movies, peep-show machines and magazines in America, worth $8 billion. He was named repeatedly as an "organized crime" figure who was working with the nation's major crime families.

The Mafia in Ohio

In 1982, Ohio Governor James Rhodes formed a Law Enforcement Consulting Committee composed of sheriffs, police chiefs, state highway patrol, liquor control and prosecutors, to investigate and report on the presence and activities of organized crime in Ohio.

Rhodes was a big man with country boy charm. He liked to joke to reporters that his Eagle Scout opponent in a Republican primary was "the kind of guy who gets out of the shower to take a leak." When asked about his foreign policy, he replied, "Beat Michigan." He was not just the most popular Republican in Ohio; he was the most popular politician by far. Rhodes swept up newspaper endorsements as easy as he pocketed campaign cash.

But he seemed to be an unlikely crusader against the Mob. A 1969 article in *Life Magazine* showed that his investigation of organized crime might lead right back to his own desk: Rhodes himself had troubling links to Mafia bosses in Ohio.

The *Life* headlines said:

The Governor... and the Mobster
Leniency for a Hoodlum, Slush-Fund Income

Next to a big picture of a smiling Jim Rhodes holding a baseball bat and wearing a Cincinnati Reds cap, the magazine displayed prison mugshots of "one of the smartest and meanest Mob leaders in America," Yonnie Licavoli.

Ohio Governor James Rhodes in 1978 at a meet-and-greet outside the Cincinnati Club on Garfield Place in Piatt Park. His ethics and Mob connections were questionable, but his ability to get things done was not. Alex Burrows, *The Cincinnati Enquirer.*

Like the Mob boss of Newport and the Cleveland Four, Moe Dalitz, the Sicilian Mafioso Licavoli had been a member of the brutally violent Purple Gang in Detroit. In 1935 he was sentenced to life in prison for the murders of a rival underworld boss and three other men. Then in January 1969, Governor Rhodes suddenly reversed three decades of Ohio governors and commuted Licavoli's sentence to second-degree murder, making him eligible for parole. It was a curious about-face, reversing Rhodes's own previous rejection of parole for Yonnie.

Life reported one possible explanation: "For more than ten years it has been known in underworld and law enforcement circles that a quarter of a million unmarked Mob dollars existed in a 'spring Yonnie' fund, available to anyone who could facilitate his release."[78]

A spokesman for the governor tried to explain that Licavoli had been rehabilitated and was now "a different kind of man, cut free from bad associations, nonviolent and philosophically different." But that was spitball spin. Yonnie was still Yonnie. The younger brother of Cleveland and Tucson Mafia boss Pete Licavoli, and uncle to James "Jack White" Licavoli, Yonnie was still running numbers rackets from his prison cell in Ohio. His prison record was "in fact, outrageously bad," *Life* reported.

The story also revealed interesting news to most in Ohio: Governor Rhodes had a history of illegal slush funds that he dipped into for private clothing, houses, cars and other luxuries. The magazine found that Rhodes used $63,000 in campaign donations to build a house, and had to pay $85,000 in penalties for unpaid taxes.

Obviously, this was a politician who would get itchy fingers when the Mob offered $300,000[79] to "spring Yonnie."

When *Life* reporters visited his office to ask questions, Rhodes ducked into hasty meetings and avoided them. With so much support from the press in Ohio, "The governor is unaccustomed to coping with any sort of adverse publicity," the *Life* story said.

Then Rhodes reversed direction again and sent Licavoli back to prison from a hospital where he was staying after he faked a heart attack. A year later, when everyone had forgotten the national embarrassment of the *Life Magazine* story, the old gangster was paroled. But Rhodes paid the price, losing a primary for the U.S. Senate.

Rhodes sued *Life*, then dropped the suit. Forced out of office by term limits in 1970, he waited until 1974, then ran again. He sued the

---

[78] "The Governor and the Mobster," *Life Magazine,* May 2, 1969.

[79] More than $2.3 million in 2022.

State of Ohio to finally win an Ohio Supreme Court ruling that allowed him to be governor again without violating term limits. He won the race for governor by defeating Democrat incumbent John Gilligan of Cincinnati, and served two more four-year terms.

Against that backdrop, the governor's new organized crime task force in 1982 made sense—to repair his dented reputation with public relations Bondo.

When it was released, the Report to the Governor of Ohio on Organized Crime made fascinating reading.[80]

It began with an appetizer of state history about a Zanesville, Ohio bootleg liquor still, busted in 1935, that could turn out 5,000 gallons of 190-proof alcohol every twenty-four hours—all controlled by the Cleveland Four Mob, run by the boss of Newport, Kentucky and owner of the Beverly Hills Country Club in nearby Southgate, Moe Dalitz. Then the report connected the dots from Dalitz to organized crime in the 1980s.[81]

"These profiteers have continued to build their monopolistic organizations to the point that they now rape the Ohio economy for millions of dollars of untaxed revenue," the report began. "For the first time, these people and businesses are named in a widely encompassing public report."

It said the state was divided into seven La Cosa Nostra area codes: Toledo (Detroit LCN); Cleveland-Akron (Cleveland LCN); Steubenville (Wheeling, West Virginia Mob); Columbus (local organized crime groups affiliated with the Cleveland Mob); Dayton-Middletown (Toledo, Columbus and Cincinnati); and Cincinnati (Covington and Newport, Kentucky organized crime).

"Organized crime, the largest business in our free society, is thriving throughout Ohio," the report said. "Once thought to be only an

---

80 Organized Crime: report to the governor of Ohio, The Law Enforcement Consulting Committee, 1982.

81 Dalitz and his Cleveland Four Mob controlled or owned most of the illegal casinos and nightclubs in Newport until 1961, when Attorney General Robert Kennedy went to war against the mob, starting in Newport. Dalitz moved to Las Vegas where he built the first destination casino, the Desert Inn, and became the "Godfather" of Las Vegas. *Forbidden Fruit: Sin City's Underworld and the Supper Club Inferno,* Peter Bronson, 2000, Chilidog Press.

influence in northern Ohio, organized crime now has spread its tentacles, reaching out and impacting every corner of our state."

These were not the gangsters of the past in Newport, such as Dalitz, Red Masterson, Sleep Out Louie, Screw Andrews, Charles Lester, Tito Carinci and Pete Schmidt. The modern Mob families in 1982 had become "criminal cartels ... corporations of corruption, indeed, quasi governments."

For example, the report described how "24 bars, topless clubs, residences and a vehicle" were burned in Columbus as the Mob moved in to take over through "assaults and extortion." It said, "If the owner refused to sell, he was beaten or the bar was torched." At least two killings resulted. There were seventeen shell corporations skimming and laundering money. It was Newport all over again.

One of the Columbus adult nightclubs named in the report was Larry Flynt's Hustler Club. The headquarters of Flynt's growing magazine empire was also in Columbus, and he lived in the upscale Bexley neighborhood, making him a neighbor of the Ohio governor's mansion.

To illustrate the Mob's methods of political corruption, the report included the handwritten confession of James Traficant to the FBI: "During the period of time that I campaigned for sheriff of Mahoning County, Ohio, I accepted money from Orlando Carabbia, Charles Carabbia, Joseph Naples and James Prato. This money was given to me with the understanding that certain illegal activities would be allowed to take place in Mahoning County after my election, and that as sheriff I would not interfere with those activities."

Traficant was acquitted by claiming the bribes were part of his own "undercover investigation" of organized crime. He served as sheriff, then was elected to the U.S. House as a Democrat, representing Youngstown. He was re-elected four times but was expelled from the House in 2002 after he was convicted of racketeering, bribery and tax evasion. Even after that, many in withering, Rust-Belt Youngstown would have voted for him again anyway. "He may be a crook," voters liked to say, "but he's *our* crook."

The report also gave Ohio another reason to dislike the University of Michigan. Nearly all of the LSD in Ohio, it said, came from the same source: Ann Arbor.

And Ohio found what other states and cities already knew: The biggest Mafia pornographer in the state was Reuben Sturman, owner of Sovereign News in Cleveland, whose "empire is estimated to include fifty distribution companies and over 700 retail outlets throughout the United States, Canada and at least forty foreign countries."

Sturman was Cleveland's local godfather of porn, but he answered to the big bosses in the Gambino family in New York. In trial testimony, Sturman said the Cleveland Mob attempted to get a cut of his profits, but quickly backed off when the Gambino family said "hands off." For years, local prosecution of Sturman was handcuffed by an injunction from a federal judge who routinely blocked enforcement of obscenity laws.[82]

Sturman was finally convicted and sent to prison in 1995 after more than ten years of trials. At age 70, he was sentenced to twenty-nine years in prison for tax evasion (millions stashed in Swiss bank accounts), bribery, jury tampering (his young wife offered sex or cash to a juror) and extortion. At the time of his sentencing he was worth more than $100 million.

The son of Russian immigrants had started out selling comic books and candy. He said he never thought porn was wrong or right. It was "just a product to sell." He bragged that his enormous legal expenses were "just another cost of doing business."

And he could easily afford it. The markup on porn products, the report said, was 1,800 percent.

According to testimony by "Jimmy the Weasel" Fratiano, "When Sturman has a problem, he goes to DiBe." Robert DiBernardo, a.k.a. "DiBe," was a captain in the Gambino family—one of the ruling families

---

[82] One of Sturman's dealers, John Krasner, was called "the Prince of Pornography," who had a record of robbery, narcotics and gambling. He was backed by the Philadelphia Mob in a rivalry battle that included kidnapping, bombings and finally his Mob-style execution in 1979 in Fort Lauderdale, Florida. "Mafia & Porn," Kris Milligan, February 3, 2000.

in New York. "If DiBe wanted Sturman to do something, he would do it," the Weasel said.

DiBe's name would come up again later in the FBI's "Miporn" investigation of the Mob in Miami.

Cincinnati's Blue Angel Mob

The Cincinnati area "has several of the traditional (Mafia) persons of whom police are aware," the report said. One was "the son of an executed Mafia Don" who moved into Cincinnati from Buffalo, New York, and ran the biggest heroin ring in Ohio.

"Big Al" Anastasia, boss of the Mafia's Murder Incorporated.

The unnamed "Mafia person" in the report was Emberto "Little Al" Anastasia, son of "Big Al" Anastasia, a hit man for the Genovese crime family who was called "The Master of Murder" and "Lord High Executioner."

Big Al was executed in 1957 as he sat in a barber's chair at the Park Sheraton Hotel in Manhattan. The hit was ordered by Vito Genovese, police said.

The story of Big Al Anastasia's son in Cincinnati was more interesting than the governor's report let on. It began in 1960, when a bid was made to buy the Blue Angel night club at 608 Walnut. The place was a classy hotspot for jazz and comedy.

But one paragraph in a news roundup noted that Cincinnati Police were "disturbed" by the night manager of the Blue Angel—young Al Anastasia, 28.[83]

The buyer, Joe Bellamah, insisted Anastasia "will have no money in the venture," Al Schottelkotte reported in his *Enquirer* column, "Talk of the Town."

But Cincinnati Police Chief Stan Schrotel knew what the press did not: He blocked the liquor license and the truth came out. The money

---

83 "Monkey Business," Al Schottelkotte, *The Cincinnati Enquirer*, August 12, 1960.

for the purchase was supplied by Anastasia—part of the Genovese Mob, which was one of New York's most powerful crime families.

A front man, Bernie Fassler, put his name on the application and it was finally approved, but the "silent partner" who owned the club was still "Little Al" Anastasia.

"The first real sign of organized crime in Cincinnati that I became aware of was when Al Anastasia tried to buy the Blue Angel," former Vice Squad cop Jimmy Simon recalled. "Schrotel would not give him a license so he hired Bernie Fassler to be front guy. I know this story intimately and accurately because I got it directly by Bernie. Bernie was a fun guy but he always walked the edge of the line."

In April 1961, Anastasia bought Junior's restaurant across the street from the Blue Angel, at Sixth and Walnut. The sellers were Lee and Michael Comisar, owners of the famous five-star Maisonette restaurant. The "gangland" connection was no secret. It was mentioned in a story about the sale.[84]

One of the short-order cooks working in Junior's was James Perry Cravens, Simon said. "Al Anastasia was running drugs. JP Cravens could not even read or write, but his daily net was $20,000 on selling heroin.

"I worked that narcotics case. I had informants provide me with information about Cravens and Anastasia together. JP's girlfriend was Jackie Parmer, queen of all the drug dealers."

When Simon and the vice squad busted Cravens in 1971, the front page of *The Enquirer* showed a table covered with rows of shotguns, rifles and handguns seized at one of his houses. The raid on April 30 netted 27 ounces of heroin, bulk cocaine, 36 rifles and shotguns, 2 machineguns, 41 handguns, police radios and $35,000 in cash. Cravens went to court wearing a full-length mink coat. He had two Lincolns, two Cadillacs, three women—including Jackie Parmer—and four homes. On paper he owned a cleaning service, several pony kegs and bars and worked as manager of the Crown Bar on McMillan Avenue.

---

84 "Junior's Sold to Anastasia by Comisars," *The Cincinnati Enquirer*, April 18, 1961.

CHAPTER 10 • GETTING WISE TO THE WISEGUYS

In 2022, Simon looked back and laughed about how the stash of drugs and weapons was found. "Roger Hummeldorf (a vice cop) stumbled going up the steps. He was not the most athletic guy. And when he stumbled he found the false door in the steps that led to all the heroin and guns."

Cravens, who wore a mustache and an afro haircut with a big gold medallion around his neck, looked a bit like comedian Richard Pryor in photos taken as he was booked at the police station. He and thirty-six others were arrested on a 329-count indictment. Cravens posted a $500,000 bond, but was convicted in 1977 and sent to prison for forty years. The biggest Mob racket in Cincinnati was narcotics.

"JP wore silk shirts with fur collars from Rome. He was very street smart," Simon said.

Later, the Blue Angel was sold to Larry Flynt and became the Hustler Club. "There was just a line of crooks in that place," Simon said. He and the vice squad soon had their hands full dealing with Flynt.

Such as the night a cop on patrol saw a young woman on the street, crying and holding her face. He picked her up and took her to the hospital, where Simon interviewed her. "She told me the whole story, but refused to testify because she was terrified."

The woman told him she was working as a prostitute "dancer" for Flynt. "She went into the Hustler Club and tried to quit. They took her into the alley behind the place and threw acid in her face. They told her, 'Tell your friends this is what happens when you f--- with us.' I went down to the bar and tore the place apart. I wanted to make it clear to those guys we wouldn't put up with that stuff around here."

Like detectives Robert Meldon and Thomas Streicher Sr. before him, he was sending a message. "Most people today would not understand what it was like in the 1970s. I couldn't get away with that today," Simon said. "You had to be there, to live through it, to describe it."

Simon worked undercover on a Hamliton County-Cincinnati Police investigation of prostitution in massage parlors owned by Flynt in Ann Arbor, Michigan. "We made arrests, but nobody would testify against the Flynts. They were evil people. They would mess you up so fast. We knew those guys were as corrupt and crooked as organized crime could be."

The governor's report said Larry Flynt was connected to a Mob deal for vending machines in Dayton and Columbus. But by 1982, after Cincinnati's relentless court battles with Flynt, the report said adult bookstores, X-rated theaters, massage parlors and strip clubs "are not problems" in Cincinnati, "primarily because of the determined efforts of the Hamilton County Prosecutor (Si Leis)."

By comparison, Columbus had nineteen adult bookstores and topless bars.

"Cincinnati was our model," said Benjamin Bull, who traveled the country for CDL to help prosecutors battle the porn industry. "That was part of our message. Cincinnati had successfully eliminated all hard-core porn. It was banned, prohibited and prosecuted under existing obscenity statutes."

The CDL teams were in a legal arms race against the best lawyers the Mob could buy, constantly refining strategies and tactics, Bull said. "We were really in demand by local prosecutors. We taught the Department of Justice how to prosecute these cases."

He traveled as far as Hawaii to be a featured speaker at the American Bar Association convention.

"What really gave rise to the whole effort was Cincinnati. And credit for that goes to Carl Lindner, who supported it, and Charlie Keating. Before his reputation was tarnished, Keating was a driving force with a vision—to stop porn and rid communities of those bad elements."

Bull recalls a meeting in Keating's office that was interrupted three times in forty-five minutes by calls from U.S. Senators asking his support or advice. "He was well respected, prominent, beloved in many circles."

Bull and other CDL lawyers rarely lost in court. "But even if you prosecuted people like Larry Flynt and did not get a conviction, it was of huge value to bring what he was doing into the light of day, to galvanize opinion, show people who he was and force them to draw conclusions," he said. "Except among Flynt's very liberal friends in the media, most opinions about him were not favorable."

CHAPTER 10 • GETTING WISE TO THE WISEGUYS

What Charlie Keating and Si Leis started in their first prosecutions of *Vixen* in 1969 and Larry Flynt's *Hustler* in 1976 was now gaining national momentum. Keating and his CDL lawyers rescued declining cities, redeemed neighborhoods, restored quality of life, fumigated sleazy sin strips and put hard-core pornographers and sex traffickers behind bars.

But the cost was steep for Keating. He poured in his own money in the early years. His reputation was under constant attack, especially in the press. His children were threatened. His daughter was assaulted.

"Larry Flynt thrived on having enemies," Bull said. "If he didn't have them, he would create them. His number-one public enemy was Charlie Keating. And Charlie's number-one public enemy was Larry Flynt."

As their battle escalated, things were about to change radically for Larry Flynt. And Keating would get a powerful new ally: President Ronald Reagan.

Boogie Nights

11
Butchie, Rocco and Meese

In January 1972, two oily hipsters called "Butchie" and "Rocco" checked in to The Voyager Motel on Biscayne Boulevard in Miami. The Voyager had once been a glamour star among Miami hotels, designed by the same architect who created the swanky Fontainebleau Hotel. But the original 1957 Voyager, with its giant entry arch and Jetsons roofs, was now as dated as tailfins on a junkyard Cadillac. It had become the "Norma Desmond" of Miami hotels. Butchie and Rocco didn't care that it was a rundown rendezvous for one-night-stands, drugs deals and hookers. They just needed a room with a bed and heavy drapes.

Less than a week later, they left with enough "film in the can" to make the most famous porn movie of all time. They had no idea it would be so successful.

Their low-rent budget of $22,500 was financed by Butchie's father, Anthony Peraino, an underboss in the Colombo crime family in New York. "Butchie" was the street name of Louis Peraino. "Rocco" was

The Voyager Motel on Biscayne Boulevard in North Miami was showing its age by the time it became the filming location in 1972 for the most successful porn movie of all time. Wikimedia Commons, Library of Congress.

Gerard Damiano, who used the alias "Jerry Gerard" and appeared in the film credits as "Al Gork."

Their star was Linda Lovelace, whose real name was Linda Boreman. The movie was *Deep Throat*.[85]

The plot was about as sophisticated as a blue joke told by Redd Foxx. The dialogue could have been invented by illiterate mouth-breathers between bites of clam linguini in a Mob strip club—because it was. The roles were stock porno characters: "Bearded Man on Couch," "Nurse," "Delivery Boy." But critics were thrilled that it had dialogue at all. It was "the first stag film you could see with a date," according to popular film critic Roger Ebert, who apparently knew almost nothing about women or dating. He gave it two thumbs up.

According to the FBI, the film grossed at least $100 million. The Mafia producers claimed $600 million—because they used the movie to launder money through their X-rated theaters.

Deep Throat was rated in the top ten for earnings for seven weeks, outgaining nearly everything but the James Bond movie *Live and Let Die*. Truman Capote, Barbara Walters, Jack Nicholson, Frank Sinatra and Johnny Carson all boasted that they had seen it. Jackie Onassis, the gold standard for "in-crowd" fashion, went to the premiere. The *New York Times* newsroom staff watched it together.[86]

President Richard Nixon had just been re-elected on promises to restore law and order in the wake of race riots, anti-war protests, soaring crime and liberal courts that handcuffed the cops. *Escape From New York* became an instant cult classic for the way it depicted the dystopian future most of America expected. The "New Right" was on the rise, bringing a grass-roots backlash against chaos, rebellion and decadence.

But it was also the Golden Age of Porn, which had its own laundered alias: "Porno Chic." The most hard-core, XXX-rated pornography was now so mainstream, *Deep Throat* became a household name as the

---

85   "Organized Crime Reaps Huge Profits From Dealing in Pornographic Films," *The New York Times, October 12, 1975.*

86   Try to imagine how that would fly with the newsroom diversity committee today.

anonymous source for *Washington Post* reporters whose Watergate reporting helped to unravel Nixon's presidency.

The success of the movie shocked the world. And the Mob moved in like a predator smelling fresh blood.

The director was paid off with $25,000 — barely more than the cost to make the movie. Then he was muscled out by his Colombo crime family backers. Another porn producer who got in bed with the Mafia sympathized: "I made a deal with the devil. I got what I deserved."[87]

The star, Linda Lovelace/Boreman, did not even get that much. She was paid $1,250, which was taken away from her by her pimp and wife-beater husband, Chuck Traynor.

Later she would tell the dark and ugly story of what happened behind the cameras. "Virtually every time someone watches that movie, they're watching me being raped," she said. "It is a crime that movie is still showing; there was a gun to my head the entire time."[88]

In her 1980 autobiography, *Ordeal,* she described how she was forced by Traynor to make the movie:

> "When in response to his suggestions I let him know I would not become involved in prostitution in any way and told him I intended to leave, he beat me and the constant mental abuse began. I literally became a prisoner, I was not allowed out of his sight, not even to use the bathroom ... He listened to my telephone calls with a .45 automatic eight shot pointed at me. I suffered mental abuse each and every day thereafter. He undermined my ties with other people and forced me to marry him ... My initiation into prostitution was a gang rape by five men, arranged by Mr. Traynor. It was the turning point in my life. He threatened to shoot me with the pistol if I didn't go through with it. ... They treated me like an inflatable plastic doll, picking me up and moving me here and there ... they were playing musical chairs with parts of my body. I have never

---

87 "Porno Chic: Hard-core grows fashionable – and very profitable," Ralph Blumenthal, *The New York Times*, Jan 21, 1973.

88 "Why the new movie about Deep Throat could be important," Carolyn Bronstein, *The Atlantic*, January 7, 2013.

been so frightened and disgraced and humiliated in my life. I felt like garbage.

"I engaged in sex acts in pornography against my will to avoid being killed. The lives of my family were threatened."

The movie was not popular everywhere. Newport, Kentucky was once the "Sin City" of the Midwest in its glory days of Mob rule, where more than 300 prostitutes were counted in one mile and nearly twenty strip clubs and X-rated theaters lined the streets. But Newport reformers battled all the way to the Supreme Court to ban *Deep Throat* and dozens of copycat films like it.

In 1973 the FBI raided Cinema X in Newport and seized *Deep Throat*. Porn lawyers claimed it had "redeeming social value" as a type of "sex education." One "expert witness" even said it was sympathetic to women. Juries took a look and said, "Hell no." A judge who had to watch it wrote:

> "The film runs from one act of explicit sex into another, forthrightly demonstrating heterosexual intercourse and a variety of deviate sexual acts, not 'fragmentary and fleeting' ... it permeates and engulfs the film from beginning to end. The camera angle, emphasis and close-up zooms (give) maximum exposure in detail of the genitalia during the gymnastics, gyrations, bobbing, trundling, surging, ebb and flowing, eddying, moaning, groaning and sighing, all with ebullience and gusto. There were so many and varied forms of sexual activity one would tend to lose count of them."

In the Newport case, U.S. District Judge Mac Swinford fined the distributor, Harry Mahoney, $72,000 and sent him to jail for three months. Mahoney was a major pornographer from Durand, Michigan, known as the reclusive "Howard Hughes of Porn." He owned adult bookstores, peepshows, strip clubs and X-rated theaters all over the Midwest, including the Monmouth Street Novelty and Bookstore and Cinema X Theater in Newport.

A 1977 report by the U.S. Department of Justice showed his connections to La Cosa Nostra families: the Colombo family in New York and DeCavalcante family in New Jersey:

CHAPTER 11 • BUTCHIE, ROCCO AND MEESE

In the 1970s, the "sin strip" in Newport had 17 topless clubs, including Sparkle Plenty's on Monmouth Street. As the sign said, "No Experience Necessary – Will Teach." When Newport passed an ordinance requiring dancers to cover specific body parts, the dancers retaliated with transparent Band-Aids. *Cincinnati Post*, Kenton County Library archives.

> It is believed that Harry V. Mohoney of Durand, Michigan, is one of the largest dealers in pornography in the United States ... He is alleged to have a close association with the LCN. Colombo and the LCN DeCavalcante, both of which are very influential in pornography in the eastern United States. In Michigan, Mohoney is known to hire individuals with organized crime associations to manage his businesses (which) consist of sixty known adult bookstores, massage parlors, art theaters, adult drive-in movies, go-go type lounges and pornographic warehouses in Michigan, Indiana, Illinois, Kentucky, Tennessee, Wisconsin, Iowa, Ohio and California. He is involved in the financing and production of pornographic movies, magazines, books and newspapers.... He has a working relationship with DeCavalcante's representative Robert DiBernardo and has met with Vito Giacalone and Joseph Zerilli of the LCN Detroit.

Newport wasn't just battling porn. It was battling the Mob that had held the city hostage since the 1920s. After repeated setbacks, Newport won its court battle and closed down Cinema X in 1982. When the screen was taken down, police found hidden cameras that were aimed at the audience. They had been used to take pictures of local VIPs on both sides of the Ohio River that separates Cincinnati from Northern Kentucky—raw materials for extortion and public corruption.

By the early 1980s, feminist leaders Andrea Dworkin, Catherine MacKinnon and Gloria Steinem joined the anti-porn battle and protested that movies such as *Deep Throat* were degrading and cruel to women. They teamed up with Linda Boreman after her book came out. Super-lawyer Alan Dershowitz, who represented one of the porn actors in the movie, called them "feminist fascists."[89]

Once again, the Mafia deployed its platoons of high-cost litigators and buttered the courts with cash. Judges in obscenity cases suddenly caught "Newport Eye," blinded by liberal ideology or bribes. When a New York judge called *Deep Throat* "a nadir of decadence," ruled that it was obscene and imposed heavy fines, an appeals court reduced his fines and the press attention only fueled the popularity of the movie, proving the lesson that dates back to *Genesis*: Forbidden fruit is irresistible.

In fact, that was the business model for organized crime. It started with Prohibition, when gangsters cashed in on a thirsty nation's demand for bootleg booze. Then they added gambling, prostitution, loan sharking, corruption, extortion, numbers rackets, drugs, murder-for-hire and, finally, porn. After *Deep Throat,* a flood of similar Mob-financed movies made millions that were funneled back into organized crime.

An FBI informant reported a conversation in Peraino's office in Florida, where cash from the hit movie was pouring in. The informant told his handler, "You are not gonna believe this. We got so much damn money in the main office up here, we can't move around. The money is getting in the way. We got it in garbage bags stacked up in here. We don't even count it anymore.... We weigh it."

---

[89] In 2019, Dershowitz was accused of being one of the "clients" of the Jeffrey Epstein porn ring that was accused in court testimony of providing underage girls to various celebrities and VIPs including Bill Clinton, Bill Gates and Prince Andrew. Young women testified that they were used as "sex slaves" at Epstein's luxury estates or on his private jet, while Epstein made secret tapes for blackmail. Dershowitz was Epstein's lawyer. Epstein allegedly killed himself in prison, but the "suicide" was so brazenly phony it created a nationwide meme, "Jeffrey Epstein did not hang himself."

Some of the millions from porn movies was redirected into a "legit" Hollywood film company owned by the Mob that made more socially redeeming movies such as *Texas Chainsaw Massacre.*

Larry Flynt was beginning to look like a visionary—a trailblazing porn pioneer.

The Miporn sting

In 1976, a pair of Dade County (Miami, Florida) Sheriff's deputies opened a phony business in an airport warehouse, called Golde Coaste Specialties. On paper, they were selling blue jeans. But they let it be known they were in the mail order business for porn. The warehouse was wired for sound and video and the customers lined up. When they realized they had sharks on the line that they couldn't haul in, they called the FBI for a bigger boat.

Three FBI agents took over the sting operation, led by a veteran of the porn wars, Bill Kelly. It was named Miporn (Miami + porn). For almost three years, two of the agents traveled to Las Vegas, Honolulu and other cities and states, mingling with their new friends in the "adult" industry. They partied with call girls, drove rented Cadillacs and dressed like "made guys" in designer jeans, open collars, gold chains and flashy suits. Cocaine, sex and booze were all props for the roles they played as Mafia porn princes, like the *Donnie Brascos* of dirty movies.

On Valentine's Day in 1979, 400 FBI agents reeled in their catch: They served fifty-four search warrants on forty-four suspects in thirteen cities. One of the suspects had a heart attack when the feds showed up and caught him trying to destroy documents. He died, "saving the government a lot of money," an agent quipped.[90]

Like the Hollywood portrayal of FBI agent Joe Pistone *(Brasco)*, the Miporn agents struggled to negotiate their split personalities. One of them, Patrick Livingston, lived the Mob life so long he had delusions that he was "omnipotent and could get away with anything," a psychiatrist said. Welcome to Mob World.

---

90 "Firm Run by FBI Breaks National Smut Conspiracy," Charles R. Babcock and Scott Armstrong, *The Washington Post,* February 15, 1980.

His marriage fell apart and he was caught shoplifting in a department store. Lawyers defending the porn Mob gleefully seized on his troubles to attack Livingston's credibility as a witness. "I think it will make my job easier," said porn lawyer Herald Fahringer, who had previously defended Larry Flynt.

Sure enough, in December of 1982, a federal judge dismissed all forty-two indictments. In spite of incriminating tapes and solid evidence collected during the undercover operation, the judge said Livingston had "a serious credibility problem."

"There *is* a Santa Claus," Fahringer crowed as his Mob clients were set free.

The Supreme Court reversed the lenient federal judge in 1986, and reinstated some of the convictions. But the initial decision was typical of the "crime coddling" courts that caused a "law and order" backlash. There was no question the defendants were guilty.

FBI agent Roger Young, who worked on Miporn, said, "There is no such thing as 'just' an obscenity case. They ran into child pornography, stolen property, illegal weapons, money laundering, prostitution—many, many violations."[91]

The big Mob fish hooked in Miporn included the Perainos of the Colombo family in New York, who had bankrolled *Deep Throat*. The great white shark was Robert "DiBe" DiBernardo, a "respectable" family man in Long Island who coached Little League. His neighbors knew him as a "real estate investor." In fact, he was the boss of Star Distributors, the Mafia's biggest porn distributor on the East Coast.

More than that, DiBe was the boss of the underworld's porn industry nationwide. He answered to Gambino boss John Gotti, known as "the Teflon Don" for his miracle non-stick surface when it came to indictments.[92]

---

91   Interview with Roger Young, a retired FBI Agent who specialized in child pornography and obscenity cases, Morality in Media, Catholic News Agency, April 18, 2022.

92   DiBernardo's name made national headlines in the presidential campaign of 1980, when the Democratic Party's candidate for vice president, Geraldine Ferraro, was linked to DiBernardo through her husband.

In 1986, DiBe was awaiting trial on child pornography charges when he disappeared. The story of his murder came out in 1991, when "Sammy the Bull" Gravano turned against the Mob and revealed his role as a hit man for the Gambino and Colombo crime families.

Gravano said he murdered nineteen Mafia targets, including former Gambino boss Paul Castellano. His testimony that Gotti ordered him to kill DiBernardo finally convinced a jury to convict the Teflon Don of conspiracy to commit murder and other charges.

Gravano said that on June 5, 1986, he and another hit man he called his "Luca Brasi"[93] invited DiBernardo to a meeting in the basement of Gravano's construction company. Gravano's assistant hit man pretended to go for a cup of coffee, grabbed a gun that was hidden in a cupboard and came back to shoot DiBe in the back of the head.

DiBernardo's body was never found. But his neighbors who thought he was "in real estate" may have finally been right—at least by the Mob's definition, meaning buried in a landfill.

The Meese Report

The final report was 571 pages of research, hearings, legal analysis and testimony from victims of pornography. The press ridiculed it or ignored it.

The same year the Mob's porn boss was killed, President Ronald Reagan asked his Attorney General to launch a new investigation of pornography and organized crime in America, following a pattern established in the 1960s: Democrats in the White House ignored porn or worked to legalize it, while Republican Presidents investigated and prosecuted the porn industry.

In May 1986, eleven men and women of various eclectic backgrounds were asked to "determine the nature, extent and impact on society of pornography

---

93 From *The Godfather*, proving even Mob hit men like Mob movies.

in the United States and make specific recommendations to the Attorney General concerning more effective ways in which the spread of pornography could be contained, consistent with constitutional guarantees."

President Reagan's "Meese Commission" was born. It was an ordeal the members would never forget. They reported:

- "My knees buckled and tears came to my eyes."
- "I ask you, America, to strike the chains from America's women and children, to free them from the bonds of pornography, to free them from the bonds of sexual slavery..."
- "We can use this wonderful gift (of sex) to create or destroy, to rule or be ruled, to honor each other or debase each other."
- "A person who learned about human sexuality in the 'adults only' pornography outlets ... would learn that sex at home meant sex with one's children, stepchildren, parents, nephews, nieces, aunts, uncles and pets, with the neighbors, milkmen, plumbers, salesmen, burglars and peepers ... that people take off their clothes within the first five minutes of meeting one another...."[94]

Attorney General Ed Meese did not write or participate in the conclusions, but the results that came out in 1986 were called the Meese Report by the press, just as President Johnson's commission was named the "Nixon report." The Meese Report was a 580-page rebuttal to the discredited 1970 LBJ/Denmark commission that insisted porn was "harmless."

The seven men and four women who served on the Meese Commission for six years waded through dark, fetid swamps of soul-staining evil. Every creepy, slithering, sick fetish and perversion was examined and tagged for their report. They cataloged hundreds of smut magazines and more than a thousand films with titles that abused the imagination.

---

94 Final Report of the Attorney General's Commission on Pornography, Rutledge Hill Press, Nashville, Tennessee, 1986.

CHAPTER 11 • BUTCHIE, ROCCO AND MEESE

They did not rely on academic "experts" and social science professors imported from Denmark. They heard testimony from the American victims of child pornography, abuse, rape, prostitution and the porn industry.

"The incest started at the age of eight," one said. "My dad would say that if it was published in magazines that it had to be all right."

"Pornography was our textbook. We learned the tricks of the trade by men exposing us to pornography and us trying to mimic what we saw," said a former prostitute.

They heard from victims of "porn rape," abuse and coercion, whose stories sounded a lot like what Linda Boreman/Lovelace described during the making of *Deep Throat*.

The commission reported that at least 60 percent of the women used in pornography were victims of incest or childhood sexual assault. "They are frequently raped, the rapes are filmed and they are kept in prostitution by blackmail."

The Danish expert who claimed porn was harmless in 1970 was exposed as a fraud. "Rapists are fifteen times as likely to have had exposure to 'hard core' porn during childhood," the report said. Eighty-one percent of sex murderers interviewed by the FBI said their "biggest sexual interest was reading pornography." More than half of rapists said they were "incited to commit an offense" by porn.

The testimony from victims was shocking, graphic and heartbreaking.

Where the 1970 report could find "no evidence" that porn was connected to the Mob, the 1986 version cited dozens of studies and investigations by local law enforcement agencies that demonstrated almost complete control of the porn industry by organized crime.

FBI agent Bill Kelley, who led the Miporn investigation and others, said: "In my opinion, based on twenty-three years of experience in pornography and obscenity investigations and study, it is practically impossible to be in the retail end of the pornography industry without dealing in some fashion with organized crime."

They found that profits were as obscene as the movies. Magazines distributed by the Mob that cost fifty cents to produce sold for $10.

The report described the profile of the typical woman in a porn magazine or film: She started in prostitution when she was seventeen. She had run away from home to escape sexual abuse. She was a victim of "every form of rape, sexual assault and battery."[95]

The women whose images were sold in $10 porn magazines or in skin flicks made millions for the Mob, but were paid almost nothing. Many, like Linda Boreman, were forced, blackmailed, beaten or threatened to work.

Murder, arson, extortion and prostitution were attached to the porn business like fleas on a stray cat. Porn was getting more violent and more damaging to satisfy the insatiable demand by porn addicts for new thrills, the 1986 report warned.

And even then, porn was moving to new platforms on cable TV and video store rentals. That made the earlier 1970 report "starkly obsolete," the Meese Commission said.

President Johnson's 1970 panel of professors and ACLU lawyers had urged repeal of all porn laws and said everyone should be able to see whatever they wanted without regard to harming children.

The 1986 report urged immediate action to protect children with stronger laws. It said the growing pornography problem was aggravated by failure to enforce existing laws, and local prosecutors needed federal help because they were each trying to wage war against a well-financed national network of organized crime. That was the same thing Charlie Keating discovered and warned about back in 1969.

The 1970 commission held almost no hearings. The 1986 commission traveled from city to city for several public hearings and invited victims, the public and the press to attend and participate. Unlike the 1970 commission cloaked in *omerta* (silence), the 1986 group was transparent to the public.

And the national media responded with scorn and a shrug—the old Newport Eye. "Slouching toward censorship," was the headline over an

---

95 ibid

attack by the top lawyer at the ACLU.[96]

The only member of the legitimate press to regularly cover the Meese Commission meetings and hearings was syndicated columnist Michael McManus, who wrote the introduction to the report.

"I was shocked to discover that almost the only people I saw (at meetings) were writers for *Playboy, Penthouse* and *Forum* magazines and representatives of the ACLU," he wrote. "Therefore, it was no surprise that most reporting was shallow and quick to quote the predictable critics, such as the ACLU or *Penthouse* Publisher Bob Guccione."

The porn Mob put up $900,000 for a campaign to discredit the report.[97] That was not covered by the press, either. But when the report came out, most of the press was quick to scoff and dismiss it without reading it. What most Americans probably remembered from headlines about the report was the clever photo, carefully framed to show Attorney General Edwin Meese holding up a copy of the report in front of a twelve-foot statue of Lady Justice—which had one breast exposed. Not everyone in the Reagan administration was a great communicator. But manipulating one photo to ridicule years of thankless, traumatizing work by the commissioners was media malpractice.

It did not stop there.

Columnists said the commission report was "unscientific" because it did not include any of the 1970 social scientists and academic "experts," only direct testimony from actual victims of porn.

A typical editorial cartoon showed Meese on a ladder with a firehose, trying to put out the flame on the Statue of Liberty—obtusely equating porn with free speech.

An ACLU lawyer was widely quoted as saying the sky was falling and the Meese Commission wanted to take America to "the sexual Dark Ages."

---

96   SIECUS (Sex Information and Education Council to the U.S.) Report, May 1986, Barry Lynn, legislative counsel, American Civil Liberties Union.

97   Final Report of the Attorney General's Commission on Pornography, Rutledge Hill Press, Nashville, Tennessee, 1986.

Time Magazine fanned paranoia of "sex busters" and "a new moral militancy."

Porn had become partisan. The national porn speedometer would swing back and forth depending on who had their foot on the political accelerator in the White House. When Democrats had control, it was "Porn to be Wild." When Republicans took over, their goal was to make America "Porn Free."

Much to the dismay of the media, American voters had sent an unequivocal message in 1980 by dumping Democrat Jimmy Carter for Republican Ronald Reagan. And Reagan knew that the press did not speak for the people. He supported the Meese Commission by assigning a federal task force to ramp up prosecution of obscenity.

In 1987, President Reagan announced the Child Protection and Obscenity Enforcement Act, to "give our sons and daughters the simplicity and beauty that at American childhood should entail."[98]

Reagan put the focus on crime, by pointing out that "organized crime controls the vast majority of the multibillion-dollar obscenity market."

Jerry Kirk of College Hill Presbyterian Church in Cincinnati, president of the National Council on Pornography Abuse, was a leader in creating the nation's new laws to stop child pornography. "By declaring war on child pornography and illegal obscenity, the president takes the focus off censorship and puts it on enforcement of the law," he said.

Predictably, the press had panic attacks.

The *Washington Post*, for example, protested that prosecuting pornographers in multiple states at the same time was "unfair." From a story published on January 11, 1993, "U.S. Crusade Against Pornography Tests the Limits of Fairness":

- Meese set the tone for the Justice Department's anti-pornography crusade with his selection of prosecutors for the task force who had a special enthusiasm for obscenity cases.

---

98 Message to the Congress Transmitting Proposed Legislation on Child Protection and Obscenity Enforcement, President Reagan, November 10, 1987.

CHAPTER 11 • BUTCHIE, ROCCO AND MEESE

- The first director of the force was a prosecutor who had lobbied for anti-pornography legislation in North Carolina, and occasionally signed official correspondence "Yours Truly in Christ." Two lawyers hired had formerly worked for a militant anti-pornography group, the Arizona-based Citizens for Decency Through Law (CDL), founded by conservative Arizona financier Charles H. Keating Jr., who contributed part of his considerable fortune to fighting pornography. Keating since has been convicted of multiple counts of fraud in the unrelated savings and loan scandal.

- Although there was no formal relationship between the government and the now-defunct CDL, the organization from the early 1980s played a major role in conceptualizing the anti-pornography campaign, and some of its lawyers later helped carry it out as Justice Department officials. The group's causes and targets became virtually indistinguishable from those of the Justice Department.

The story also credited—or blamed—Bruce Taylor of CDL for suggesting tactics that some called "the most effective prosecutions in the history of the Department of Justice."

> In 1983, CDL general counsel Bruce A. Taylor wrote to Reagan describing his vision of a nationwide prosecution campaign against pornography, in which specific government attorneys in specially chosen locales around the country would be assigned the task of indicting pornographers.
>
> With the department's cooperation, Taylor—recently described by current task force head Patrick Trueman as one of the country's most effective experts in obscenity law—gave lectures to federal prosecutors in which he described them as "crusaders for morality," and coached them on trial tactics. He offered help with legal briefs and drew prosecutors' attention to potential witnesses willing to complain about pornography.

The *Post* story was typical of press coverage. To summarize the media indictment: Prosecutors who fought pornography were "enthusiastic." Some were Christians. CDL, from its humble start in Cincinnati, had become powerful enough to lead the way, eventually enlisting the help of the Department of Justice, thanks to President Reagan. And worst of all, the "crusade for morality" was effective.

As usual, press outrage was hypocritically selective. There were no similar objections when ACLU activists manipulated the 1970

The newsletter for Citizens for Decency Through Law circulated widely and reached as far as the White House, where it helped influence President Reagan, *the Washington Post* complained.

presidential commission to *legalize* pornography. There were no fussy complaints when oil or tobacco companies were prosecuted in multiple states. But having conservative, faith-based leaders involved in the battle for morality was sinister and "unfair."

Cincinnati Enquirer Editorial Page Editor Thomas Gephardt, a conservative known as "Mr. Whig," captured the media's attitude when he wrote that it was "infinitely pleasanter to have leprosy than it is to utter a few kind words for the Attorney General's Commission on Pornography."

The strategy of press critics, he wrote, was mockery ("Who wants to be laughed at?"); name-calling ("hypocrite," "fanatic" or "busybody"); amateur psychology ("There's something 'wrong' with anyone who makes an issue of pornography"); and insinuation ("speculating on the pornography collections assembled by anti-pornography crusaders").

"So you see, your peace of mind will be infinitely better served if you simply ignore the pornography issue," Mr. Whig concluded. "Only your conscience will suffer."

He was right. But most of the press chose to ignore the ugly side of pornography, without any apparent incontinence of the conscience.

Ironically, one of the songs on the soundtrack for *Deep Throat* was titled, "I Wanna Be Your Slave." It should have set off alarm bells about the women and children who were being forced into bondage as sex slaves of the porn industry. But the press and the ACLU were too busy making fun of that "pair of boobs," Ed Meese and Lady Justice.

NOT IN OUR TOWN · PETER BRONSON

Stairway to Heaven

12

In Walked Jesus

A rabbi, a Catholic priest and an Episcopalian pastor go into a bar....

Larry Flynt could have been telling a dirty joke or describing a cartoon for the next issue of *Hustler*. Magazine staffers who were gathered for their editorial planning meeting leaned in and wondered, *Where's the punchline?*

"There will be a rabbi there and a—what's that religion that starts with an 'E,'" he asked in his gravelly smoker's growl.

"Episcopalian."

"Right, an Episcopalian priest."

It was no joke. Flynt was describing his vision—no, *revelation*—for a new, born-again version of *Hustler*. The meeting was described by Rudy Maxa in a *Washington Post* story on January 8, 1978, "Hustling for the Lord."

"But I don't want you to think I'm going to sit down with biblical scholars and let them run the magazine," Flynt said as the staff squirmed and bridled. "I'll use them for reference. If I have any questions I'll just fall right down on my knees and ask Him what to do."

So, no punchline. He's serious. And who's the publisher? A panel of holy men or God Himself?

There would be no more photo "spreads" of women alone, he told them. Sex would hereafter be presented in a "natural, healthy way," with a man included.

Cartoon character "Honey the Hooker" would be just "Honey," about "a woman coping with the neuroses of society," Flynt said.

As the staff grumbled and started to protest, Flynt stood up and started passing out orange pamphlets. "Look," he said, "I want you to go to your rooms and read this."

His wife, the new $500,000 publisher, started to ask, "What about the cartoons—"

"I can't, not now," Flynt cut Althea off. "Look, I want you to go to your rooms and read this. There's no use talking about something when you don't know what you're talking about."

What he was talking about was a brochure from the Christian Patriots, a group that promoted "Christian Nationalism" to oppose government sabotage of liberty and natural rights in the Constitution. The orange pamphlet urged followers to take a urine and saliva test that claimed to diagnose current and future diseases, even cancer. There was no mention if the test could diagnose lunatics.

It was December 2, 1977, just nine months after Flynt's conviction on obscenity and organized crime charges in Cincinnati. Set free on bail during his appeal, Flynt had flown his staff and the author of the pamphlet to Colorado Springs, and wanted all his staffers to take the Christian Patriots urine tests.

The staff adjourned to read the pamphlet and returned in only a few minutes. The verdict was a hard "No." They refused, citing their own natural rights and employment contracts. They also may have been worried about the inventor of the miracle test, who was in prison for practicing medicine without a license.[99]

Who is this Bible beater pretending to be Larry Flynt? they must have wondered.

It was definitely not the Larry Flynt who was the darling of the liberal press and intellectual elites. Not the guy who smoked six packs of cigarettes and drank a fifth of scotch every day. Not the guy who bragged about bedding a dozen women a week, every week, claiming 6,000 women over ten years. This new holy-roller Flynt was not the guy who was celebrated as a martyr by Norman Mailer and Woody Allen. Not the guy who became a heroic defender of the First Amendment to the left.

---

[99] "Hustling for the Lord," Rudy Maxa, *The Washington Post,* January 8, 1978.

CHAPTER 12 • IN WALKED JESUS

This guy was talking about his "calling" to recruit more Christian Patriots—a group so far right they made Simon Leis sound like Simon & Garfunkle.

The new Larry Flynt had a vision from God: He would publish a *Hustler Magazine* that would be popular with 1.8 million subscribers who lusted for smut—*and still* be acceptable to devout Christians. It was truly a "Mission Impossible," like attempting to mix fire and dynamite without an explosion, or building a church shared by Orthodox Jews and Islamic Fundamentalists. The whole world watched in disbelief as Flynt launched his new "born-again" *Hustler* with "new and improved" Christian smut.

"First Born Again Issue!" proclaimed the July 1978 cover, featuring naked Adam and Eve from the backside, surrounded by a lion, a horse, an ox and a wolf, all staring at the nude couple like *Hustler* subscribers ogling a centerfold: "Genesis: Shocking Look at the Garden of Eden."

Any clueless Christians who bought it looking for devotionals would be disappointed to find the usual poster-sized foldout of a nude couple in energetic positions, articles promoting masturbation, and the regular amateur-hour "Beaver Hunt" pictures that were sent in by readers for a $50 bounty. The only noticeable difference: The captions under pictures of female masturbation were written "in consultation" with

Biologist and psychologist Alfred Kinsey was a thoroughly creepy man. His research on human sexuality was later debunked as fraudulent and flawed, but it made a big splash in the 1950s, used as ammunition for the 'anything goes' sexual revolution that Kinsey and his team led by example. Wikimedia Commons, public domain.

real "experts," including a PhD coauthor of the widely publicized 1948 Kinsey Report on sexual behavior that fraudulently presented prison inmates—including rapists and child molesters—as representative, normal, healthy Americans.[100]

What in the Wide World of Sports had happened to Larry Flynt?

Newspapers nationwide sent reporters to find out. Few had as much access as Flynt's friend Maxa. But they all told mostly the same story about Flynt being "brought to Jesus" by President Carter's sister, the evangelist Ruth Carter Stapleton. Johnny Cash and comedian Dick Gregory had supporting roles, like apostles who passed baskets at the miracle of loaves and fishes.

It was great copy, but not the whole story. Stapleton may have been the "closer," but the conversion of Flynt began earlier.

In the beginning, the mustard seeds of Larry Flynt's faith were planted when he met The Reverend Bob Harrington, known in New Orleans as "The Chaplain of Bourbon Street." They hit it off like Jack Daniels and Coke. Skeptics nodded and figured, "It takes a hustler to know one."

Reverend Bob was a regular guest on TV talk shows hosted by Merv Griffin and Phil Donahue. He wore tailored suits, designer ties and flashed more gold rings, diamonds and bracelets than King Solomon's pawnshop. "God wants you to have the very best of everything in life," he liked to say—which sounded a lot like God wanted *him* to have the best of everything.

When it was suggested that famous atheist Madalyn Murray O'Hair

---

[100] Kinsey documented graphic child sexual abuse by working with—and not reporting—serial pedophiles. He wrote in one of his reports, "It is difficult to understand why a child ... should be disturbed" by being molested or looking at adult nudity. "According to one biographer, 'Kinsey decreed that within the inner circle men could have sex with each other; wives would be swapped freely, and wives, too, would be free to embrace whichever sexual partners they liked.' Kinsey himself engaged in various forms of heterosexual and homosexual intercourse with members of the Institute staff, including filming various sexual acts in the attic of his home." "Alfred Kinsey: A Brief Summary and Critique," Alan Branch, The Ethics and Religious Liberty Commission, May 21, 2014.

knew more scripture than Reverend Bob, he quipped, "But I know the author."[101]

The Reverend Bob's friendship with Flynt blossomed. He agreed to be interviewed for an issue of *Hustler*. And Flynt attended one of Reverend Bob's tent-revival "Think Positive" rallies, where he joined speakers onstage such as Paul Harvey and President Carter's best friend, the scandal-clouded banker Bert Lance. Flynt only received "polite applause" from the Christian crowd for his rambling unprepared remarks, reports said. But he was so impressed by the event he bought Reverend Bob a $155,000 motor coach, "To drive across America and make people feel good," according to an inscription on the side of the bus.

"That's when I knew something was happening," Reverend Bob said after getting the free bus, "because the Bible says a man's heart is where his treasure is." Reverend Bob made sure his treasured golf clubs rode on the bus too.[102]

The Lord works in mysterious ways his wonders to perform.

And nothing was more mysterious than Larry Flynt's conversion on the weekend before Thanksgiving in 1977, on a private jet flying from Columbus, Ohio to Colorado Springs with his new best friend Ruth Carter Stapleton. They were introduced by a *60 Minutes* producer, and Stapleton invited Flynt to dinner with her husband at their country club. They stayed up and talked long into the night—while others at the country club probably stayed awake long into the night wondering what they had seen: *Was that the Smut King with the evangelist?*

In *The Washington Post*, Maxa quoted Flynt's description of his rebirth in Christ.

> The feeling began as a warm, tingling, powerful sensation. Flynt could feel a slightly medicinal taste rising from his throat. He was frightened but outwardly calm as the vision appeared: a man laughing heartily and calling himself Paul stood with Jesus Christ.

---

[101] Chaplain of Bourbon Street Dies at 89, Baptist Press, July 5, 2017.

[102] "Hustling for the Lord," Rudy Maxa, *The Washington Post*, January 8, 1978.

> "I promised to give up my wife for Him," Flynt said. "I promised to see myself castrated, to look down and see myself with no sexual organs and look up and say, 'Yes, God, it's okay, if that's Your will, that's fine.' I spoke in tongues. There were animals eating at my neck, like baboons and monkeys, gnawing at me. He told me my calling: to bring peace on earth. And He told me there had been a distortion of His Word, which confirmed my thing on religions but only one God...."

It lasted for hours.

Suddenly, Larry Flynt was in demand from a different crowd. His invitations to speak about the First Amendment at universities were now replaced by phone calls with Johnny Cash and former Watergate conspirator Chuck Colson, who had started a prison ministry after serving time in a federal prison himself. Flynt went on Jim Bakker's *PTL Club* TV show. He gave his testimony of personal salvation at Braeswood Assembly of God Baptist Church in Houston, Texas, with Stapleton at his side. He told about his vision of the Apostle Paul with Jesus as he prayed on the plane. He said he was delighted to realize that if a notorious sinner such as Paul could persecute Christians and still be forgiven, there was hope for Larry Flynt, who called himself "the worst of the worst."

Pastors, priests and rabbis debated and watched the epic spiritual battle for the soul of Larry Flynt. Was it real, or another publicity stunt? Could someone who was so deep in darkness step into the light? Would the dark side surrender without a fight?

"The whole world is watching for me to fall from grace," Flynt said. And like a man on a highwire, he put on a thrilling show for the crowds watching below. He windmilled his arms, flailing for balance; each wobbly toddler step was greeted by cheers and jeers as he gyrated to regain his footing—one step forward, another two seps back....

He announced he would need a bigger jet for his new mission from God. His old $2.2 million Israeli-built Jet Commander, called the "Pink Panther" or the "Pepto Bismol Jet," would not be big enough to carry all his new friends, evangelists, born-again celebrities and Christian Patriots. He needed a Boeing 727, he said.

CHAPTER 12 • IN WALKED JESUS

But then he announced that it had to be painted pink again, to remind everyone of the code word for the extra-porny photos that set *Hustler* apart from *Playboy* in the skin magazine trade.

But wait, there's more... in that pink plane, the very vehicle for Flynt's spreading empire of porn, he would hang an oil painting given to him by Stapleton: Jesus laughing.

He decreed, "We will no longer hang women up like pieces of meat." Then he put the quote on the cover of *Hustler* next to a photo showing the bottom half of a naked woman, upside down in a meat grinder—displayed as a piece of meat being shredded into sausage.

Just weeks after his widely publicized salvation, he stopped in at his old hangout, The Brass Mule strip club in Newport, Kentucky, to watch a performance by "Morganna" the Kissing Bandit, who became famous when she ran onto the field during a Cincinnati Reds game to kiss Pete Rose. Flynt said he saw no problem with visiting a strip club. "There are more integrated bordellos than churches," he said.[103]

He talked to Stapleton almost daily and praised her for leading him to salvation. But then he ran a cartoon cover showing her brother, President Carter, looking at *Hustler* with his eyes popping. "The President's Sister Shows Pink," the cover said.

Jesus wept.

Larry's magazine staff and his old friends were freaking out. He was acting bughouse crazy. He adopted a health-food organic diet and fasting routine recommended by Dick Gregory. After mocking and hating politicians for years, he spent $200,000 on ads nationwide to seek prayers for Senator Hubert Humphrey, who was dying of cancer. He gave the staff $650,000 in bonuses and surprised Althea with a $275,000 house in Evergreen, Colorado for Christmas. He talked about plans to publish an illustrated Bible, and wanted to produce a Christian version of the popular TV miniseries *Roots*. He called himself "the eighth wonder of the world."

---

103 "Flynt Views Morganna, but Sees No Conflict," Norm Clarke, *The Associated Press,* February 17, 1978.

Then, just before Christmas, a month after his public conversion, the inner circle staged an intervention. "Larry Flynt's family had a different sort of holiday surprise in mind," *Columbus Monthly* reported.[104] "They were completing arrangements to have Flynt locked up and committed" because of his "increasingly erratic, unpredictable behavior."

Althea angrily denied being involved. Larry fired his brother Jimmy, "Because he could not accept my conversion to Christ." The effort to legally declare him incompetent was abandoned and Flynt called a top-level meeting to announce that, "I'm Larry Flynt and I'm back. I'm going to run this company and no one else is. I pay you good wages and I demand loyalty to *me*. There are plots going on in this company. There are conspiracies going on behind my back."[105]

To most of the world, the old Larry Flynt who sold his soul to make millions by exploiting naked women was completely "sane." But the new Flynt who turned his back on that to be forgiven by Christ was "nuts."

Althea Flynt in 1977. She denied being part of an attempt to have Larry committed for his 'increasingly erratic' behavior. Bob Free, *The Cincinnati Enquirer.*

---

104 *Columbus Monthly,* June 1978.

105 "Did Flynt's Family Try to Commit Him?," syndicated columnist Bob Greene, June 14, 1978.

CHAPTER 12 • IN WALKED JESUS

Skepticism of his conversion stuck like gum on a shoe. Reports said the White House believed that President Carter's sister was being hustled for publicity. Others speculated that she was hustling Flynt for contributions to a religious retreat she was building in Dallas.

Althea's reaction ranged from diffident to indifferent. She fell asleep while Larry discussed the Bible with his new friends. When she saw Christians greeting Larry at an airport, she was overheard saying, "Oh, no, they're going to try to convert me." Her attempts to read scripture with Larry were derailed because he couldn't resist focusing on the "begats" and who "knew" each other. The King Larry Version of the Bible always seemed to be X-rated.

While Larry was on a mission from God, Althea stepped in as the new publisher of the expanding Flynt empire that included *Hustler,* the even more crude *Chic* skin magazine, mainstream *Ohio Magazine,* and *Slam,* a humor magazine vying to compete with *Mad Magazine* and *National Lampoon*. Her idea of a "bottom line" was entirely different from Larry's. Where he was obsessed by pink, she focused on green.

After watching the reaction to the born-again *Hustler*, Althea said, "In walked Jesus, and out walked millions."

Reeling in the Years

13

'The Wizard of Odds'

THE CINCINNATI ENQUIRER, 1978—Jake felt like Lloyd Bridges in *Sea Hunt*. He was diving deeper and deeper into his research, down into the weedy, dark sea floor of local headline history. Then, just as he spotted a treasure chest of gold in a sunken shipwreck... the phone rang and he had to come up for air.

We will return after these messages, he thought, reaching for the phone.

It was Jim Gardner. "What are you working on for tomorrow?"

"It's that file you gave me, the 'Brains Beckley' clips."

"That's what you get for asking about the Newport College of Criminal Knowledge," Jim said. "Sounds like fun. Sort of makes Screw Andrews look like a farm club rookie, right?"

"Fun like quicksand. Here I was, all set to write an easy little column about the mismanagement of the Ohio Lottery and now I'm so deep in the background jungle I need Tarzan to throw me a vine."

"I'm pretty sure Cheetah works in sports, so the Ape-Man must be swinging around there somewhere. When you're done with him send him to the Copydesk. We're ass-deep in alligators."

"What's going on?"

"Clarabell threw a donut at Cliff the editorial writer in the break room."

"Clarabell" was Karen Bell, who thought she was the newsroom's gift of Gloria Steinem. She wore her hair in a reddish-blond frizzy shrub that could have been an "afro" if she were black. One day she walked past the Copydesk in a tie-dyed, billowy blouse over awning-striped elephant bellbottom jeans. Judy took a long look and said one word that stuck like superglue: "Clarabell." The clown on morning TV.

Jake secretly thought Clarabell wore miniskirts just so she could mutter "Chauvinist pig!" whenever a guy made the mistake of looking at her legs or holding a door. So he always made sure to hold a door for her. Her angry glare was worth it every time.

Karen spent more time meddling in other people's work than covering her own beat as the "Environmental Reporter," and came to the newsroom every day determined to make the world a better place—but only according to her own blurry blueprint. Her heart bled for the Vietcong, stray cats and starving Africans, but not necessarily in that order. Punch insisted she probably would run over fifty starving Ethiopian refugees with a firetruck to save one kitten in a tree. Her assignment as courts reporter had been suddenly adjourned when Jim noticed that in Karen's stories, every cop was a criminal and all the criminals were saints.

But she was president of the Cincinnati Journalists' Chapter of the National Organization of Women (CNOW), which was a smart career move. The meetings only drew a handful of frowning feminists and one lonely, hopeless TV weatherman. But the corporate executives who were taking over *The Enquirer* were terrified of CNOW and all the other grievance groups, so they had imposed "hiring targets"—a.k.a. unethical, illegal affirmative action quotas—for "women and other minorities," stubbornly ignoring the fact that women were not a minority. The quotas were poison for newsroom morale, but the cash incentives for Gannett news executives who filled their quotas were irresistible. So Clarabell was fireproof.

"Good thing it wasn't Murray the atheist," Jake said. "He would bean her with a fritter. And how can anyone get mad at Cliff? He's so mild mannered he makes Don Knotts look like Dirty Harry with road rage."

The editorial department was a quiet refuge of thoughtful discussions and well-reasoned opinions—also known as God's Waiting Room or The Gray Lady's Graveyard—where nice, unremarkable and cooperative reporters went to await retirement. But the conservative voice of unsigned editorials on the "publisher's page" caused a simmering hostility among anti-establishment reporters and editors, who believed the First Amendment was written with a loophole: "This offer not available for 'right wing' opinions." Reporters retaliated by putting a brick on the left side of the scales—and they outnumbered editorial writers 20 to 1.

"What set her off?" Jake asked.

"She objected to an editorial that endorsed the death penalty for those guys who killed that Cincinnati cop, Charles Burdsall. Cliff politely suggested that she could write a letter to the editor."

"Let me guess. I'll bet she said, 'That's not funny.' Like that joke: 'Question: How many feminists does it take to change a lightbulb? Answer: That's not funny.'"

Jim laughed. "She told him she was embarrassed that she worked for a newspaper that supported capital punishment."

"What did Cliff say?"

"He said, 'That makes two of us. I'm embarrassed you work here too.' And that's when she hit the launch button."

"Glazed or jelly? Did she hit him?"

"Raspberry-filled. She missed and hit the wall. The breakroom looks like the scene of an aggravated homicide. Cliff got flustered and said, 'You couldn't hit a rock with the broad side of a barn.'"

"Nice line. I'll bet we see that in an editorial one of these days. I didn't know Cliff had that in him. Might be the first time the editorial staff finished an opinion with something besides 'we can only hope' or 'time will tell.'"

"Could be. But right now I can only hope that time will tell me about your column for tomorrow. What happened at Silly Hall?"

"Compared to the battle of the breakroom, it was a yawner. They had some three-piece suits visiting from Las Vegas to make a pitch for casinos in Ohio. The mayor was almost as excited as that time he thought a voting machine was an ATM for votes."

"Las Vegas? Sounds like the syndicate boys are getting serious. Were they wearing fedoras and overcoats with wide lapels?"

"Actually, they looked more clean-cut than a brand manager at Procter & Gamble. Conservative, tailored suits, every blow-dried hair in place, no pinkie rings or violin cases. When they promised millions in tax revenue, I thought half the council members would jump over the table and give them a big sloppy kiss."

"And we need casinos because the state lottery has done so well at improving education?" Jim asked, imitating Johnny Carson making fun of President Carter in the plummy voice of "Art Fern."

"Exactly. Test scores are worse. And the schools still demand tax hikes at every election. Unless a lot of losers have learned the hard way to quit buying lottery tickets, I don't think it has done anything at all for education. But all the politicians say it's for the children."

"So anyone who raises questions must hate kids and teachers," Jim said. "Only a fool would dare."

"Like me," Jake said.

"Sounds like the clips I gave you could be helpful. Beckley was a man ahead of his time," Jim said. "They called him 'The Wizard of Odds.' If he was running the lottery, all the teachers would be driving Cadillacs and they wouldn't have to worry about student test scores. They could send them all to Yale and Harvard."

"God help us if that happens. If our new managing editor brings up his 'Harvard College' degree one more time in a staff meeting, I think I will barf. One of those nitwits is three too many."

Jim didn't disagree, but said, "Look, what I called about, in case you want to jump on it, Larry Flynt just got shot in Georgia."

Jake paused to take a sip of coffee. He could hear Jim's Zippo clicking shut on the other end of the line as he lit a cigarette. Jake said, "Yeah, Jerry Lamprey stopped by to tell me. He's sure some Christian redneck Republican did it. His words, not mine."

"Who knows," Jim said, "Flynt seems to have a talent for making enemies. Did you hear that he went down to Georgia and rented a bookstore to sell his crotch novels, just to stick a thumb in the eye of the local prosecutor? He stood on the courthouse steps and called the prosecutor a jerk. I think he was begging to be prosecuted to get more attention. And now this. I guess he got the wrong kind of attention this time. Be careful what you ask for..."

"Didn't he say the other day that he felt safer in Georgia than he did in Cincinnati? Talk about irony," Jake said. "Jerry says when they find the guy who shot Flynt, Si Leis will have him extradited to Cincinnati—just so he can give the shooter a medal for public service."

"That's why Jerry works in the toy department with Tarzan and the other sportswriters."

"Well, I figured he should know because he's spent more time at the Hustler Club than some of the dancers."

"And here I thought Jerry spent every waking moment in meetings so he can listen to the sound of his own voice agreeing with management."

"Yeah, what's with all the meetings lately on diversity and inclusion? They make it sound like a cult religion. I'm always afraid they will start passing out the Jim Jones Kool-Aid."

"My theory," Jim said, "is that newspapers have meetings because they can't pick their nose. That's the polite version, just in case someone from the diversity and inclusion police is listening."

"So if I write about Flynt tomorrow, do I have to go to a news meeting to discuss it?"

"The Magic Eight Ball says, 'Signs point to yes.'"

"Then I think I'll take a pass on the Flynt shooting until we get some better sources than Jerry."

"You'll never get anywhere in the idiot-orial game if you wait for facts," Jim said. "Personally, I can't wait to hear what Gil Beckley would say about new casinos brought to you by the same mobbed-up guys who made Newport the national headquarters of layoff betting."

"Too bad he's not around to tell us since he inconveniently got whacked. And I don't think there's much public appetite for casinos after what happened at the Beverly Hills Supper Club last Memorial Day."

"Forget about all that local Mob history of arson and murder," Jim said, using his facetious Art Fern voice again. "It was an accident. Or wiring. Or something. All the experts are sure that forty years of organized crime had nothing to do with it."

Jake smiled. The Supper Club fire was one of their favorite subjects. Jake's father wouldn't talk much about it much, except to say it was just another Mob nightclub burnout gone wrong. And his father would know. He changed the subject. "Hey, Jim, speaking of the sensitivity police, do you think they will tear down the latest busted heads in the break room?"

"You mean the traffic report, 'Teenager Rear-Ended by Priest?' That was good."

"And here's one from yesterday's *Post*," Jake said. "Some guy assaulted a cop when his wife got busted for smoking pot at a rock concert. The headline says, 'Loveland Man Can't Handle Wife's Bust.'"

"Damn," Jim said. "Sometimes I wonder if copy editors do those on purpose. Look, I gotta go. But next time I see Jerry headed for your office, I'll wait five minutes and give you an escape call."

"Great idea," Jake said. "I'll do the same for you. Just say, 'Sorry, Jerry, I gotta take this call and it could take a while.' Perfect. If you see any flying donuts, don't forget to duck."

Jake hung up the phone and turned back to the clips. He picked up a story from *The Miami Herald* dated 1965.

Gil 'The Brain' Beckley

"King of the Layoff Bettors Lives in Miami Too," the headline said. It was written by Hank Messick, the fearless *Louisville Courier-Journal* reporter who covered the Mob in Newport like Marilyn Monroe's skintight sequined dress when she sang "Happy birthday, Mr. President." It left just enough to the imagination to make your eyes pop.

Messick had followed the mobsters to Miami when Newport was fumigated after the Ratterman blowup.

Next to headlines about the Pope meeting LBJ and "Battle Flares in Vietnam," Messick reported that the whole Newport gang had relocated to Miami, except for Cleveland Four boss Moe Dalitz, who lived in his Las Vegas casino-hotel, the Desert Inn. By 1965, the old Dalitz gangsters Morris Kleinman, Sam Tucker, John Croft, Trigger Mike Coppola and Gil Beckley were running a national gambling syndicate out of the Fontainebleau Hotel.[106]

---

106 "King of Layoff Bettors Operates in Miami Too," Hank Messick, *The Miami Herald*, September 19, 1965.

CHAPTER 13 • 'THE WIZARD OF ODDS'

Newport Police raided a betting ring at Eighth and Monmouth in 1950 and found a snarl of telephone lines. The operation was probably part of the national layoff-betting empire run for the Mob by the Wizard of Odds, Gil Beckley. Herb Heise, *The Cincinnati Enquirer.*

Newport, which had reported $7.5 million in *reported* wagers in 1960, according to IRS records, had dropped to $2.2 million after the "underworld figures" left town, while Miami betting suddenly exploded as soon as they landed in Florida like migrating buzzards.

That gambling surge was mainly Beckley, who fled Cincinnati and Newport on May 9, 1960—the morning after the George Ratterman frame-up backfired on the Mob. And look who was sitting at the next

George Ratterman was a star quarterback at Notre Dame and played in the NFL before he ran for sheriff. The Newport, Kentucky Mob tried to destroy him with knockout drops and a stripper, but it backfired.

table when mobster Tito Carinci put chloral hydrate knockout drops in Ratterman's scotch-and-soda at the Terrace Hilton in downtown Cincinnati: Gil Beckley.[107]

In a sidebar, Messick provided a glossary of Mob lingo: "ACTION: Gambling, crooked or otherwise. COUSIN: Telephone company employee who fraudulently arranges long-distance service for gamblers. LAYOFF BETTING: Procedure whereby bookmakers insure their bets by sharing them with other gamblers who have bigger bankrolls. RATTERMAN COCKTAIL: A drink containing knockout drops."

Jake wondered what would happen if he ordered a Ratterman Cocktail at the Terrace Hilton. They probably would pretend they never heard of it. But Slow-Foot Bill, the bartender at the Alibi Club in Newport, would know how to make one.

He read on. Beckley, the story said, had arrived in Newport in 1950 and quickly became the biggest layoff betting bookie in the country, working at Bobben Realty, the front company owned by brothers Bob "Big Porky" and Ben "Little Porky" Lassoff.

It was a long, well researched piece of reporting, showing the paper's daring effort to expose the Mob. Messick quoted Bobby Kennedy, who was attorney general at the time, calling out Beckley just nine days after the Ratterman story made national headlines. Kennedy used Beckley as his prime example of organized crime in gambling.

"These people conduct their business by telephone," Kennedy said. "When local authorities get close to them, they merely pick up stakes and move to another jurisdiction." He traced Beckley around the Midwest, to Newport, then Canada, and back to Newport until the Ratterman extortion attempt backfired.

Other clips reported that Beckley was a close associate with some notorious gangsters: former Xavier University football player and Newport thug Carinci (who engineered the Ratterman plot at the direction of Mob lawyer Charles Lester); sports "fixer" Lefty Rosenthal (whose life in Las Vegas was the basis for the movie *Casino*);

---

[107] Ibid.

CHAPTER 13 • 'THE WIZARD OF ODDS'

Headline from the *Miami Herald* on October 29, 1969. Carinci, at right, was known as 'Tito' Carinci in Newport, one of the gangsters who plotted the failed frame-up of Sheriff candidate George Ratterman. When they were run out of Newport, some of the Mob went to Las Vegas, others relocated their gambling rackets in Miami.

and "Trigger Mike" Coppola (the brutal hit man in Messick's book *Syndicate Wife*).

Trigger Mike was a whole black book of mobster connections: Charles "the Blade" Tourino from Havana, Joe Adonis, Meyer Lansky, names like "Sammy Foots," "Sharkey," and Coppola's main guy, "Fat Tony" Salerno. Fat Tony was connected to the three big New York City crime bosses: Frank Costello, the Lucchese crime family and Vito Genovese.

Trigger Mike ran numbers rackets in Harlem, gambling in Miami and narcotics all over the East Coast. In his spare time he beat his wife and earned his nickname with his hair-trigger temper.

"Fat Tony," on the other hand, was not fat at all, Jake noted. He was five foot eight and weighed 175 pounds, according to an FBI report.[108]

In 1966 the FBI conducted thirteen raids in nine cities, including Beckley's luxury apartment at the Blair House in Miami, where the agents got in by pretending to deliver a case of scotch whiskey. They found the "blue box" Beckley used to get free phone service from phone company "cousins," who were bribed to erase the records of thousands of phone calls each year so they would not attract FBI and IRS attention. Beckley's customers included Texas oil billionaire H.L. Hunt.[109]

His regulars knew Beckley as "Dad." But his Mob name was "The Brains." He became a mentor to others in the national gambling network,

---

108 FBI Vault documents.
109 "13 FBI Raids Smash Vast Gambling Ring," Hank Messick, *The Miami Herald,* January 9, 1966.

such as Lefty Rosenthal and William Clyde Demming of Fort Thomas, Kentucky, who took over the Mob's Cincinnati gambling franchise when Beckley fled to Miami.

Demming kept a house in Silverton in Cincinnati, under an alias. But one of his runners, Emil "Jelly" Wehby (who tipped the scales at about 300 pounds), made too many calls to the Silverton address from Las Vegas. The feds showed up at the brick two-story house and caught Demming with bags of betting slips and cash. His "handle" of money in play on daily bets was $400,000.

A *Cincinnati Post & Times Star* story from 1967, "Gambling Here Has Mafia Touch," connected Beckley to Carlos Marcello, the New Orleans Mob boss who was named as a suspect in the JFK assassination in 1963.[110] Beckley also worked directly for the Genovese crime family in New York, supervised by underboss "Fat Tony" Salerno.[111]

Suddenly Cincinnati discovered that the Mob was not just a Newport problem. Bigtime Mafia bosses Marcello, Genovese and Salerno were all connected to Cincinnati. Like the *Post* readers in 1967, Jake was surprised.

The next clip reported an FBI investigation of Beckley for fixing fights and NFL football games. He was so good at it, the National Football League hired him to smoke out rigged games. "If I know something's wrong, I'll give you the name of the club, but I won't give you the names of the players," Beckley agreed.[112]

Beckley, a "nationally prominent gambling figure," was convicted for racketeering in 1967.[113] Somewhere along the line he cut a deal to testify.

When the feds investigated a New England Mob racket run by the Patriarca crime family, Beckley was one of the government's star witnesses. Then in 1970, Beckley vanished, and a massacre of his closest associates quickly followed, with seven hits. One was found stuffed in the trunk of his new gold Cadillac, shot in the face and chest. Another

---

110 Report of the U.S. House Select Committee on Assassinations, 1979.

111 "Gambling Here Has Mafia Touch," *The Cincinnati Post,* December 6, 1967.

112 "Conglomerate of Crime: The Mafia Story," *Time Magazine,* August 1969.

113 U.S. Department of Justice Memorandum, "Department's Disclosures of FBI Surveillances Having a Bearing on Prosecutions," March 23, 1967.

CHAPTER 13 • 'THE WIZARD OF ODDS'

was found riddled with bullets in a Detroit alley. A third was shot and tossed from a car on the freeway. Beckley was never found. He was last seen heading for an airport in Canada with $1 million in a suitcase.[114]

According to one report, Las Vegas comedian Jack Carter said he was told that Beckley was dismembered and put in a garbage can that was thrown in the ocean—the same way the Mafia eliminated gangster "Handsome" Johnny Rosselli in Florida in 1975 after he threatened to talk about his work with the CIA to assassinate Castro and JFK.[115]

Jake looked again at the *Post* story from 1967. It started on Page One and jumped twice to inside pages, running maybe 3,000 words. That was gutsy, he thought. But no byline. Which was probably smart. Stories about organized crime in Cincinnati were harder to find than a bank open on Sunday. As his father liked to say, "Heartburn can be fatal—especially if you give it to the wrong people."

Jim was right. If Beckley's crew had a daily handle of $400,000 in Cincinnati, just imagine what they could do with a numbers racket lottery for the whole state.

He decided to write the column for laughs. He began:

Stung by criticism of declining school performance, the Ohio State Lottery For The Children has announced a new director, Gilbert "The Brains" Beckley.

Unfortunately, Beckley was indisposed and unavailable for comment since his premature demise in a Mob hit in 1970. But partners in the Organization that Beckley worked for were in town yesterday to make the city an offer it can't refuse: a lottery jackpot in tax revenues if City Council will support legalized casino gambling in Ohio.

Councilmember's eyes lit up like cherries in a one-armed bandit as they stood in line to welcome the gambling windfall with both hands....

---

[114] Dan Moldea, *Interference: How Organized Crime Influences Professional Football,* Open Road Media, 2014.

[115] *Forbidden Fruit: Sin City's Underworld and the Supper Club Inferno,* Peter Bronson, Chilidog Press, 2020.

Sympathy for the Devil

14
The Smut King and the Mafia

The bullet that struck Larry Flynt weighed less than an ounce. It was hardly bigger than a pencil eraser. But in the millisecond it entered his body it destroyed his world like a personal atom bomb.

Freelance reporter Neil Shister, working for Larry Flynt's newspaper the *Atlanta Gazette*,[116] was there and described the shooting of Flynt and his lawyer Gene Reeves in a story published the next day:

> "I was about twenty feet behind them. I heard a loud report and I looked to see if a car had backfired. There was the smell of gunpowder. The street was very quiet. I didn't see anybody. I didn't see the car.
>
> "I looked over at Larry and he was holding his stomach and sort of crumpling over; there was a stain on his shirt. He was wearing a blue pinstriped suit and a very white shirt. My first thought was that someone had thrown a tomato at him or thrown some garbage on him. I ran up to him, his shirt was open and I could see two big holes. Apparently, the bullet had entered his right side and exited (left). He was bleeding but not profusely, and part of his intestine was visible in the wound. He was lying on his back in obvious pain. He really wasn't saying anything."

Flynt lost nearly everything but his life that day. He lost the use of his legs. "I'm going to walk," he vowed, "it's just a question of whether it will be on land or water." But he never walked again.

He lost himself. He would never be the same again, never be pain free, never be the man he was. Never again indulge as he had in his all-consuming obsession with sex.

---

[116] In January 1978 Larry Flynt also bought *The Plains Monitor*, the local newspaper in President Carter's hometown of Plains, Georgia (pop. 684).

And those closest to him believed he lost his mind.

For three years he almost vanished. He moved to Bel-Air, California, a suburb of Los Angeles, where he lived in an estate he bought for $2.5 million (about $11 million in 2022 dollars). The twenty-room house, formerly owned by pop singer Sonny Bono, was next door to Johnny Carson. But Flynt only saw his new neighbor by watching *The Tonight Show*. He never went out.

He locked himself behind a 500-pound steel door and sat watching TV around the clock, lying in bed or sitting in his gold-plated wheelchair, using an electronic push-button device to open and close the heavy security door for nurses, meals, bodyguards and Althea. The few who saw him said his skin was as pale as a bloodless corpse. He kept the heavy blinds drawn shut on the sunniest Southern California days and would sometimes turn up the air-conditioning high enough to wrap himself in a blanket and drink hot chocolate in front of a blazing fire in July. Flynt was retreating deep into the darkness.[117]

He and Althea ingested massive amounts of drugs and surrounded themselves with a squad of armed security guards, an alarm system and an attack dog.

Today, he would be diagnosed with Post Traumatic Stress Disorder. But while Sigmund Freud and others had studied the damage of violent trauma to mental health, PTSD was not listed by the American Psychiatric Association Diagnostic and Statistical Manual of Mental Disorders until 1980. At the time Flynt was shot in 1978, little was known about the psychological damage to gunshot victims beyond the old definitions of "shell shock" in World War I and "battle fatigue" in World War II.

Since then, studies have found that gunshot victims have "significant long-term declines in physical and mental health," and often spiral into severe substance and alcohol abuse aggravated by unemployment and disability.[118]

---

[117] "For Flynt: Sex, drugs, pain," Rudy Maxa, *The Miami News,* December 7, 1983.

[118] Physical and Psychological Outcomes 8 Months after Serious Gunshot Injury. *Journal of Trauma,* October 2002.

CHAPTER 14 • THE SMUT KING AND THE MAFIA

Flynt started taking Dilaudid, a powerful opioid painkiller, and swiftly graduated to several injections daily. When the tide of pain flooded over the dam of Dilaudid, he followed the injections with a Brompton Cocktail, which originated in 1896 at the Royal Brompton Hospital in London. The updated recipe: morphine or heroin, cocaine, Thorazine, high-proof alcohol and chloroform, mixed with cherry syrup.

Flynt's Brompton Cocktails were 60 percent morphine, 30 percent cocaine and 10 percent high-octane gin.

He spent $22,000 a year on drugs, legal and illegal. Most were prescribed by unethical doctors. Althea spent that much each week on cocaine—about $75,000 a week in 2022 dollars.

And still, Flynt told a reporter in 1982, his leg pain was unrelenting and agonizing, "...like standing up to my thighs in boiling water while someone with a claw hammer ripped the meat off my bones."

He said he was certain he was shot by the CIA, because he had raised questions about the assassination of President Kennedy and offered a $1 million reward for information about it.[119] TASS, the Soviet news/propaganda agency, reported as fact that Flynt was shot because he questioned the assassination.

Interviewed in his hospital bed in Columbus, Ohio just weeks after the shooting, Flynt said, "I knew who did it even before I was shot. The CIA did it, the same people who assassinated President Kennedy, his brother Bobby, Martin Luther King Jr. and Malcom X... I knew it was going to happen sooner or later. I just thank God my life was spared. I mean to walk out of here."[120]

Most law enforcement officers believed he was shot by the Mob. They had good reasons.

Just two days after he was shot while on trial for obscenity in Lawrenceburg, Georgia, the *Atlanta Constitution's* lead editorial asked, "Who shot Larry Flynt and his attorney Gene Reeves?" It concluded, "If the would-be killer turns out to be an agent of organized crime, the

---

[119] "Shot by CIA, Flynt Charges," *The Associated Press,* May 18, 1978.

[120] Ibid.

tragedy of Larry Flynt will serve as further evidence that the dirty book trade is closely related to underworld activities and all the violence that goes with them."[121]

Most in the media scoffed at the Mob connections, like the *Wall Street Journal* editorial that said organized crime charges against Flynt were just piled on by a vindictive Cincinnati prosecutor. The evidence said otherwise.

In May, almost three months after the shooting, the local prosecutor in Gwinnett County, Bryant Huff, announced that the investigation would follow links to organized crime. The motives: "internal business problems within his company, business problems across the country and the role of organized crime in pornography."[122]

Huff traveled to Columbus, Ohio to interview Flynt in the hospital. For months, Flynt, Althea and others in their organization had foolishly refused to be interviewed by police. After the visit, the prosecutor said Flynt had reconsidered his CIA theory and now had "an open mind" about a Mob hit. Althea and the Hustler company offered a $100,000 reward for information leading to the arrest and conviction of the shooter. The misdemeanor obscenity charges against Flynt in Georgia were dropped. And the fear that would consume Flynt behind his 500-pound steel door in Bel-Air began to creep in.

A few months later, in September, suspicions about the Mob were raised again by a car-bombing at the home of Althea's brother-in-law, William Rider. His Toyota Land Cruiser was dynamited as it sat in the driveway at his Columbus, Ohio home. Rider, a regional sales manager for Flynt Publications and a former Columbus Police narcotics officer, was unhurt.[123]

Then in November, exactly eight months after Larry Flynt was shot, a key executive in the Flynt *Hustler* empire was shot in the chest while getting out of his car in Columbus. Walter William Abrams, 33, was

---

[121] "The Flynt Shooting," *The Atlanta Constitution*, March 8, 1978.

[122] "Flynt Probe to Shift," *The Associated Press*, May 26, 1978.

[123] "Violence Against Flynt Publishing Empire Unexplainable, Police Say," *The Associated Press*, November 134, 1978.

CHAPTER 14 • THE SMUT KING AND THE MAFIA

with Larry's brother Jimmy Flynt when he was shot by a sniper with a high-powered rifle. The bullet narrowly missed Abrams's heart, and he lived.

Jimmy, who drove Abrams to the hospital, said, "I could tell you the CIA done it, but all that's bull. If I can't give you the facts, I won't give you nothing."[124]

Police said there was almost zero chance the shooting was a mistake. Abrams was shot as he exited his car in his assigned parking spot with his name on it. Columbus Police said Abrams was reluctant to help them. They hinted at Mob motives, such as a possible feud over porn territory.

"Maybe we're cutting into all the underground porn, maybe we're hurting those guys," Larry speculated when asked about Mob hits. "But I know all those guys personally."

Even after Flynt himself confirmed his Mob connections, most of the press maintained the fiction that he was just the self-made independent operator of a raunchy magazine, defending the First Amendment.

But then in July, *The Cleveland Press* dropped a bomb that reverberated like the dynamite under Ridder's Toyota Land Cruiser. The story showed how Larry Flynt's Hustler Clubs in Ohio were financed by the Mob.[125]

The story was uncovered during the paper's five-month investigation into Cleveland charities that were being used as fronts by the Mob to run loan-sharking for taverns. The story identified Seaway Acceptance Corporation, a loan company, as a Mob organization; Seaway was involved in pinball and vending machines throughout Ohio.

Seaway issued "loans" to a VIP list of mobsters and Cleveland political figures, including Big Jim Dickerson, the "unofficial mayor" of Cleveland and second in command at the state lottery; Mafia boss Big Ange Lonardo, brother-in-law of Cleveland Mafia boss John Scalish; and Mervin Gold.

Gold was especially interesting. His business partners included an

---

[124] "Flynt Executive Shot; Condition Satisfactory," *The Associated Press*, November 8, 1978.
[125] "Seaway helped Flynt build a porn empire," Walt Bogdanich and Walter Johns Jr., *The Cleveland Press*, January 28, 1978.

The Cleveland Press exposed Larry Flynt's underworld connections in 1978, and other papers both national and across Ohio picked up the story, such as these headlines from the *Dayton Journal Herald*. The story made a brief splash, but only the Cleveland Press followed up.

international gunrunner, a numbers kingpin and racketeer, and Mafiosos who stole $8 million in securities from Canada that were funneled to the CIA to finance the overthrow of Castro during the Bay of Pigs invasion. Gold was beaten to death in 1963. In 1975, an investigation of the CIA led by Vice President Nelson Rockefeller heard testimony that Gold was murdered by the Mob because of his involvement in the CIA-Mafia plots, which were funded with cash from Seaway.[126]

And that Mob front was also where Larry Flynt got his start. Not from his own initiative, hard work and "hustle," as most of the media reported. After failing at more than a dozen bars in the Dayton area, he was lifted out of bankruptcy with the generous help of La Cosa Nostra.

---

126 Ibid.

CHAPTER 14 • THE SMUT KING AND THE MAFIA

The Cleveland Press reported that Larry Flynt "received what law enforcement authorities say is 'substantial' financing from Seaway."

The first story showing Flynt's backing by the Mob was published on January 28, 1978. It was picked up by newspapers in Ohio and played in short stories on inside pages. After that, it was widely ignored. The media had their story about the self-made porn king and First Amendment crusader, and they stuck to it like bugs on a bumper. But then in July, after Flynt was shot, *The Cleveland Press* ran a more detailed report.[127]

"Looking over Flynt's checkered past, evidence clearly shows that Flynt entered business where mobsters traditionally have exerted great influence, such as nightclubs, vending machines and pornography," said the *Press*, an afternoon daily that ceased publication in 1982.

The story provided ample evidence, citing a confidential report leaked from the Ohio Attorney General's office:

- Seaway confirmed the loans to Flynt, and the Attorney General's report said Seaway was controlled by organized crime.
- Flynt associates told investigators that Flynt was in debt for $250,000 to Seaway and the Mob, paying interest at 12 percent, about twice the current interest rate charged by banks.
- When Flynt reneged on payments, "He subsequently received a personal visit from the finance company," the *Press* reported. The loan collectors were two "hoodlums." A streetwise lawyer negotiated a deal to save Flynt and his brother from beatings, or worse, from the Mob enforcers.
- Mortgage records showed Flynt had borrowed another $150,000 in 1974 from AAV, a mobbed-up Cleveland vending machine company that loaned cash to nightclubs. One of the board members of AAV was secretive Cleveland millionaire Sam Klein, who had been identified in Las Vegas as an associate of New Jersey Mafia boss Jerry Catena.

---

127 "The Mob kept popping up in the career of Larry Flynt," Walt Bogdanich and *Dayton Journal* reporter Steve Adams, *The Cleveland Press*, July 5, 1978.

Shortly after his conversion to "born again" Christian, Flynt returned to one of his favorite bars in Newport to visit Bess "Mom" Raleigh, owner of the Brass Mule and Brass Ass topless nightclubs. Gerry Wolter, *The Cincinnati Enquirer.*

- A Dayton reporter recorded Flynt's boast that he relied on the underworld for money: "I don't care who I borrow from."
- Just as investigators had suspected in the 1960s, Larry Flynt was connected to the Mob in Newport, Kentucky. In the 1970s, Flynt had provided operating funds to the Brass Ass nightclub in Newport, "a nightclub long frequented by underworld figures," the *Press* said. "He would always show up at the Brass Ass late at night, maybe 2 or 2:30 a.m., because the place was an afterhours joint," a former Kentucky lawman said. "They'd lock it up and then party inside."
- Flynt admitted he had been "an associate" of Newport mobsters, including "Trigger Mike" Coppola, pimp Carl "Slick" Fournash and Frank "Screw" Andrews, the boss of Newport for the Vito Genovese crime family in New York City.
- The story reported that Flynt was a bankrupt failure in the Dayton bar business until he made connections to borrow from the Cleveland Mob in 1968—the same year he began to expand his Hustler Clubs across the state. His rise to fame and riches was financed by the Mob, the story said. And the Mob bosses had to be very uneasy about Flynt's sudden conversion to born-again christianity.
- Flynt said the CIA and the FBI had tried to assassinate him. "But there is, of course, another theory. Not any less dramatic, only

more believable," the story said. "This theory does not involve the image of a playful pornographer, but rather a formerly bankrupt, brawling businessman who traveled in the roughest sort of worlds, populated not by the born-again Christians or First Amendment advocates whom Flynt more recently had been courting, but by Frank 'Screw' Andrews, 'Trigger Mike' Coppola and Carl 'Slick' Fournash."

As the story broke, Flynt was still in the hospital, spinning out of control. Popular syndicated columnist Bob Greene was among the first to interview him as he recovered from his wounds. Greene, who grew up in the upscale Bexeley suburb of Columbus, Ohio, where Flynt had a home, later would lose his job at the *Chicago Tribune* because he had an inappropriate relationship with a high school girl. But in 1978, Bob Greene was a big name in newspapers all over the nation, and he became a friend of Larry Flynt.

"They had prepared me for it to be bad, but it was way worse than I had imagined," Greene wrote. "He was strapped into a sitting position. Tubes ran in and out of his body, feeding him medicines and removing wastes. Morphine and barbiturates had turned his eyes into cue balls. I thought he could not see me.

"But he did, even though his eyes would not focus. He began to weep and then to sob. 'Bob,' he said, 'I want to go home.'"

Then Flynt whispered, "They shot me."

"Who?" Greene asked.

"It doesn't matter who did it, it only matters what did it. What? What?"

Before Greene left, Flynt vowed that his faith in Christ was real. But that was soon gone too.

By August, six months after the shooting, he was still in the Dodd Rehabilitation Center at the Ohio State University Medical Center, protected by an armed guard outside his door. "The former bantam rooster swinger has been reduced to an immobile paraplegic who must be helped by nurses and aides," the *Fort Myers News-Press* reported. "His once sharp memory seems to have faded a bit."

And so did his faith.

Flynt's salvation was already widely debated. And that debate continued for years, up to and beyond his death.

Some skeptics quoted The Parable of the Sower, from Luke: 4-8:

> "A farmer went out to sow his seed. As he was scattering the seed, some fell along the path; it was trampled on, and the birds ate it up. ⁶ Some fell on rocky ground, and when it came up, the plants withered because they had no moisture. ⁷ Other seed fell among thorns, which grew up with it and choked the plants. ⁸ Still other seed fell on good soil. It came up and yielded a crop, a hundred times more than was sown."

Translated: Larry Flynt's salvation was trampled or choked by the thorns of drugs, porn and the people around him who worshipped drugs and porn.

Others quoted 2 Corinthians, 5:17: "Therefore, if anyone is in Christ, he is a new creation. The old has passed away; behold, the new has come."

Translated: Larry Flynt's "old man" never passed away; he was never a "new creation."

"The Bible teaches us that only God knows our heart as to salvation," said a devotional from Live Prayer Church in St. Petersburg, Florida.[128] "One thing is 100 percent certain, Larry Flynt poured out raw sewage into our culture for over five decades. Pornography is not a victimless issue! Only God knows the untold number of lives he contributed to ruining with his filth, the number of marriages and families that were destroyed."

The press preferred the un-saved Flynt. After he renounced his faith in Christ, *Los Angeles Magazine* declared that Larry Flynt was an "American saint."[129]

In 2012, *Truth Magazine* published a column by editor Mark Mayberry that provided a biblical answer to the question of Flynt's salvation:[130]

---

[128] Bill Keller, Live Prayer Church, St. Petersburg, Florida.
[129] "Larry Flynt's Life in Contempt," Ross Anderson, *Los Angeles Magazine*, March 4, 2021.
[130] "The Years of the Wicked Shall be Shortened," Mark Mayberry, *Truth Magazine*, July 3, 2012.

CHAPTER 14 • THE SMUT KING AND THE MAFIA

"Larry Flynt's suffering has largely come as a result of his own free choice to live in defiance of the will of God. The scriptures clearly forewarn mankind that sin leaves one's life a shattered mess.

"As we witness the fall of Larry Flynt, we are also reminded that the Devil works to destroy the souls of man by promising fun, joy, happiness and prosperity. He delivers sorrow, heartache, death and destruction."

"The good news of Christ is that forgiveness is available to every sinner, whether he be the self-righteous Pharisee (Lk. 18:11-12), the woman caught in the act of adultery (Jn. 8:1-11), the drug pusher, or the kingpin of a pornography empire.

"Forgiveness is conditioned upon repentance—a resolution to turn away from the practice of any sin and to turn toward the love and service of God. Larry Flynt cannot be a born-again, saved, pornography publisher. If Larry Flynt is born again or saved, he will become the former pornography publisher!"

Flynt ignored the debate as he wandered deeper into the thorns. He compared Billy Graham to Hitler. He began taking barbiturates for his pain and received weekly deliveries of unidentified pills from comedian Dick Gregory. "Even we don't know what some of those pills are," said one of his doctors.

In September, Althea and Larry said they were tired of the "narrow-mindedness" of Columbus, Ohio and moved to the Bel-Air estate in the "Land of the Lotus Eaters." Their new home was decorated like the Clampetts' mansion on *The Beverly Hillbillies,* with a red velvet-lined elevator and a red Rolls Royce in the driveway that had mink floormats. In 1980, a SWAT team from the Los Angeles Police raided his home to rescue him after a former bodyguard claimed Flynt was being drugged against his will by his staff. Shots were fired. Nobody was hurt. The case was dropped. Larry was clearly being drugged—but *he* was doing the drugging, with enthusiasm.

Drugs had become his new salvation. Althea said they took drugs together so she could be like him. "It was like a religious ceremony," she said.

They kept nurses standing by with a supply of Narcan to yank them back from the edge of death when they drifted off in overdoses. They discussed suicide. Larry wanted Althea to assist. She angrily refused, saying she had done everything she could to keep him alive when he was shot: "I didn't care if all I had was your head in a fishbowl!"[131]

In 1982 Larry announced that he was an atheist and decided to give up any hope of walking again. He had two surgeries to sever his spine and cauterize the nerves that kept him in agony, choosing to lose control of his bladder and bowels to stop the pain.

The "Born-again" version of *Hustler* died after a few issues. It became more raunchy and outrageous than ever. In 1980, *Penthouse Magazine* Publisher Bob Guccione won a libel and invasion of privacy lawsuit against Flynt and *Hustler,* for publishing a photo "likeness" of Guccione in a homosexual act, and insinuating that he had given his girlfriend an STD.

The jury awarded damages of $39 million.

Guccione's attorney told the jury, "Larry Flynt with a printing press is like giving a pyromaniac an acetylene torch."

Most people find salvation after they hit rock bottom. Larry Flynt flipped the script. He tried salvation first, *then* took the steep plunge to the bedrock bottom of his personal crater.

---

[131] Rudy Maxa story. Washington Post, Dec. 7 1980.

15
Kamikaze Larry: The FBI File

Washington, DC
March 9, 1984

INFORMATION CONCERNING FLYNT'S PLAN TO BLOW HIMSELF UP DURING HIS APPEARANCE BEFORE THE U.S. SUPREME COURT IN NOVEMBER, 1983

On March 1, 1984, [NAME REDACTED] voluntarily appeared at the U.S. Attorney's Office, Washington, DC, with his attorney and furnished the following information to FBI Agents from the Washington Field Office.

[REDACTED] Larry Flynt's trip from California to Washington, DC for his appearance before the U.S. Supreme Court. When the entourage arrived in National Airport, they were met by [REDACTED], Mitch WerBell, and Gordon Novel....

He stated that Flynt had asked both Gordon Novel and Mitch WerBell to fill the tubes of his wheelchair with C-4 plastic explosives and rig it up to a button so he could detonate himself while appearing before the U.S. Supreme Court and thereby kill himself and all the members of the court. Additionally, he requested WerBell and Novel to make him a "kamikaze" vest.

He wanted it to be fashioned of C-4 and impregnated with needles so that when it detonated the needles would be propelled like fragments from a grenade. He stated both men refused and WerBell arranged to switch wheelchairs without Flynt's knowledge, just in case Flynt had gotten someone else to build the bomb.[132]

---

132 The FBI Vault: File of Larry Flynt.

The Letter Head Memorandum (LHM) is buried in Larry Flynt's FBI file, which was obtained from the FBI Vault under the Freedom of Information Act. The story it tells is unbelievable—*almost*. With Flynt, nothing is too wild to be credible. According to a still secret FBI informant who was part of Flynt's posse of bodyguards, Flynt plotted to detonate a suicide bomb in the U.S .Supreme Court.

The men he asked to help him plot what would have been the worst assassination in U..S. history are nearly as incredible as the plot itself. Their stories could be characters in Vince Flynn thrillers. Both can be found like Waldo, blending into the background scenery behind deep-state conspiracies, the JFK assassination and scandals involving abuse of power by the CIA and FBI.

The Wizard of Whispering Death

In one of his rare pictures, Mitchell WerBell III wore camo fatigues, a handlebar mustache and a red beret on his shaved head, holding a sniper rifle in his hands and a fat stogie in his mouth. He looked like every Hollywood version of the action-movie soldier of fortune, mercenary, arms dealer, spy—because he was all of that and more. The real thing.

Before John Wayne in *Green Berets,* Sylvester Stallone in *The Expendables* and Arnold Schwarzenegger in *Commando,* WerBell owned the trademark on that cigar-chewing image. It's more likely that Hollywood modeled its special forces action-figures on WerBell

Soldier of Fortune Mitchell WerBell III was a true-life action figure who refused to help Larry Flynt assassinate the entire U.S. Supreme Court. Wikimedia Commons.

than the other way around. Art imitated life because his life was so extraordinary.

He was born in Philadelphia in 1918, the son of an exiled Czarist cavalry officer who sided with the "White Russians" to fight against the communist revolution that swept Russia in 1917. During World War II, Mitchell WerBell joined the OSS (Office of Strategic Services), which later became the CIA. He was sent on secret missions in China under the command of OSS founding officer Major General John Singlaub, and served alongside Howard Hunt, the CIA agent who became famous as one of the Watergate "plumbers" sent by President Nixon's aide John Dean to plug leaks about the hotel break-in that ultimately forced Nixon to resign.[133]

The WerBell legend as an international man of mystery has more twists than James Bond in an Oliver Stone remake of *The Manchurian Candidate.*

After the war, WerBell moved to Atlanta, Georgia and ran public relations for a local department store, then opened his own PR firm. Meanwhile, he became a mercenary adviser to dictators, including Fulgencio Batista, the Mafia's man in Cuba before the Castro communist revolution. In 1966, he was hired to engineer an aborted invasion of Haiti called Operation Istanbul—which was financed by CBS and filmed as a documentary that was never shown on TV.[134] Yes, a TV network plotted and paid for the overthrow of a foreign government as "news" entertainment.

In the late 1960s WerBell invented a silencer called "Whispering Death." It was so effective the U.S. Army adopted it and snipers used it on long range recon patrols to target Vietcong and North Vietnamese Army officers in Vietnam. WerBell was given the rank of Major General so he could tour Vietnam and demonstrate the Whispering Death to special forces soldiers there.[135]

---

[133] "Mitch WerBell: You Couldn't Make This Stuff Up," Will Dabbs, *GunsAmerica Digest,* November 28, 2021

[134] "Agnew Assails CBS Special," *The Tech*, March 23, 1971.

[135] "Cobray: Turning the Tables on Terrorists," Tom Dunkin, *Soldier of Fortune*, Jan. 1, 1980.

He invented the suppressor for the "MAC-10" (M10) mini-machine-gun and produced and sold it with his own arms company, SIONICS, which grew into an international arms dealing business.

He opened a paramilitary training center near Atlanta called Cobray, where he ran a bootcamp for security details from foreign governments, private companies and wealthy executives. He was invited to participate and plan coups in the Bahamas, Panama and Guatemala—among the ones that are known. He said Coca-Cola paid him $1 million to put a stop to kidnapping threats against its executives in Argentina.[136]

WerBell told the kidnappers, "We will kill you. We will go after your wife. We'll kill her."[137]

When WerBell was charged with being part of a drug smuggling conspiracy in 1976, his lawyer said he may have been involved in "guns, revolutions, maybe even assassinations," but never drugs.[138] Murder, yes, but no to drugs.

Asked about speculation that he may have been involved in the assassination of JFK through his CIA connections, sniper silencers or trainees, he said, "We don't play with people like that (Jack Ruby). I mean, it's as simple as that. This guy Ruby, he called, I didn't know who the hell he was, but that was years ago."[139]

Very few people knew more than Mitch WerBell about the secrets of the CIA, the Mob and America's dark side of international power. "There's a helluva lot I ain't said yet, and there's a helluva lot I ain't gonna

---

[136] "How Coke Runs a Foreign Empire," *Business Week,* August 15, 1973.

[137] *For God, Country and Coca-Cola,* by Mark Pendergrast, Basic Books, 2000.

[138] "Michell WerBell – The Man Who Was Involved in Everything," Ian Harvey, *Vintage News,* October 17, 2018.

[139] *The Last Investigation,* Gaeton Fonzi, Thunder's Mouth, 1993. Fonzi interviewed WeBell at his Powder Springs, Georgia compound and training camp in 1977. He wrote: "Trained as a paratrooper and a guerilla warfare expert, he established himself as a stalwart secret agent and came out of the China-Burma theater of operations as a dues-paid life member of the Old Boys network of American secret intelligence—the superspy fraternity that included CIA Directors Allen Dulles, William Casey, Richard Helms and (CIA agent) E. Howard Hunt, among others."

say yet," he said. "I've been in so many places, so many countries, so many revolutions, it's beginning to get all mixed up in my mind…"[140]

'I put the dress on J. Edgar Hoover'

Even the name of Gordon Novel sounded like fiction. He was clean-cut and squared away in a dark suit, Slim-Jim tie and white shirt, every hair in place with help from Brylcream or Vitalis. He could have been Don Draper's stunt double in *Mad Men*.

Novel grew up in New Orleans and married his own "Betty Draper," Miss New Orleans 1958. For a while he owned a drag strip and ran auto shows. Then, like WerBell, he seems to show up everywhere.

In 1961 he was caught with a gang that stole firearms and explosives from an armory owned by the private Schlumbarger Company in Louisiana. With him were Guy Bannister and David Ferrie. Bannister supplied weapons for the Bay of Pigs invasion in 1961; Ferrie was a CIA agent or freelancer, who was a friend to Lee Harvey Oswald and worked as a pilot for New Orleans Mafia boss Carlos Marcello.

Novel insisted the guns and explosives were stolen for the CIA as part of Operation Mongoose, authorized by JFK to overthrow Castro. He said they had a letter from Attorney General Robert Kennedy that gave them a "Get Out of Jail Free" card. The letter was never found, but Novel was not prosecuted and did get out of jail free.[141]

Novel turned to electronics, to manufacture and install eavesdropping "bugs" for foreign governments, domestic companies and politicians. He was hired as an investigator, then became the missing "mystery witness" in the sensational 1969 investigation of the JFK assassination by New Orleans District Attorney Jim Garrison, who was played by Kevin Costner in the Oliver Stone movie *JFK*.

In fact, Novel was a mole, sent to infiltrate and undermine the Garrison investigation by the LBJ White House, he said in 2019. "I've been connected with Ramsey (Clark) since 1967. When I was at the

---

140 Ibid.
141 "The Garrison Commission on the Assassination of President Kennedy," William W. Turner, *Ramparts Magazine,* January 1968.

White House, he was attorney general and I got the task of kicking the shit out of Garrison. I thought I put him on the ash heap of history until Oliver Stone came, took his ashes and remolded them into the JFK movie."[142]

In the same interview, Novel boasted about a 1993 PBS *Frontline* documentary, *The Secret Life of J. Edgar Hoover*. In the documentary he said a CIA officer had showed him a picture of FBI Director J. Edgar Hoover engaged in a sex act with his chief deputy and housemate Clyde Tolson. The documentary also said Hoover placed bets with the "Prime Minister of Crime," Frank Costello, boss of the New York Mafia.

The *Frontline* episode reported that Costello and Mob kingpin Myer Lansky also had copies of the Hoover photos "and used them to ensure the FBI did not target their illegal activities."[143] Hoover complied. He stubbornly denied the existence of organized crime until he was forced to admit it by Attorney General Bobby Kennedy in 1961.

"Remember, I'm the guy who put the dress on Hoover," Novel said. "And just so you know, I don't think much of J. Edgar Hoover and his FBI."

Novel, who was personally involved with some of the people alleged to be involved in the assassination, said the Mob killed JFK. He also said he was working for the CIA, then later denied it. His "legend" is almost too tangled to follow. Which is the point.

Unaware that he was a mole, Garrison hired Novel as his chief of security. When he discovered that Novel was a CIA agent who may have been involved in the assassination, Garrison subpoenaed him as a material witness to his investigation, to testify in the trial of alleged conspirator Clay Shaw ("Mr. X" in the Oliver Stone movie).

---

142 "Gordon Novel on the JFK Assassination, Jim Garrison & J. Edgar Hoover," Tim Ventura, *Dialogue & Discourse*, December 20, 2019.

143 "Documentary details Hoover's alleged homosexuality,'" Diane Werts, *Newsday*, February 9, 1993. "In the Frontline documentary Susan Rosensteil says on camera that she saw Hoover dolled up in a black chiffon dress, high heels and false eyelashes and being called 'Mary' at a clandestine rendezvous with her (Rosensteil's) own husband, the late philanthropist and longtime Hoover crony Lewis Rosensteil, who she says was bisexual."

Novel immediately fled to Columbus, Ohio in 1967, with a possible stopover at CIA headquarters in Langley, Virginia. Novel, former owner of a topless bar in New Orleans, was now a neighbor of Columbus celebrity Larry Flynt. When and where Flynt met Novel is unclear, but Columbus is the likely place. They shared an interest in strip clubs.

Garrison filed theft charges against Novel for stealing documents from the investigation when he fled. But his extradition to Louisiana was blocked by Ohio Gov. James Rhodes—who would only allow it if Garrison promised not to ask Novel about the assassination of JFK.

Garrison was flabbergasted. He called it, "One of the most incredible things I've ever seen." In a *Playboy* interview in October 1967 Garrison said, "In other words, it's OK for me to send a man to jail on a burglary rap, but I mustn't upset him by inquiring if he killed the President. I'm all in favor of protecting a defendant's civil rights, but this is straight out of *Alice in Wonderland*."[144]

The *Life Magazine* exposé of Gov. Rhodes's connections to organized crime was published two years later, in 1969. If the Mob did assassinate the President, it would be more than inconvenient for Novel to testify about it; Rhodes's refusal to allow extradition was at least very helpful to the Mob, the White House and the CIA.

When Garrison called Novel a CIA agent in the *Playboy* interview, Novel filed a $10 million libel lawsuit against Garrison and *Playboy*. It was dismissed.

Next, Novel was hired as investigator for flamboyant automaker John DeLorean in 1982, where he uncovered an attempt to frame DeLorean for cocaine trafficking—a case that would involve Larry Flynt and lead to his nearly explosive appearance in the U.S. Supreme Court.

A decade later, in 1993, when federal agents opened fire at the Branch Davidian compound in Waco, Texas, Novel reviewed the video record and found anomalies in infrared film recordings that he said proved the federal agents fired first on April 19, when they had denied shooting at the compound. He became part of the lawsuit against the federal

---

144 "Playboy Interview: Jim Garrison," *Playboy Magazine,* October 1967.

government led by former LBJ Attorney General Ramsey Clark. Despite his shadowy past—or maybe because of it—Clark hired Novel as chief investigator in the case.[145]

Apparently, blowing up the Supreme Court was too much even for hardened killers and spooks such as WerBell and Novel. Murder? Yes. Assassinations? Yes. Overthrowing governments? Okay. But blowing up the entire U.S. Supreme Court? No way. They refused. When Flynt arrived at the Supreme Court, his car was searched and U.S. Marshals found two handguns in the trunk. One of Flynt's bodyguards was arrested and charged. To avoid prosecution, he informed the FBI about Flynt's plans to wear a suicide vest in his exploding wheelchair.

After years hibernating in the dark as a reclusive addict, 1983 was the year Flynt finally came out of his Bel-Air cave—like a rabid wolverine with a grudge.

Full of rage, high on drugs, mentally unstable and craving attention, he left a wake litigation, incendiary headlines and destruction. Even without a suicide vest, "Kamikaze Larry" blew up emotionally and detonated rhetorical pipe-bombs wherever he went.

The DeLorean Tapes

Late in 1983, two dozen U.S. Marshals were sent to Flynt's Bel-Air compound to drag him to federal court. He was being held in contempt, threatened with a $420,000 fine for refusing to divulge where he got the sensational "DeLorean Tapes" that he had leaked to the media.[146]

According to the prosecution, DeLorean had resorted to trafficking cocaine to save his DeLorean Motor Company in Northern Ireland. He was busted in an FBI sting as he tried to sell $24 million in cocaine to an undercover agent posing as a drug dealer.[147]

---

[145] "Charges by private eye spur probe in WACO," Dick J. Reavis, *San Antonio Express News*, January 23, 2000.

[146] "Court Gives Flynt Immunity in DeLorean Videotapes Case," *The Associated Press*, December 10, 1983.

[147] Where does an auto company executive get $24 million in cocaine? From the Mob. Who did DeLorean know with Mob connections? Gordon Novel.

CHAPTER 15 • KAMIKAZE LARRY: THE FBI FILE

John DeLorean in 1971. He was a star at General Motors as developer of the Pontiac GTO and Chevrolet Vega, among others. He left to start his own DMC DeLorean company in 1973.
Chevrolet Publicity photos/ Wikimedia Commons.

The videotapes leaked by Flynt showed DeLorean telling the FBI agent, "It's better than gold."

The tapes also showed that when DeLorean began to get cold feet on the deal, the undercover FBI agent asked him if he would rather see his daughter's head smashed in. It was not good PR for the FBI.

Flynt claimed he paid $25 million for the tapes. But he refused to say where they came from. The source was probably Gordon Novel, who had been working as DeLorean's chief of security before he went to work for Flynt. He would have known that Flynt and his magazine made a willing and reckless platform to embarrass the FBI.

It worked. DeLorean was found not guilty on grounds of entrapment in 1984. But his *Back to the Future* car company was bankrupt by then. He had to sell his 434-acre estate, which was turned into Trump National Golf Club Bedminster by future President Donald Trump.[148]

The FBI files show that the Department of Justice in Washington was very interested in Flynt. The FBI was already investigating his wild claim that he had videotapes of President Reagan, Attorney General Edwin Meese and White House Chief of Staff Michael Deaver having sex with a hooker.[149]

The FBI took a look and decided the tapes were either nonexistent or so vague they could have been anyone. Part of that Flynt file, however, shows that the Assistant U.S. Attorney in Washington, DC used the investigation to seek information about the recent death of WerBell.

WerBell died at UCLA Medical Center in Los Angeles in December

---

[148] "Trump buying Bedminster golf course," *New Jersey Hills*, September 12, 2002. The PGA Championship was scheduled at Trump National for 2022, but the PGA canceled it under pressure from anti-Trump protests.

[149] FBI file on Larry Flynt.

1983. A field agent in Los Angeles checked it out and reported to the DC office that "the physician who attended to WerBell ... stated that congestive heart failure was the result of chronic obstructive pulmonary disease." Autopsy results were not obtained "since there were no unusual or suspicious circumstances."

That would change dramatically.

'Have that man arrested!'

On November 8, Flynt had the first of many explosive confrontations with the U.S. Supreme Court. With his plans for a suicide bombing thwarted, Flynt resorted to "F-bombs" instead.

"F--- this court!" he yelled at the justices, calling them "Eight (bleeps) and a token (bleep)." The first obscenity was a seven-letter word beginning with "A," but not "acrobat." The second referred to the first woman on the court, Justice Sandra Day O'Conner, with an exceptionally offensive obscenity.

"Marshal, have that man arrested!" Chief Justice William Brennan thundered.

"I will see that it's done," the marshal replied.

As marshals swarmed Flynt and bum-rushed him out of the courtroom in his wheelchair, he spewed an acrid cloud of spittle and obscenities. One of the marshals saw him reach inside his jacket and thought that Flynt would grab a weapon or his colostomy bag to throw it at the justices.[150] Or maybe he was so high on drugs he thought he could trigger his suicide-bomb wheelchair.

U.S. Supreme Court portrait of Chief Justice William Brennan, 1976.

---

150 Ibid.

CHAPTER 15 • KAMIKAZE LARRY: THE FBI FILE

FBI records said nothing even remotely like it had happened in more than two hundred years of Supreme Court history.

Flynt had arrived that day wearing a black T-shirt emblazoned with "F--- This Court." The case was a libel suit, *Keeton vs. Hustler Magazine.* Kathy Keeton was *Penthouse* Publisher Bob Guccione's co-publisher and live-in girlfriend. Her lawsuit began in 1980, triggered by five *Hustler* issues in 1975-76 that implied she had gotten an STD from Guccione.[151]

Justice Sandra Day O'Conner, the first woman on the U.S. Supreme Court, got the full Larry Flynt treatment. He called her an obscenity in court, and repeated it in writing when she politely asked him to stop sending her copies of Hustler Magazine. *Wikimedia Commons.*

A few weeks after being hustled out of the Supreme Court, Flynt was back in court again in Los Angeles for the DeLorean case. He wore a U.S .flag as a diaper. The FBI files describe what happened:

"After Flynt was wheeled into the courtroom and placed directly in front of the magistrate, Flynt removed from beneath a towel on his lap a folded red flag, spit upon it and threw the flag at the bench in the direction of the magistrate. At the same time, Flynt unleashed a torrent of profane and obscene language."

The remarkably patient magistrate recessed the hearing and gave Flynt a second chance. Flynt apologized—then did it again and was removed. After a third chance and another explosion of curses and spitting, he was held in contempt and sentenced to 60-days in jail.

The magistrate also ordered him to undergo a 90-day psychiatric evaluation. At the end of it, he was found to be mentally competent to be

---

151 Flynt lost and was eventually ordered to pay $39 million in damages.

held in contempt. It was official: Larry Flynt was sane but contemptible.

His storm of rage continued. Before the year ended, he was overheard ordering his entourage to blow up a church. He sent *Hustler* subscriptions to the Supreme Court justices and crudely insulted Justice O'Conner again when she politely asked him to stop. He announced that he was running for president with Russell Means of the American Indian Movement, handing out campaign buttons that showed a woman's naked legs wrapped around the Capitol. Informants said he offered WerBell $1 million to kill Hugh Heffner, Guccione, Frank Sinatra and *Reader's Digest* Publisher Walter Annenberg.[152] He threatened to blow up the U.S. Capitol and threatened to kill President Reagan.[153] And according to courtroom testimony under oath, he poisoned Mitchell WerBell.

The murder of Mitch WerBell

The story came out six years later in 1989, as part of a separate, tangled murder-for-hire trial that involved a cocaine dealer, a Hollywood movie and Flynt's bodyguards. It was the sensational "Cotton Club Case," named after the flop movie directed by Francis Ford Coppola.

The key witness in the case was William Rider, Althea Flynt's brother-in-law and Flynt's chief of security.

When Flynt moved to Bel-Air, Rider hired twenty-five bodyguards to enforce security. Two of them apparently moonlighted on murder-for-hire jobs and were paid to kill *Cotton Club* producer Roy Radin, 33, over a dispute with his cocaine dealer about movie profit shares.[154]

Rider secretly taped the bodyguards as they told him about the murder. Radin's 300 pound body had been found in a remote Los Angeles canyon, shot in the head repeatedly with a .22 pistol.[155]

---

152 "Alleged Flynt Plot to have Sinatra, others killed, reported," *The Associated Press*, October 27, 1988. No motives for the hits were offered. The Los Angeles Sheriff who investigated said, "I've been led to believe that Larry Flynt has a propensity to try to harm people he sees as his enemies, whether business arrangements or whatever."

153 FBI file on Larry Flynt.

154 "Cotton Club Witness Is Linked to 2 Murders," Dennis McDougal, *The Los Angeles Times*, June 30, 1989

155 Radin wore fedoras and promoted comedy shows starring Milton Berle, George Gobel and Shecky

Michael Pascal, whose security company provided bodyguards to Flynt, testified that he visited WerBell in the hospital with Gordon Novel, as WerBell was dying.

WerBell said, "They put something in my drink."

"Who got you?" he was asked.

Pascal said, "He named Mr. Rider and Mr. Flynt. He asked us to get them, Flynt and Rider. He was talking to Gordon Novel, holding his hand and he said, 'For me, get them.'"

According to Pascal, Rider and Flynt put 4 to 6 ounces of digoxin into WerBell's drink during a cocktail party at Flynt's Bel-Air home. The normal dose is one milligram. An excess can trigger fatal heart attacks. WerBell collapsed at the party and was taken to the hospital, where he died a few days later.[156]

Pascal said the motive was that WerBell refused to train Flynt's bodyguards at his training camp in Georgia. However, it seems just as likely that Flynt may have suspected WerBell as the informant who told the FBI about his plan to blow up the Supreme Court. And WerBell was also the "hit man" who was given a $1 million check to kill Sinatra, Hefner, Guccione and Annenberg. The check was never cashed; maybe WerBell alerted police about Flynt's hit-list, or maybe Flynt was afraid that he would.

By 1989, when the Cotton Club Case came to trial, Rider was no longer working for Flynt. He had been fired and was accused by Flynt of raping Flynt's 14-year-old daughter. Rider sued and was awarded $8.6 million in damages from Flynt in 1989.[157] But during the Cotton Club trial he was put in witness protection because he had been told that Flynt had offered a $70,000 bounty to kill him.[158]

Green. Gobel told Johnny Carson on the *Tonight Show*, "Roy Radin knows as much about show business as a pig knows about church on Sunday."

156 "Defense Challenges Credibility of Key 'Cotton Club' Witness," Linda Deutsch, *The Los Angeles Times*, June 30, 1989

157 *Rider v. Superior Court (LFP Inc.)*, California Court of Appeals, 1988.

158 "Cotton Club Witness Says Flynt Has Contract Out on Him," Dennis McDougal, *The Los Angeles Times*, June 22, 1989.

Even by Larry Flynt's nonexistent standards, 1983 was a scorched-earth disaster of rage, obscenity and insanity. Flynt said he was no longer in pain since his surgeries and was no longer using drugs. Years later he admitted that he had never stopped.

Soul Man

16
Flynt vs. Falwell

In the early 1980s, the decade of *Magnum P.I.* mustaches, blow-dried razor cuts, jackets with pushed up sleeves and shoulder pads on women, an Italian liquor company launched a $3 million ad campaign to sell Americans an expensive imported red liqueur that tasted like a blend of cough syrup, orange peels and mildew. It was a tough task. But their New York advertising agency, Sachi and Sachi Compton, rose to the challenge with a magazine campaign that was almost as successful as Volkswagen's "Think Small" ads.

Americans may not have liked the Italian Robitussin, but they talked about the ads.

"First of all, Campari was a very popular product, really, throughout western Europe," adman Robert Jordan explained in court. "It really was not much of a factor in the beverage business in the United States and had not been tried by very many people. It has a rather unique bitter flavor, and as a consequence it is something of an acquired taste. In other words, if you try it, the first time you may be somewhat ambivalent about it. But, perhaps, the second time you drink it you get to like it a little more. Perhaps some of the same way people feel about olives—some of them do."[159]

And sex. Olives and sex. That was it. You could almost see the lightbulb flash on in their ad agency creative meeting. *Let's see... olives, orange peels, rancid butter, bad pickles... how do we make it sexy? Eureka, that's it! Sex! The secret ingredient is sex! We get these sexy celebrities to talk about Campari and make it sound like they're really talking about sex!*

---

[159] Excerpts from the Testimony of Robert Jordan, Famous Trials, December 5, 1984.

Presto! The Italians had new ads for Campari in all of the uptown, sophisticated magazines: *New Yorker, Cosmopolitan, Playboy, Vogue...*

Jill St. John talks about her first time

St. John: My first time was in the Tre Scalini, that adorable sidewalk café in Rome.

Interviewer: Oh, really? Right out in the open?

St. John: Sure. You see, I'm basically an outdoorsy type person.

Interviewer: I see. You must tell me all about it.

St. John: Well, we were just relaxing after a hard day shooting, just me and the crew. It happened with the stunt man.

Interviewer: The stunt man? That sounds a bit risky.

St. John: Oh, it wasn't really. You see, he was Italian and they just seem to know about these things.

Interviewer: Go on.

St. John: He was very romantic. He leaned close and gently. "Well," I said, "I've never been shy about anything before." He gave me a charming grin, then ordered a Gingerly for me, that's Campari and ginger-ale and soda, and a Campari and soda for himself.

Interviewer: A little mix of Italian and American. How interesting. How was it?

St. John: Very satisfying, after that long, hot day. See, it was deliciously light and so refreshing, a very special experience.

Interviewer: Did you ever have it again?

St. John: Of course, many times. It's not the kind of thing you try once and then you forget about it. I've gone out with some outstanding men and they all know one or two new ways to enjoy it. I prefer the Exotic, that's Campari with grapefruit juice.

The ad man, Jordan, was asked the kind of obtuse questions lawyers have to put on the record:

"Was there a double meaning in the text?"

"Yes, there was," Jordan answered. "And that was essentially a kind of humorous, tongue-in-cheek, attention sort of device. That's right."

"And the tongue-in-cheek, attention getting device, while ostensibly about the liqueur had as its double meaning what?"

"Well, frankly, first sexual experience."

When Larry Flynt saw the ad, he got the joke. And stole it.

In two issues, November 1983 and March 1984, he ran his own nearly identical Campari ads in *Hustler Magazine*.

Jerry Falwell talks about his first time

Falwell: My first time was in an outhouse outside Lynchburg, Virginia.

Interviewer: Wasn't it a bit cramped?

Falwell: Not after I kicked the goat out….

Interviewer: But your mom? Isn't that a bit odd?…

It went on and on. This time the punchline was more of a curb-stomping: Falwell was depicted as an incestuous drunk hypocrite, and his late mother was a whore. It was not "tongue-in-cheek," it was more like venomous forked-tongue slander hiding behind the mask of parody.

Was *this* what Jefferson, Madison, Franklin and the Founding Fathers had in mind in 1791 when they made freedom of speech the First Amendment to the Bill of Rights?

Jerry Falwell didn't think so. He read about the *Hustler* ad in a magazine on a flight home to Lynchburg, Virginia and called his lawyer as soon as he landed. He had two words:

"Get him."

But that was not easy. Public figures such as Falwell had almost no protection from libel and slander. In the 1964 *Times v. Sullivan* case, the U.S. Supreme Court declared open season on public figures and gave an unrestricted hunting license to the press. After 1964, the *victim* of slander had to prove it was untrue, and that it was done with "actual malice." Falwell not only had to prove it was false, he had to prove that

Flynt's motive was hate, not humor. The bar was set so high an Olympic pole vaulter couldn't clear it on the wings of angels.

But that's why the ad man was being grilled in court. The Reverend Falwell had somehow cleared the bar twice in lower courts, winning $200,000 in damages from Flynt. *Hustler v. Falwell* was Flynt's appeal of that verdict to the U.S. Supreme Court.

In court, Jordan was asked if Campari protested about copyright infringement to Flynt. He said they wrote Flynt a letter to complain but received no response. They were probably not heartbroken about the added "attention getting" exposure from the showdown between Flynt and Falwell. They would get free advertising in every news story about the battle. The press obliged and covered it like Godzilla vs. King Porn. Those naughty liquor ads would now be Exhibit A in a landmark Supreme Court case that would decide how far the First Amendment can be stretched before it breaks like a hurled highball glass of Campari.

Falwell was not a man who was easily provoked to litigation by the relentless insults by the media. As a founder of a Christian college, Liberty University, a televangelist and founding pastor of Thomas Road Baptist Church in Lynchburg—one of the first to be called a "megachurch"—Falwell was already a public figure with his own TV show. After years of abuse, his skin was as thick as a King James Bible.

Jerry Falwell, 1985. Deborah Thomas, Wikimedia Commons.

The focus of most attacks was his leadership of the conservative Moral Majority, whose name itself made liberal-secularist heads explode like cherry bombs. The Moral Majority became the Fort Sumpter of the "culture war" by organizing Christian support for President Reagan and conservative family values.

Falwell was pro-life and preached the inerrancy of the Bible on homosexuality, infidelity and other sins. But he also preached the Gospel: Hate the sin, but love the sinner, like Christ. "I don't agree with your lifestyle," he told gay protesters. "I will never agree with your lifestyle, but I love you."

He was mocked for saying in 1999 that the purple Teletubby, "Tinky Winky," was a gay role model.[160]

When talk show host Ellen DeGeneres came out of the closet as a lesbian, Falwell nicknamed her "Ellen Degenerate." The left and most of the media carpet-bombed him. But he remained mostly amiable about it and apologized.

Speaking to the press on the steps of the U.S. Supreme Court during a break in the *Hustler* case, he said, "My wife and I have an album at home. We collect all the cartoons about Jerry Falwell. I've been harpooned by everybody at least once and we've been amused by every one of them.

"I have never been incensed by a political cartoon or any other kind of a cartoon other than Mr. Flynt, when he suggested that as a minister of the Gospel that I have been involved incestuously with my late mother, who died at age 82 some years earlier, a godly woman whose memory has never been blemished by anyone, and when he suggested that my mother was a whore, a prostitute. I cannot imagine any red-blooded male in any nation on earth not being incensed by that."[161]

He sued Flynt for invasion of privacy, libel and intentional infliction of emotional distress. A jury dismissed invasion of privacy and libel, but awarded The Reverend Falwell $200,000 for emotional distress. That was upheld on appeal, so Flynt appealed again to the U.S. Supreme Court.

Supreme Court observer Stuart Taylor called the case "the liveliest argument the Court has heard in recent memory."

Even Chief Justice William Rehnquist laughed when Flynt's lawyer inadvertently mocked his own client by arguing, "Hustler is saying, Let's

---

160 Critics said the idea of gay characters in children's shows was preposterous. But 23 years later, a Disney executive bragged about secretly introducing "queerness" and transgender grooming into children's movies.

161 "Falwell v. Hustler," Stuart Taylor Jr., *The New York Times,* December 3, 1987.

deflate this stuffed shirt. Let's bring him down to our level.'"

Justice Scalia wondered if anyone should be dragged so low they were on a level with Larry Flynt. "Good people should be able to enter public life" without suffering such extreme abuse, he said. But he voted with the rest of the justices to overrule Falwell because without a jury finding of libel—which was almost impossible—there could not be emotional distress from libel.

The Supreme Court trusted the subjective judgment of juries to set community standards on porn. But it did not trust juries to set the boundaries on free speech. And this time, the issue was speech (the parody of a public figure), not obscenity (*Hustler* Magazine pictures*)*.

The Founders could not have imagined someone like Flynt and his magazine if they were tripping on LSD cocktails spiked with magic mushrooms. But they probably would have agreed with the court. They were absolutists—fundamentalists like The Reverend Falwell—when it came to free speech.

James Madison, who wrote the Bill of Rights, said, "Knowledge will forever govern ignorance, and a people who mean to be their own governors, must arm themselves with the power knowledge gives. A popular government without popular information or the means of acquiring it, is but a prologue to a farce or a tragedy or perhaps both."

Thomas Jefferson was less flowery: "The press, confined to truth, needs no other legal restraint; the public will correct false reasonings and opinions on a full hearing of all parties; an no other definite line can be drawn between the inestimable liberty of the press and its demoralizing licentiousness."

In case anyone missed the point he added: "Were it left to me to decide whether we should have a government without newspapers or newspapers without government, I should not hesitate a moment to prefer the latter."

The Supreme Court ruled 8-0 in favor of Flynt. Newspapers and broadcasters had joined Flynt's appeal, to protect their freedom to offend, so the media cheered the decision. But in the language of the classically educated Founders, it was a Pyrrhic victory.

CHAPTER 16 • FLYNT VS. FALWELL

In the public mind, the press had climbed in bed with the most degenerate public figure in America and defended his slander of a good man and widely respected religious leader.

"'I think the First Amendment gives me a right to be offensive,'" Flynt said. "To live in a free society, you've got to pay a price, and the price is toleration."

He was right. First Amendment protection was not provided for Hallmark greeting cards and happy chatter on morning talk shows. It was there for the most offensive speech, to protect all viewpoints and opinions from censorship.

But many Americans wondered: How much do we have to tolerate? Does the First Amendment give the media the right to destroy someone's life and reputation without accountability? It would take a generation to find out with a case from Cincinnati.

In 2019, a Covington Catholic High School student, Nicholas Sandmann, who was visiting Washington, DC on a school field trip, was confronted by a drum-banging Native American protester, apparently because Sandmann was wearing a souvenir "Make America Great Again" hat displaying the slogan of President Donald Trump.

The 16-year-old high school freshman was dragged through the media meatgrinder based on a misleading, maliciously edited snip of video. He was accused of being racist, of "smirking" and being part of a crowd that surrounded the protester. The truth was in fact the opposite of what the press reported, as any reporter not blinded by anti-Trump bias could have easily discovered. The unedited film showed that the protesters were bullying and shouting vile insults at the high school kids, and the drum-banger approached and confronted Sandmann.

Parents who would be appalled and outraged if the same thing happened to their own children on a school fieldtrip viciously attacked Sandmann because they were consumed by hatred of Trump.

Sandmann said he wore an awkward smile because he was trying not to provoke the man banging a drum in his face, and trying not to embarrass himself, his school or his community. "My life changed forever in that moment. The full war machine of the mainstream media revved up into attack mode. They did so without researching the full video of the incident."

What happened to Sandmann was a new definition of what Jefferson called "demoralizing licentiousness" on a free-speech playground without fences, built by Larry Flynt.

Sandmann sued the Washington Post, CNN, NBC and other media companies for hundreds of millions. His lawsuit alleged:

- The *Washington Post* led "a mainstream and social media mob of bullies which attacked, vilified and threatened Nicholas Sandmann, an innocent secondary school child."
- Sandmann was targeted because he was white, Catholic and wearing a MAGA hat he bought as a souvenir on his first trip to Washington.
- The *Post* ignored basic standards of journalism "to advance its well-known and easily documented, biased agenda against President Donald J. Trump by impugning individuals perceived to be supporters of the President."
- Sandmann was subjected to "public hatred, contempt, scorn obloquy and shame," "severe emotional distress," "permanent harm to his reputation" and a lifetime of "constant concern over his safety and the safety of his family." He and other Covington Catholic students, including some who were not even on the trip, were threatened and slandered.

Many of the media companies settled to avoid trial. The amounts they paid were kept secret. The same newspapers and TV networks that demand transparency and clamor about "the public's right to know" to expose the scandals of other corporations and public figures, covered up the amounts they paid to avoid their own embarrassment. The public's right to know stopped at the door to the newsroom.

The Sandmann case was another reason for declining trust in the press. Since it was first measured in 1972 at 68 percent, public trust in media had cratered to 16 percent by 2022.[162]

Many in America thought what happened to Sandmann was media malpractice, and it's fair to assume from the settlements that they were right. Some on the Supreme Court began to reconsider the *Times v. Sullivan* license to libel. They suggested it was time to hold the media accountable.[163]

Justice Clarence Thomas wrote, "The proliferation of falsehoods is, and always has been, a serious matter. Instead of continuing to insulate those who perpetrate lies from traditional remedies like libel suits, we should give them only the protection the First Amendment requires."

Justice Neil Gorsuch agreed: "Large numbers of newspapers and periodicals have failed. Network news has lost most of its viewers. With their fall has come the rise of 24-hour cable news and online media platforms that 'monetize anything that garners clicks.'

"What started in 1964 with a decision to tolerate the occasional falsehood to ensure robust reporting by a comparative handful of print and broadcast outlets has evolved into an ironclad subsidy for the publication of falsehoods by means and on a scale previously unimaginable."[164]

Thomas Jefferson and James Madison might be disgusted by Larry Flynt's sick humor in the parody of Falwell, but they would probably accept it as the price to be paid for freedom of speech. They would be more disturbed by the steep decline of ethical standards in the press and rise of censorship by the government, social media, entertainment, academia, big tech companies and even newspapers and broadcast media. Madison and Jefferson would not even recognize the twenty-first century "news business" that Justice Gorsuch described: media platforms that "monetize anything that garners clicks."

---

162 The news for the press keeps getting worse. In July 2022 the annual Gallup Poll of trust in institutions reported another steep decline: 16 percent for newspapers and 11 percent for TV news. Congress was lowest at 7 percent.

163 In 2022, Justice Clarence Thomas urged the U.S. Supreme Court to revisit the "almost impossible actual malice" standard because it has allowed the media "to cast false aspersions on public figures with near impunity."

164 Dissent in Berisha v. Lawson libel case, No. 20-1063, 2021

Ironically, progressives and their cancel-culture allies in media—especially social media—have done more to censor free speech than the Moral Majority, Citizens for Decency Through Law and all the conservative sheriffs, prosecutors, judges and Presidents combined.

As James Madison might say, "Curses on the infamous knaves whose debilitated minds and fanatical partisan fevers have traduced the constitutional gift of liberty into farce—*and* tragedy."

Won't Get Fooled Again

17
Meet the New Boss

THE CINCINNATI ENQUIRER, MAY 25, 1984—"What do you know about the new publisher?" Jim asked. Jake was listening as he smeared a french-fry in a puddle of ketchup. The question was directed to Cliff the editorial writer. As a member of the editorial board, Cliff was closer to the inside stuff—or at least had more time in "the principal's office," the sarcastic newsroom name for the upper floor where "the man upstairs" worked.

Jake, Jim and Cliff were having lunch at Arnold's. It was the oldest downtown saloon in Cincinnati, and it looked like it. There was an ancient Gothic-lettered "Biergarten" courtyard for outdoor seating. The bar was hand-carved mahogany, built in 1861 before machines and power tools made everything. It was really two bars, with an open arch in the middle so bartenders could pass through and mix drinks to serve two rooms and two lines of bar stools that were always crowded. Jake liked to imagine local boys who fought in the Civil War leaning on the same scarred, varnished rail to have one last whiskey in Cincinnati before marching off to Shiloh and Gettysburg. Legend had it the place once offered more risqué entertainment in the little rooms at the top of the narrow, creaky stairs in back.

But Jim, Cliff and Jake had not chosen Arnold's for its history. It was a long walk from the Enquirer Building on Vine Street—which was just what they wanted. They did not want to be seated anywhere near the radar ears of other reporters and editors, who took lunch at the Sports Page and other diners closer to their desks.

They sat at a table in the courtyard, under the Bahama-blue spring sky. Even the pollen-moted air that dusted the tables was a big relief from the nicotine hazed newsroom. Jim ordered bourbon and water. Cliff had a Schlitz. Jake sipped a Coke.

It was 1984. Bill Keating was gone, promoted to the headquarters of the newspaper chain that was now the new owner of *The Cincinnati Enquirer*, Gannett Corporation. The city's morning daily was no longer owned by someone local who knew, understood and cared about Cincinnati. It was now just one more link in a chain of a hundred newspapers, all part of a conglomerate of TV stations and billboards, run by a small man with an extra-large opinion of himself, Al Neuharth.

Carl Lindner had sold the paper to his friend Karl Eller of Phoenix, owner of Combined Communications. But then Eller made the mistake of trusting Neuharth. While he was closing a deal to merge Combined Communications with Gannett at Neuharth's estate in Florida, Neuharth eavesdropped on Eller's phone calls[165] and used the information like a card cheat to outmaneuver Eller and push him to the sidelines.[166]

Gannett had promoted Bill Keating to corporate headquarters in Washington DC, installing Neuharth's handpicked "Gannettoid" publisher, sent from the Kmart of newspaper chains.

"I'm worried about anyone chosen by Neuharth," Cliff said. "He surrounds himself with toadies. From what I hear he is treated like an emperor and everyone around him is afraid to say anything that will get them decrapitated." It was their new favorite word, lifted from a busted head that slipped by the Copydesk goalies: "This Day in History: Fifth Wife of Henry the VIII Decrapitated."

"It sounds like the Court of the Crimson King," said Jake. Jim and Cliff looked at him blankly. "It's an album by a progressive rock band. King Crimson? Tortured guy screaming on the cover?... Never mind."

---

[165] *Confessions of an S.O.B*, Al Neuharth 1989, Doubleday Business

[166] The rigged deal sparked a feud between Neuharth and Lindner that blew up in 1998, when Gannett transferred an editor to Cincinnati who bragged that he would "get Carl Lindner." The investigative expose of Lindner's Chiquita Company backfired when the reporter was caught illegally eavesdropping on voicemails at Chiquita (just like Neuharth). Gannett and *The Enquirer* had to run front page retractions and pay Lindner a settlement that was closer to $20 million than the "$11 million" reported by the *Enquirer*.

CHAPTER 17 • MEET THE NEW BOSS

"It sure sounds painful," Jim said. "Why don't you move up to first class and listen to some Chet Baker and Bill Evans?"

"Well, as far as I know, Neuharth doesn't torture anyone," Cliff continued. "Unless you count corporate meetings. They are very big on meetings and conferences and meetings to discuss more conferences. They also do corporate on-site visits they call 'cattle shows.' They send top execs out to the newspapers to terrorize everyone and inspect the local troops to see if anyone is worthy to start shinnying up the greasy corporate promotions pole."

Jake was surprised to find that Cliff, the mild-mannered editorial writer, had the heart of a rebel under his buttoned-down collars and tan Brooks Brothers poplin summer suit. He was hard to classify. He was only a few years older than Jake, but seemed a decade more mature than most of Jake's friends. His hair was short, combed and clean-cut, shouting "square." But then there were those wire-framed glasses that said he was hip. Jake knew from Jim that Cliff was a Vietnam veteran who had come home in rough shape, but never talked about it. "Who wants to be known as the baby-killing boogeyman who might shoot up a Kroger," Jim had half joked. "We may have been forgotten after Korea, but at least we weren't treated like psychos for serving our country."

So Jake was glad to find that Cliff shared his own loathing of meetings and the pole climbers who actually enjoyed them.

"On the positive side, our new publisher came up through the newsroom," Cliff said hopefully.

"That's bad news," said Jim, shaking his head. "They are the worst."

"What makes you say that?" Jake asked. "Aren't *we* from the newsroom?"

"Bingo," Jim said. "And *we* would make terrible publishers. People from the newsroom have no concept of business or serving their community, they are all about themselves. Newspapers have always promoted people to their ultimate level of incompetence—I'm living proof. But a publisher from the newsroom? That's like putting the top crab in the bucket in charge of the fishing boat. Ridiculous."

"Speaking of promoting incompetence, how are you getting along with Clarabell as managing editor?" Cliff asked.

"You just made my point," Jim said. "Imagine someone like that as publisher, if you can without losing your Greek spaghetti."

"We might have to," Jake said. "I hear Gannett has her on the fast track. She's the kind who thrives in that petri dish. They love her community activism."

Cliff shook his head. "Every day I say a prayer of thanks that the editorial department is not under newsroom supervision. The other day she told me we should not run any syndicated columns from conservatives like Walter Williams because they're 'wrong.' True story. I started to say something about our First Amendment obligation to give readers a variety of viewpoints, but decided to save my breath in case I had to run from a flying fried cake."

"Did you tell her to write a letter to the editor," Jim asked, winking at Jake.

Cliff made a face that looked like the tortured guy on the album cover. "Not a chance in hell. I'm still having nightmares."

"What else do you know about the new man upstairs?" Jim asked.

"Well, from what I hear from people he has worked with, get ready for the 'Crimson King,' as Jake says. These Gannett guys use all the Harvard MBA buzzwords about 'stakeholders,' 'buy-in' and 'teamwork,' but their favorite hammer in the toolbox is intimidation, just like Neuharth. They keep everyone off balance, looking over their shoulders like the prisoners in *Cool Hand Luke*."

"Whut we have heah is a failyuh to comMUNicate," Jake imitated in a bad southern drawl.

"These Gannett guys have no lives outside the office," Cliff went on. "If you're not there for ten or twelve hours a day, you're slacking. And they call you at home, on the weekend, on vacation—as if they want everyone to be just as miserable as they are."

Jim put down his sandwich. He knew the type. There was an officer in Korea like that: way over his head in the deep end, covering it up by being a coldblooded hard-ass. Jim used say the guy was like a canteen.

CHAPTER 17 • MEET THE NEW BOSS

Whatever came out always tasted like the last thing someone put in. If "Lt. Hardass" had not been shot in the first wave of Chinese attacks at Chosin, he would have gotten them *all* killed with his stupidity and indecision.

"I'm losing my appetite," he said, pushing his plate of brats and kraut away. "I miss Bill Keating already."

"Here's a question I've been wondering about," Jake said. "Why are so many people in the newsroom so liberal? I mean, there aren't enough conservatives to fill a janitor's closet."

"More than you think, maybe," Cliff said, cleaning his John Denver glasses on his napkin. "I think we might fill most of a janitor's closet. Some are just afraid to admit it."

"But why?" Jake asked.

"Look at the calendar," Jim said. "It feels just like 1984. 'Mediacrats of the world unite! You have nothing to lose but your credibility.' When the newsroom politburo is finished there will be no more politically incorrect opinions, no more conservative subscribers, only the tiny echo chamber of progressives writing for each other at Orwell's 'Ministry of Truth.' We don't write stories anymore. Now they call it a 'narrative,' which is a word that comes from fiction. And stories that don't follow the politically correct 'narrative' don't win prizes or compliments in your performance evaluation. Circulation is shrinking. Trust in the media is lower every year. I just wonder who will write the obit when the local newspaper commits suicide?"

Jake shook his head, "When I was in college, I always pictured the newsroom as a place where people had open-minded adult conversations to share ideas and different viewpoints. I always figured you could say almost anything if you knew how to do it the right way. But now...."

Jim turned to Cliff, "Isn't that what you eggheads do in the editorial department all day? Think deep thoughts and take turns saying 'whereas,' 'wherefore' and 'notwithstanding' while you smoke pipes and admire the leather patches on your elbows?"

"Well, not exactly. But we do have more latitude than you guys. We report to the publisher who knows his city... Wait, delete that. I should say we *did* have more latitude. I'm not sure what we can expect with the new guy. The only time I met him he never even made eye contact. He just kept pushing papers around his desk as if I wasn't there and he was way too important to talk to a plebe like me. Finally, he said our editorial was too 'polarizing,' whatever that means."

"What was it about?" Jim asked.

"Supporting President Reagan's effort to reduce abortion."

Jake said, "When I met the new boss at the welcome reception he kept looking over my shoulder, like he couldn't wait to talk to someone else. His eyes were darting around the room like flies in a jar. And he kept nodding and saying 'Yeah, yeah,' like whatever I said was boring old news and he already knew everything about it."

Jim lit a cigarette and changed the subject. "About Jake's question," he said. "Cliff has a theory. Tell him, Cliff."

"Why are newsrooms so liberal," Cliff said, stating the question as if he was back in debate club at Purcell High School. "First, I think our business attracts people who are anti-authority and tend to be more emotional than logical—meaning writers. And the J-schools push liberal ideology because it's the orthodox religion on every campus. Most faculties are infested with professors who have never held a real job anywhere, much less at a newspaper. They live in ivy covered bubbles where everyone thinks like they do. In fact, I agree with Jim that making the news business a credentialed profession that requires a college degree has made reporters worse. They come out of college with the idea that they are smarter and better than the common peons who read the newspaper.

"Look at the awards racket. We're as bad as those phonies in Hollywood who crave validation from their silly Oscars. Reporters chase awards for the same reason, because they're insecure. Deep down we all know we're not as popular and important as people make us feel. We just have a 'Press Card' passport into their world. Like actors, without the roles we play we're nobody."

Jake nodded, "And most award-winning stories land in your lap by accident."

CHAPTER 17 • MEET THE NEW BOSS

Jim said, "I always thought there were three types of people: The politicians and business leaders who see us as useful idiots to be flattered and manipulated; the cynics who see us as drunks in a minefield who can blow up their lives; and all the rest who naively think getting their name in the paper is their little half-popped kernel of fame from the celebrity popcorn machine. But it's never as good as they thought it would be. We always get something wrong—the name of their dog, the year they graduated... something."

"You mean like that story last week about the judge who's retiring so he can devote more time to 'philandery'?" Jake asked.

Cliff said, "Exactly. We laugh, but it was no joke for his family to be embarrassed because a reporter can't spell philanthropy. Sometimes I wonder if we do more damage than good. At our best we inform people and expose wrongdoing. At our worst we misinform, sensationalize and wreck lives. We like to compare ourselves to cops and nurses—long hours, low pay, a thankless job. But nurses and cops don't chase cheesy awards. They have the validation of saving lives. When readers complain we say, 'I guess I must be doing my job right.' Is there any other job that makes a virtue of pissing people off?"

Cliff's second Schlitz had loosened his tongue. Jake steered him back. "But how does that explain why reporters and editors lean so far left?"

"It's the path of least resistance. It's a miracle how any student can survive a college education these days without becoming a radical. The left has created the fiction that all the cool and smart people are liberals. So ipso facto, conservatives are stupid and square."

Jim said, "Ipso fatso? No more drinks for Cliff. He's starting to speak editorialese. Let me add something in English. The awards racket also enforces the liberal party line. The *New York Times* and the *Washington Post* win the big prizes and set the guardrails for the news business. Everything else is just crumbs in an empty cake pan."

Jim crushed out his cigarette and continued. "Newsrooms always leaned left. All that crap about 'afflicting the comfortable' is just class envy in a bowtie. But the Watergate generation has pushed the business hard left. Everybody wants to change the world. The scariest part is that they actually believe their left-wing propaganda is unbiased truth. And when the Clarabells get put in charge, turn out the lights, the party's over."

Jake wondered, "Maybe that whole prize racket is why it's so easy to manipulate us. They know we're chasing fame and glory so they throw us a few bones and lead us right down the path they want."

"Good point," Cliff said. "Reminds me of a story I read in 1974, unmasking 'Deep Throat' as an FBI official who was hand-feeding Woodward and Bernstein. Those guys at the *Post* didn't investigate anything. All of the hard work was done by the courts, Congress and the FBI. That wasn't reporting, it was stenography."[167]

Jim nodded. "It all started with allowing anonymous sources. Getting inside information makes us feel important. We fall in love with the source and can't see how we're being used, then refuse to look at anything that might undermine our secret source."

Jake asked, "So what can we do?"

"I'm not optimistic," Jim said. "Gannett is crazy for quotas. The newsroom is being balkanized—there's an editorial word for you, Cliff. We have militant women journalists, Latino journalists, black journalists and gay journalists and they all push their political agendas and get more radicalized by going to annual conventions of radicals that we

---

[167] "Did the Press Uncover Watergate?" by Edward Jay Epstein, *Commentary Magazine,* July 1974. *Vanity Fair* was credited with revealing the identity of "Deep Throat" in 2005. That was untrue. Mark Felt, second in command at the FBI, was first named by Epstein as the source for the *Washington Post* in 1974. Epstein wrote: "The prosecutors at the Department of Justice now believe that the mysterious source was probably Mark W. Felt, Jr., who was then a deputy associate director of the FBI, because one statement the reporters attribute to 'Deep Throat' could only have been made by Felt. (I personally suspect that in the best traditions of the New Journalism, 'Deep Throat' is a composite character.)"

Epstein's answer to his column's headline: "In the end, it was not because of the reporting of Woodward and Bernstein, but because of the pressures put on the conspirators by Judge John Sirica, the grand jury, and Congressional committees that the cover-up was unraveled. ... At best, reporters, including Woodward and Bernstein, only leaked elements of the prosecutors' case to the public in advance of the trial. ... the fact remains that it was not the press which exposed Watergate; it was agencies of government itself. So long as journalists maintain their usual professional blind spot toward the inner conflicts and workings of the institutions of government, they will no doubt continue to speak of Watergate in terms of the David and Goliath myth, with Bernstein and Woodward as David and the government as Goliath."

pay them to attend. Readers aren't blind. They can tell the nutcases are running the nervous hospital."

Cliff nodded. "I call it the Law of Radical Entropy. Eric Hoffer says mass movements start out with good causes, then get hijacked by radicals and fanatics. When the fanatics get power, they will do anything to keep their grievance going long after the goal has been achieved."

Jake said, "It reminds me of that famous quote: 'The herd of independent minds.'"

Cliff nodded, "Harold Rosenberg, 1948. He was talking about the press."

"Now you're starting to sound like the Copydesk," Jim said.

"I did my tour of duty with Punch and Judy," Cliff said. "The Mekong Delta was less stressful."

Jim pushed his chair back. "Gentlemen, we are the last of the Mohicans, if I am allowed to say that—we're the counter-counter-culture." He waved for the check. "We'd better get back before Clarabell tries to fire us so she can fill some more quotas. My anonymous sources say she would really enjoy that."

As they stood to go, Cliff asked Jim, "Are you marching in the American Legion Memorial Day parade on Monday?"

Jim said, "Yep. Wouldn't miss it. I wouldn't be here if not for some of my buddies who didn't come home… " He paused.

Cliff filled the awkward silence. "Me too. We don't need any awards to validate that."

Fear the Reaper

18
The Devil Went Down to Georgia

Vicki and Nancy were hitchhiking on I-79 in West Virginia on a sunny, warm June day in 1980 when a black, jacked-up 1971 Chevy Nova with mag wheels slowed and pulled onto the shoulder ahead of them. They picked up their backpacks containing everything they had, and ran after it. Vicki took the front seat and Nancy climbed into the cramped, hot, black-vinyl backseat.

They had no idea they had just stepped from sunlight into fatal darkness.

The young women were like many lost refugees of the counterculture in the '70s and early 80s. The polite label was "free spirit." They were wilted flower-children, runaways or dropouts, kids who got "turned on" using drugs and left college, high school or boring jobs to see the country and follow the hippie siren song of "love, peace and happiness."

"If you're going to San Francisco..." the radio beckoned.

They soon learned that "love" was just grubby old leering lust, "peace" only lasted until the next hash pipe or needle, and "happiness" had been abducted by desperate poverty, shared mattresses, bad trips, body lice, pushers and predators.

Vicki was 26, Nancy was nineteen. But they showed high mileage. The grime of being on the road from Arizona (Nancy) and Iowa (Vicki) was baked into their skin, hair, fingernails and clothing.

The constant stress of gas station restrooms, finding a meal, riding with strangers and no place to sleep had worn them as thin as their unwashed socks. But they were still hopeful. They were almost there: the Rainbow Gathering in the West Virginia mountains—a back-to-nature Woodstock without electric guitars, promising all the gauzy dreams in the dogeared Love-In catalog: harmony, freedom, lots of drugs, no rules, no work and back-to-nature outdoor toilets.

"Be sure to wear some flowers in your hair..."

"This is a cool lookin' car you got,"[168] Vicki said, hoping to break the ice. The driver looked safe. Shoulder-length dirty-blond hair, flared slacks, long sideburns and sunglasses. He was youngish, probably hip. One of those guys who gets high on the weekends but only lets his freak flag fly at half-mast; definitely not Frank Zappa; more like a blue-collar Stephen Stills. They made small talk about his car. Then the driver started asking creepy-weird questions about dating black men.

Vicki half-defiantly said she had. Nancy picked up the vibe and said she probably would. They knew what he meant by "dating." But they didn't know where he was going with it. It made them uneasy.

They didn't know it, but their answers were wrong. The driver immediately made up his mind: "So at that point I decided to waste both of them and, uhh, lured them out into the woods, you know," he confessed seventeen years later.

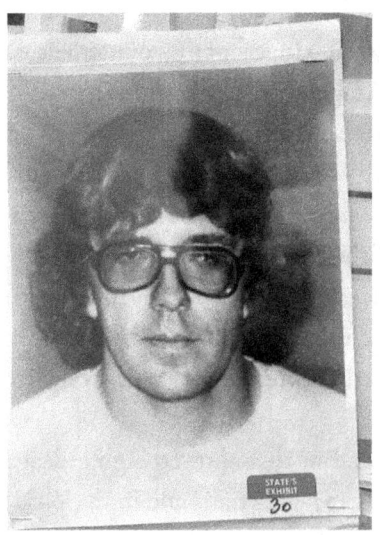

Joseph Paul Franklin in a picture taken near the time of his arrest in October 1980, about four months after he murdered two young women hitchhikers.

First he pulled off the highway at a convenience store to gas up. Then as they left he found a two-track dirt lane and turned off the road. The girls were getting nervous.

"It was a very isolated area, nobody around at all. So, uhh, I ordered them out of the car and they refused to do it." He reached under the driver's seat and pulled out a huge .44 magnum revolver.

"I wanted them to believe that I was planning on raping them, you

---

168 Transcripts of confession by Joseph Paul Franklin, 1997

know," he said. "Yeah, I told them that. That's the only way I could think of to get them out of the car. I didn't wanna tell 'em I was going to kill 'em. ... You know, that would have been even worse." He laughed, imagining how that would have paralyzed the frightened girls.

He watched and waited as Vicki and Nancy cringed against the car doors, trying desperately to get away without getting out, their eyes wide and white with fear. The driver said, almost reasonably, "Look, get out or I'm going to have to shoot you right here." They didn't move. He said it again, "Get out or I will shoot you."

Later he recalled, "You know, I could have just said, 'Hey, look. I'm a serial killer, you know what I mean? I will really kill you if you don't get out." He laughed again. "So anyway, I just decided, you know, when I realized they weren't goin' to move I just went ahead and shot the one immediately right there in the front seat."

He shot Vicki in the chest, then swung the powerful, deafening handgun back to Nancy and shot her in the side of the head as she cringed in the corner of the small backseat.

As Vicki was dying in the front seat, he looked into her eyes to watch the light fade away and shot her again in the chest, then turned the gun back to Nancy and shot her twice more in the head.

As the echoes of the gun blasts faded, he calmly grabbed them by their collars and dragged the two bodies out of the car. He laid them in the grass, looked at his victims briefly, then got back in the car and drove away. He took their backpacks down another dirt road nearby and threw them on a pile of trash. He checked the car and found a piece of bone in the backseat, but not as much blood as he expected. The side of the car had stopped the bullets, leaving a small, raised bump on the outside of one door. He cleaned up the blood, took the big revolver apart and buried it.

The girls' bodies were found at dusk the same day, June 25, 1980, by a passing motorist.

The "Rainbow Killings" made national headlines. They were unsolved for thirteen years, until Jacob Beard, 47, was convicted of the murders. No matter how he was bullied, badgered and grilled, he insisted he was

Judge Melissa Powers at her desk in 2022, surrounded by files from the Franklin case, her notes on legal pads and old cassette tapes of his confession.

innocent. He was. Two men who told detectives that Beard pulled the trigger had been given immunity to testify against him. Their confessions had been coerced by the police.

The serial killer who murdered Nancy Santomero and Vicki Durian was Joseph Paul Franklin, the same serial killer who had shot and paralyzed Larry Flynt in 1978.

He confessed in 1997, on death row in Missouri, waiting to be executed for the 1977 sniper murder of a St. Louis man, Gerald Gordon. Gordon had been outside a Synagogue where Franklin shot several people, aiming to kill Jews like his idol, Adolph Hitler.

Sitting across from Franklin as he confessed was Melissa Powers, an assistant prosecutor for Hamilton County.

Back in Cincinnati, Powers had an impressive record for felony convictions but was assigned to one of the worst offices at the courthouse: a windowless room so small it could have been a supply closet. The prison cell in Missouri where Franklin confessed was barely smaller.

During the confession he was shackled at his waist and wearing chain hobbles on his ankles. His hands were cuffed. A prison guard stood just outside, watching through a two-way mirror. There was a panic button behind Powers to call for help if she needed it.

But for all that, she still felt very alone with Franklin and she was scared. "I had to remind myself to breathe," she said twenty-five years later, in 2022.

CHAPTER 18 • THE DEVIL WENT DOWN TO GEORGIA

"The most shocking thing was his skin. It had no pigment. He was so white he was almost translucent." Powers had never seen anyone who had been locked so long without an exposure to the sun. "That made it very real," she said.

In a way, his lack of color was fitting. By 1997, Franklin was known as the "Racist Killer" who hunted black victims and mixed-race couples with a sniper rifle. Most of his murders were carefully planned as part of his White Supremacist plot to start a race war, or at least kill as many blacks as he could. The most radical racist hate groups were too tame for Franklin.

But prison was another world. Franklin lived in fear of black inmates; he was especially afraid to be jailed in Cincinnati, for good reasons that Powers would soon confirm. In Missouri, he was kept in isolation for his protection. But the lack of sunlight left him whiter than white. From his bunker in Hell, Hitler would have approved.

As Powers sat in the Supermax Potosi Prison southwest of St. Louis, her journey seemed as much a product of random chance as the murders of those two hippie hitchhikers in 1980.

"One day Joe Deters called me to his office," her story began.

Law enforcement had been trying for seventeen years to get a confession from Franklin for the racist murders of two black teens in Cincinnati in 1980. There was solid evidence that Franklin was in Cincinnati when the boys were killed. He had placed classified ads to sell a gun and an electric guitar he had stolen. A young woman who bought the guitar contacted Cincinnati Police detectives, who recovered his fingerprints on it. But just proving he was in Cincinnati when the boys were murdered was not enough.

So when Hamilton County Prosecutor Joe Deters saw Franklin on the CBS crime show *Inside Edition*, he noticed that Franklin opened up to the attractive woman who interviewed him. That gave him an idea. He called local TV reporter Deborah Dixon, who had also been following and interviewing Franklin, hoping to get his confession for seventeen years.

"As a crime reporter, I started at the beginning, in Mobile, Alabama where Franklin was raised," Dixon said. "His real name was James

Clayton Vaughn. He later changed it, taking Joseph and Paul from the infamous Nazi Paul Joseph Goebbels. He took his last name from Ben Franklin. I learned that his family called him 'Jimmy.'"

As he was being led in handcuffs past a scrum of reporters she shouted, "Hey, Jimmy," and he turned to talk to her. The connection was made.

When Deters called Dixon to share his plan, she told him, "Don't send a man."

Deters chose Powers. As a former fashion model, the blond, pretty prosecutor might finally be the key to unlocking Franklin's secrets.

"He told me about this Franklin guy," Powers recalled. "So I started looking into it. I came back and said I wanted to write him a letter, to establish rapport. At first, Joe said no, but he finally let me write it. I knew that Franklin hated the FBI and the government, so I didn't do a typed letter, I wrote it by hand, in very feminine handwriting."

She included a picture as bait. Franklin responded in two weeks.

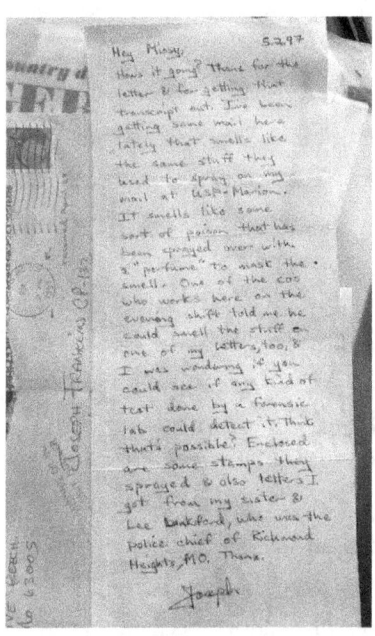

One of the letters Franklin wrote to Powers begins, 'Hey Missy,' and asks if she can test his mail to see if the prison is spraying poison on them.

In their first phone call to set up an interview, Franklin gushed, "You're so gorgeous. Uh, it'll be nice just sitting down face to face and talking with a really pretty lady."

She offered a date for the interview, but Franklin refused. That day was sacred. It was Hitler's birthday. Instead, they arranged a meeting on April 13, 1997, which was Franklin's 47th birthday.

As she entered the Death Row unit and was ushered to the cell where they met, "I was really nervous about those doors clanging shut behind me," Powers said. "I was afraid that would throw me off my game."

CHAPTER 18 • THE DEVIL WENT DOWN TO GEORGIA

Prisons have their own climate, a miasma of unwashed bodies, unflushed toilets, fear, despair, oppression, anger. The lighting is harsh, the surfaces are hard steel and stone, all designed to bury the spirit and smother any hope of escape.

Franklin would not allow videotape of the interview. "He was flat-line, speaking in a monotone," Powers recalled, "until he talked about killing interracial couples. Then he would get excited, as if he was sexually turned on."

Dixon noticed the same skin-crawling light in his eyes. "When he described killing the rainbow girls after he asked if they had dated black men, he told me, 'I knew they had to die.' As he talked about shooting the girl in the head, you could tell by his eyes that he was reliving it. He described what her eyes did, her last gasp of life. He was proud of his work."

Dixon talked to Powers before the trip to Missouri, and shared some tips given to her by FBI profilers and a criminal psychologist: Franklin craves attention and flattery; he loves being in control; he's attracted to you, you can use that; but remember, to him a lie is as good as the truth.

Powers flattered him about his well-written letters and his new prison haircut. "I was really delighted to hear from you," she said. She used words like "signs" and "omens" that appealed to his fascination with the occult.

"Are you scared to come by yourself?" he asked her several times, sensing her fear. He wanted to know her age, if she was married, where she lived. He asked for her horoscope sign and called her "Melissa."

"I'm gonna tell you something no one else knows," he would say as he began to reveal yet another of his 15 to 20-plus murders.

As he confessed to the murder of an interracial couple, he bragged about how he had learned to shoot the man first because it was easier to kill the woman that way. Women were more likely to stay to help the first victim, he explained, so they made easy targets. He showed off the large Grim Reaper tattoo on his arm and laughed about his CB handle, "Bushwhacker."

He edged his chair around closer so that he could touch her feet with his.

"I was afraid to pull away and stop the interview," Powers said. "He knew what he was doing. I was so worried. Would that evil jump to me?"

Darryl and Dante

"You know I did it," he said.

"You did what?" she asked.

"I killed those two dudes."

"In Cincinnati?"

Franklin just laughed.

Then, for the first time, he confessed how he had staked out a railroad trestle in Cincinnati, directly over a sidewalk, waiting for an "MRC" (mixed-race couple) to walk by. He had cruised through the nearby streets in his coffee-brown, 1975 Camaro.[169] He wanted to make sure the

Darrel Lane and Dante Evans, the two boys killed by Franklin in Cincinnati, were chosen for murder because they were black and they came down the sidewalk where he was waiting in ambush.

---

169 Franklin replaced the bullet-holed black Nova by selling it to an unsuspecting buyer who had no idea the car was the crime scene of the two Rainbow Killings.

CHAPTER 18 • THE DEVIL WENT DOWN TO GEORGIA

neighborhood was not "too black" because he didn't want to stand out or draw attention. He placed a scrap of white paper near a trail that led through bushes so he could spot it in the dark and climb up to the trestle. Then he returned to set up his ambush on Sunday night, June 8, 1980.

After waiting for "an hour or two" with no targets, he heard two teens as they came down the street. "So I had just decided to just go ahead and split when all of a sudden they walked up."

Dante Evans Brown, 13, and Darrell Layne, 14, were good athletes and played football together. They were laughing and shouting as

The view from the railroad trestle where Franklin waited. The bloodstain on the sidewalk was still fresh when the photo was taken and kept as evidence in his trial.

The murder scene, from sidewalk level.

they walked down the sidewalk on their way to buy soft drinks. Two innocent kids on a spring night near the end of the school year, happy and carefree. Franklin shot them with his scoped .44 caliber Ruger sniper rifle because they had accidentally stepped into his shadow of death.

"I just put the gun right on the biggest dude first, you know. And, uhm, you know, fired one shot with that .44 magnum. And, uhm, so you know I just heard somebody go 'ahh'—make a sound like, you know, they had just got shot. The other guy bolted and it was just like through a miracle that I got him, man, you know? ... As soon as he heard the (first) shot he just bolted and started runnin' and I aimed the gun without even, just in the dark there, just hope that I would get a lucky shot and hit him, you know? And sure enough it actually got him, man. It was strange."

He took careful aim and shot them both again "to make sure."

"Can you tell me why you did it?" Powers asked.

"Uhm..."

"Was there any reason?"

"Uhm, let's see. Well, my main reason at the time, uhm... uhm... let's see. I was trying to get rid of all the ugly people in the world."

"Why did you select—"

"I considered the blacks the ugliest people of all, you know."

Powers was chilled. She thought, "These boys were just in the wrong place at the wrong time and crossed paths with evil that is walking around in the world." It was a terrifying revelation. It could happen to anyone. The safe world we all live in was an illusion.

Most people float through life in a fragile bubble, blissfully unaware of evil or outright denying it even exists. Those who encounter it face to face and look into its empty, malevolent, laughing eyes, as she did, are never quite the same again. Nobody is safe. We are never prepared for the predators.

Franklin told her about killing an interracial couple in Johnstown, Pennsylvania in a similar sniper ambush two weeks after the Cincinnati killings. As he sat waiting, hidden behind bushes, cradling is .44 caliber

CHAPTER 18 • THE DEVIL WENT DOWN TO GEORGIA

Guns taken from Franklin when he was caught: two scoped Ruger rifles and two revolvers, all .44 magnum.

Ruger rifle, "I just happened to be glancing through the scope and I could not believe my eyes when an interracial couple passed by," he laughed. Arthur Smothers, 22, and his white girlfriend, Kathleen Mikula, 16, were the next random victims.

Franklin was spilling his stories now. Powers only added an occasional "Right" to keep him going.

"I put the gun on the black guy first," he said, "and he just rolled over right off the sidewalk into the gutter. ... So I racked the action and fired a quick shot at her before she could get away and I wound up missin' her. But she just remained standin' there, you know? ... to try and help him."

"Right."

"She still stayed there, did not even run, which was fortunate for me. But, uhm, I just racked the action again and put it on her again and this time I got her. And she dropped right there and I racked the action one more time and shot him again and then one more time and shot her again."

Mikula's brother said later that he didn't care if Franklin was executed. "Suffering in prison is even worse because it makes him think and think and think."

But Franklin didn't think that way.

He laughed and bragged as he dropped his third bombshell of new confessions to Powers: the Rainbow Killings.

"June was the most prolific—I mean I was most prolific as far as murders go in that month," he said, as if talking about writing songs or painting landscapes. "I committed six murders. I just decided to turn up the heat a little bit. Just started committin' more killing and, you know, just to try to force them to get me publicity because they didn't want to publicize what I was doin.'"

He also told her about shooting Larry Flynt on March 6, 1978 outside a courthouse in Lawrenceville, Georgia, where Flynt was being tried on obscenity charges. As Flynt and his lawyer returned to court after lunch at a café, Franklin shot both of them.

Flynt's lawyer, Gene Reeves, described what happened: "He and I were walking together when the shooting occurred. They didn't hit me, they hit him.[170] I think there were two shots. One of them hit him in the spine; the other one was a flesh wound that went through him and into my arm, stomach, and pancreas. But you got to realize it was a .44 magnum, which is sort of an elephant gun.

"It looked like someone picked (Flynt) up and threw him about four or five feet, because he took the impact of the bullet. He was on the ground, and I recall I got up and tried to see how he was. About that time, I passed out. Then I came to and when I did, they were taking him to the hospital. Then another ambulance came and got me.

"It blasted my gallbladder off and sat in my pancreas. I was in the hospital for twenty-six days. Of course it had a tremendous effect—all at once, I was an international news thing. I got my five minutes of fame. If I had it to do over, I'd pass."[171]

Flynt was paralyzed from the waist down and spent the rest of his life in a wheelchair.

Franklin told Powers he shot Flynt because he was outraged by *Hustler* Magazine pictures of a white woman with a black man. "He stalked Flynt in Columbus for a long time," Powers said. When he couldn't get a good shot at Flynt in Columbus, he followed him to the Georgia trial.

Dixon said, "He told me, 'I decided a year earlier I was going to kill

---

[170] When Reeves described the shooting, he and detectives believed there may have been more than one shooter, probably sent by the Mob.

[171] "Flashback: Larry Flynt shot in Lawrenceville," Josh Green, *Atlanta Magazine*, March 20013

this guy, so I stalked him for a whole year until I caught up with him.'"

Ironically, Flynt had told reporters that he felt safer in the little town near Atlanta than he felt in Cincinnati. But he could not escape the connections to Cincinnati. The man who shot him confessed to a Cincinnati prosecutor, and had already killed two kids in Cincinnati. The *Hustler* Magazine that outraged Franklin was the same issue that was presented as evidence to a jury that convicted Flynt of obscenity in Cincinnati.

Some amateur detectives have speculated that Franklin falsely confessed to the Flynt shooting because he wanted attention. Powers, who knew him as well as any prosecutor, said she has "no doubt" he did it. "He knew all the streets up there in Columbus. I was astounded at his recall and memory of the streets in the neighborhood where he stalked Flynt."

Dixon agreed. In one of her interviews of Franklin he offered to draw her a map of the areas surrounding Flynt's home in Columbus, and complained that he had tried to shoot Flynt at the North Carolina home of evangelist Ruth Carter Stapleton, but was unable to get a clear shot.

Franklin told Powers that shooting Flynt only once was a mistake. "After that Larry Flynt shooting I wanted to make sure that from then on that I pretty well emptied the magazine.[172] ... I became very upset about that, you know, about not killing Larry Flynt. I wanted to kill him really bad. I just considered that if it was just wounded, I-I was a complete failure."

After a few years in prison, he said, he had changed his mind. "He never showed remorse except for the Flynt shooting," Powers recalled. "He felt sorry for Althea Flynt."

That alone, among all his murders, was "a tragedy," he said. He had not a teardrop of sympathy for his dozens of other victims and their families.

Franklin also bragged to Powers about how he shot and wounded Washington power broker and civil rights activist Vernon Jordan in Fort Wayne, Indiana in 1980 because he was unable to get a clean shot at his preferred target, Jesse Jackson, in Chicago.

---

172 Franklin qualified it by saying he always kept at least one cartridge in the magazine to kill any cops that got in his way.

He drifted back and forth across the nation for three years, killing randomly the way a wolf selects and slaughters stray sheep: Salt Lake City; Chattanooga; Doraville, Georgia; Madison, Wisconsin… and unknown, nameless others. "He killed a lot of prostitutes," Powers said. "He would steer them into a conversation and ask, 'Would you sleep with a black man?' If they said yes, he would shoot them."

He kept a scrapbook of Polaroid pictures of his victims. Investigators believed he was impotent and took out his frustration and rage on his victims.

As the confessions continued, Franklin poured out his crimes in a black cloud, filling the tiny interview cell with darkness. "He knew I was scared," Powers recalled. "He was sort of a genius. Not smart, but clever. He was into the spirit world, getting signs from numbers, animals, omens." He passed the time in his solitary cell doing pushups and chanting to his occult deities.

"Are you afraid of me?" he asked her. "You can trust me like a brother or father. I won't hurt you."

Later he said, "I'm gonna make you famous."

The FBI's website still claims credit for catching Franklin. But it was Cincinnati Police Detectives Michael O'Brien and William Davis who put the pieces of Franklin's murders together and solved the case. When the FBI tried to hijack the case and seize the evidence collected by the Cincinnati detectives, Hamilton County Prosecutor Si Leis took their files to a grand jury to protect their work behind the cloak of grand jury secrecy. "That was brilliant," Powers said.

Franklin robbed sixteen banks to finance his killing spree and got away with it by wearing wigs and disguises. In a strange twist of fate he was arrested at the Florence Scottish Inn motel in Florence, Kentucky on September 25, 1980, when police came to arrest another bank robbery suspect at about 2 a.m. Franklin saw the police lights outside and became frantic. He pestered the desk clerk with calls to ask what was going on until the clerk became suspicious and tipped off the cops about him. They ran his license plates and spotted a gun in the car. The plate number turned up a warrant for two murders in Salt Lake City, so they arrested

CHAPTER 18 • THE DEVIL WENT DOWN TO GEORGIA

him and took him in for questioning.[173]

But after five hours, the officer interviewing him stepped out of the room to get him a soft drink and take a phone call, and Franklin escaped.[174]

Dixon reported what happened: "The Florence Police caught him with guns in his car. But he was so manipulative he talked his way into crawling out the window. Then he hitchhiked and got picked up. He said he was in a car accident and needed help. Then he stole a bike, got his hair dyed and got away. He thought that was hysterical. He was so proud of himself. In a psychotic way he was brilliant. Also sad and pathetic."

As a manhunt was launched, police learned that Franklin had been living at two motels in Florence. They interviewed friends who smoked pot and partied with him. They thought he was a great guy: intelligent, well-dressed, polite. And he loved to talk about his guns, they said.

He narrowly escaped, but the police now had his guns, his car and his fingerprints that matched the ones taken off the stolen guitar he sold in Cincinnati.

He was finally caught just before Halloween in 1980 as he left a Lakeland, Florida blood bank, where transients were paid $5 for their plasma. Fliers circulated by the FBI had described his tattoos.

Melissa Powers and Prosecutor Joe Deters at a press conference to announce the indictment of Franklin for the murders of Darrell Lane and Dante Evans Brown on April 15, 1997. Glenn Hartong, *the Cincinnati Enquirer.*

---

173   "Firing Squad Possible For Convicted Racist," *The Miami Herald,* September 20, 1981.
174   "Florence Police Speculate Suspect Still in Area," Dave Beasley and Caden Blincoe, *The Cincinnati Enquirer,* September 26, 1980.

A technician at Sera-Tec Biologicals spotted the Grim Reaper on his arm and reported it to her supervisor. He called the police.

Franklin was caught as he sold his own blood so he could continue to paint a mural of death in the blood of his victims.

When Powers walked out of the cell in the Missouri prison, she was drained and pale. She turned to one of the watching law-enforcement witnesses and said, "I just sold my soul to get that confession."

A few days later she stood next to her boss, Prosecutor Joe Deters, to announce the breakthrough. Pictures show a stark contrast. The pretty young cover-girl prosecutor with the photogenic smile suddenly looked ten years older, worn and grim, troubled and shaken. She had spent hours in a tiny cell with a merciless predator, close enough to smell his prison breath and feel his corpse-pale feet touch hers as he laughed and bragged about harvesting the lives of innocent boys, men and women, like the Grim Reaper tattooed on his arm.

How are monsters made?

Franklin was a horribly abused child, beaten so brutally by his mother that he was blinded in one eye. He was a dropout, a psychopathic serial killer and a "lone-wolf" drifter, cancered by hate.

Dixon said, "He was a sociopath in a dark, sad way because he had such a horrible childhood. He was mocked and teased his whole life. Growing up, he didn't have shoes and wore big, thick glasses." Franklin told her, "I was born that way, I don't know how to describe it, I was a born killer."

Franklin claimed he was taking orders from God. But that was a lie from the "father of lies."[175] His soul sickness came from something much darker, Powers said.

"He was just so evil. I was looking into the eyes of evil, afraid how it would affect me, how it might get inside of my head and destroy me emotionally and mentally."

---

175 "You belong to your father, the devil, and you want to carry out your father's desires. He was a murderer from the beginning, not holding to the truth, for there is no truth in him. When he lies, he speaks his native language, for he is a liar and the father of lies." John 8:44

Dixon said, "I knew that what she was about to experience would cling to her forever, like soot from a fire that won't wash off."

After Franklin's confessions, he was brought to Cincinnati to be prosecuted for the murders Dante Evans Brown and Daryl Lane. Powers was a key witness and had to testify. Franklin used every opportunity to get as close to her as possible. It made her skin crawl. One day as she sat in court, she and others noticed something strange about the lights suspended from the courtroom ceiling. All of them were stationary as expected, except one. The globe directly over Franklin was gyrating.

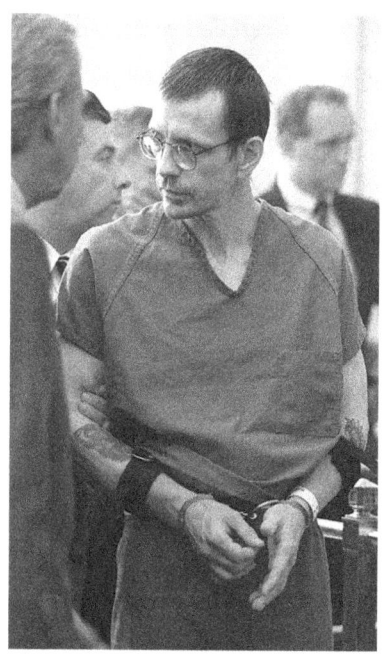

Franklin on trial in Cincinnati. Shackles cover part of the Grim Reaper tattoo on his right arm. Glenn Hartong, *The Cincinnati Enquirer.*

"There are angels and devils in our stories, and I believe the devil was at work in this man," she said.

During the trial, Powers had vivid and violent nightmares that her father and her son would be injured. Both were hurt in accidents within days, just as the dreams foretold. She finally sought help from a priest who held her hands and said, "Missy, you have to know that good always overcomes evil." At that instant she was overcome with relief and the light of God's grace. The bad dreams stopped.

Dixon had a similar experience she still can't quite explain. "I ended up after one of the interviews, I felt something so dark that I could hardly breathe. It was like somebody throwing a blanket of evil across my face. In a little place on my face the skin broke away, like a wound. I had to have a little plastic surgery. In my heart, this is what that evil blanket did to me. Maybe not. But that's what I felt."

For seventeen years, Dixon had received letters from Franklin. He told her the Cincinnati cops should pray for their souls and wrote to her that "Satan is trying to kill you," but "there's not a lot you can do about it."

She interviewed him twice in Missouri. At the end he even invited her to his execution. She declined. More than anyone, she understood what Powers went through and admired her courage.

"Melissa Powers spent hours in a room, on death row, to get the confession of record. After Deters' news conference, I found the news headline 'Beauty and the Beast' to be insulting. Melissa Powers is beautiful, but she is brave and smart. She had to play Franklin just right to get the information needed for a courtroom."

It took the jury forty-five minutes to find him guilty. He was given two life sentences, but death by lethal injection was already waiting in Missouri.

It took Powers nine years before she could talk comfortably about the case. It still bothered her in 2022 as she sat in her office as a Hamilton County Juvenile Court judge, paging through transcripts and evidence, as if the dust that had collected on old pictures and documents was still poisoned by the ghost of Franklin.

She wondered if some of the kids in juvenile court are future Franklins. Some check all the red-flag boxes: childhood trauma; beatings; never loved; cruelty to animals; fascination with firearms; bedwetters; fire starters... tomorrow's serial killers.

Juvenile Court Judge Melissa Powers keeps a framed copy of Page One from *The Cincinnati Enquirer* in April 1997, reporting her press conference after the confessions she took from Joseph Paul Franklin.

After several delays by judges who naively refused to believe Franklin's vow that he would kill again if he was not executed, Franklin was finally put to death by lethal injection in 2013.

One nightmare that Powers had in 1997 remains vivid after twenty-five years. In her dream, she held an Indian drum and had to keep banging it for some reason, on and on and on....

It did not make sense until months later. During his confession, Franklin had told her, "I'm going to give you something nobody else knows." He told her where he had dumped the girls' backpacks after the Rainbow Killings. She passed it on to detectives and thought nothing more about it until one day she asked one of them what was in the backpacks carried by Nancy and Vicki. They told her one contained an Indian drum.

"I believed those girls were speaking to me from the dead."

Night Moves

19
Political Porn

In 1994 a political parasite named James Carville mocked the women who had accused President Bill Clinton of rape by saying, "Drag a hundred-dollar bill through a trailer park and you never know what you'll find."

Larry Flynt decided to put the Carville theory to the test in the biggest trailer park on earth—Washington, DC. On October 4, 1998, Flynt ran a full-page ad in the *Washington Post*: "Have you had an adulterous sexual encounter with a current member of the United States Congress or a high-ranking government official?" It listed a phone number and offered a bounty of $1 million.

Drag a million dollars through the Washington swamp and you never know what you'll find. Thousands of calls flooded *Hustler* headquarters.

President Bill Clinton with Attorney General Janet Reno and Vice President Al Gore in 1994. Wikimedia/White House photo.

Just weeks before, the details of President Clinton's Oval Office "dates" with 22-year-old White House intern Monica Lewinsky were vividly described in the Starr Report, named after Independent Counsel Kenneth Starr. Parts of the report sounded like something from *Hustler Magazine* or the fantasy X-rated letters in *Penthouse*.

Flynt finally had found a President he could support. He rushed to save Clinton from impeachment by spending $4 million on a team of former CIA and FBI agents to dig up dirt on Republicans who were attacking Flynt's new hero, "Slick Willy."

But even his pack of trash-sniffing birddogs must have been surprised at the amount of wildlife they flushed from the DC swamp.

"There was no single factor which had a greater impact on the impeachment process than Larry Flynt,"[176] wrote author Dan Moldea, who joined Flynt's bloodhounds.

By December, Flynt's $1 million bait had hooked a giant groper.

It was Bob Livingston, the top House Republican in line to replace Speaker Newt Gingrich. When the Louisiana congressman found out his former mistress had talked to Flynt's snoopers, he hastily resigned one step ahead of the scandal squad. He confessed that "on occasion (I have) strayed from my marriage." He added, "I sought marriage and spiritual counseling and have received forgiveness from my wife and family, for which I am eternally grateful. This chapter was a small, but painful part of the past in an otherwise wonderful marriage."[177]

Representative Bob Livingston.

Before he was exiled from the swamp in disgrace, Livingston had

---

176 *Confessions of as Guerrilla Writer,* Dan Moldea, Moldea.com, June 25, 2020

177 "How Porn King Larry Flynt Dramatically Reshaped Louisiana Politics by Uncovering Two Sex Scandals," Tyler Bridges, February 15, 2021, NOLA.com, *New Orleans Times-Picayune.*

CHAPTER 19 • POLITICAL PORN

been an outspoken leader of the impeachment posse. Clinton had famously lied to the public, shaking a finger and saying, "I did not have sex with that woman Monica Lewinsky." When caught, he tortured the language with a soliloquy on what the "meaning of is, is," but it fooled nobody besides members of the press who could not get enough of the Clinton Kool-Aid.

The Starr Report proved beyond a doubt that President Clinton lied under oath and tampered with witnesses, committing criminal felonies and abuse of power. But Livingston and other Republicans focused on his more sensational sexual exploitation of a vulnerable young woman—what would later become known as a "Me Too" scandal.

When Livingston was caught in Flynt's snare, his hypocrisy became the issue for the press, a convenient way to eclipse Clinton's perjury and obstruction of justice. The Livingston scandal gave a cynical, jaded public the chance to say, "To hell with all of them. They're all crooked, lying hypocrites."

When he resigned, Livingston dared Clinton to resign too, to help heal the country. Too late. The tide of opinion had turned. Clinton brushed off the challenge.

A *New York Times* analysis said, "The shock waves of the Livingston resignation spread far beyond the West Wing of the White House, and had a sobering effect on members of Congress of both parties who might have been contemplating calling for Mr. Clinton to step down in the aftermath of the impeachment vote.

"Fearful of the entire government unraveling, very few members of Congress joined a clamor for Mr. Clinton's resignation. The President had dodged one of the most potentially hazardous moments of the entire impeachment battle."[178]

What the *Times* failed to mention was that any Republican President who sexually exploited a young intern in the Oval Office would have been tarred and feathered by the press and driven from office in disgrace. But the media defended Clinton the way Texans defended the Alamo.

---

178 "Clinton's Acquittal: The Politics – Victory for None," Lizette Alvarez, John M. Broder and Katharine Q. Seelye, *New York Times,* February 14, 1999.

Their battle cry was, "Remember, it's only about sex."

The worst of the storm had passed, but Flynt and his team of window-peeping detectives were not finished.

The next target was another leading Republican critic of Clinton, Georgia Congressman Bob Barr. He was one of the most aggressive House Managers appointed to present evidence and act as prosecutors in the looming Senate impeachment trial. Flynt's bombshell on Barr was a dud: He waved a photograph of Barr licking whipped cream off a woman's neck. It certainly looked salacious. The media loved it. But in fact, it was taken at a fundraiser that dared VIPs to do embarrassing stunts to raise money.

Flynt also revealed that Barr's ex-wife said the pro-life congressman had not discouraged her from having an abortion. Barr insisted he had opposed her decision. Another fizzle.

In response to the Flynt attacks, Barr and others demanded an investigation of Flynt and his team, for a "deliberate and concentrated effort to impede the House of Representatives from fulfilling its duties under the United States Constitution." It went nowhere. Congress was too frightened of what Larry Flynt might find next. The alleged leaders of the free world were punked by a smut hustler. Nearly everybody in the DC swamp had something slimy to hide.

The Flynt attacks were called "media terrorism," "blackmail," "jury tampering," "intimidation," "contempt of Congress" and "abetting blackmail."

And they worked. First, by taking down Livingston; second, by exposing Congress as a confederacy of phonies, philanderers, cheaters and liars; and third, with implicit Mob-style threats to Republicans to back off on attacking Clinton or Flynt would unleash his hounds to sniff out more dirt on more corrupt leaders in the House and Senate.

Flynt admitted his fishing net had dredged up embarrassing scandals among Democrats too, but refused to reveal those. Only Republicans were targeted. Moldea made the extortion explicit in an interview with *Washington Post* writer Howard Kurtz: "Some Republicans on Capitol Hill should be sending us flowers and thank-you cards. They weren't

CHAPTER 19 • POLITICAL PORN

going on TV talk shows shooting off their mouths [about Clinton], or going to the floor of Congress to seize the moral high ground. We've thrown them back in the river. We're not going to interfere with their lives. There has to be some higher purpose than tawdry sex."

He told Kurtz, "We don't want the perception that we're a bunch of terrorists and we're going to kill a hostage a week until they release the President."[179]

But that's how it looked: Keep your mouth shut about the sleazy President's sex scandal or you're next.

When Flynt announced he would name more "big fish," C-SPAN pulled the plug on his press conference, fearing libel and slander liability. "What are the chances it could get out of control?" a network official said. With Flynt? 100 percent.

The House voted to impeach Clinton, but the Senate cringed. Public opinion, influenced by the media, had turned against impeachment, and no doubt more than a few Republican senators got cold sweats about what Flynt might have in his files. They decided to support the President "for the good of the country"—and their marriages and re-election, not necessarily in that order.

They had reason to be scared. White House officials were helping Flynt's investigators with access to a metropolitan sewer district of DC dirt: a vault of secret FBI files that were seized by Hillary Clinton as

During his impeachment, President Clinton started carrying a Bible, got a dog and used photo-ops with his family to repair his image as a good husband and father.
Wikimedia/White House photo.

---

179 "C-SPAN Strikes Flynt," Howard Kurtz, *Washington Post*, January 13, 1999.

253

soon as she got into the White House. The FBI had the darkest secrets on everyone in DC, a tradition started by FBI Director J. Edgar Hoover, who built his career on political blackmail—at the same time *he* was being blackmailed by the Mob for his secret life as a cross-dressing homosexual. Former FBI and CIA agents on Flynt's team knew better than anyone where to find the most crowded skeleton closets.

Even after Clinton survived the Senate trial, Flynt could not resist and went ahead with more scandals. Moldea was proved wrong: Flynt had no higher purpose than "tawdry sex." The media loved it. Family-values Republicans trapped in the glare of sex scandals were cable-TV caviar for schlock hosts such as Geraldo Rivera. A dozen more DC Republicans were exposed in the "Flynt Report," published in March 1999. Headlines promised "Fresh Dirt" on former Speaker Newt Gingrich. Flynt's team had found out about Gingrich's "common knowledge" affair with a congressional aide during the impeachment. As Gingrich went on TV to scorch Clinton for his infidelity and immorality, he was cheating on his wife, who was in the hospital with cancer.

To voters, it was obvious: The greatest nation on earth was being run by moral cretins who made the last days of Caligula's Rome look like Vacation Bible School. There was more:

- The congressman who replaced Livingston, David Vitter, was caught using call girls provided by "The DC Madam."
- The House Speaker who replaced Gingrich, Dennis Hastert, was sent to prison for sexually abusing boys as a high school wrestling coach.
- Powerful Republican Henry Hyde, author of the anti-abortion Hyde Amendment, was caught cheating on his wife with a married woman.
- Democrat Congressman Mel Reynolds was indicted for sexual assault of a 16-year-old campaign worker, but was re-elected and served in Congress until he was convicted for assault and solicitation of child porn.

CHAPTER 19 • POLITICAL PORN

And there was Clinton. Nobody in presidential history had done more to pornify the White House and dishonor public decency. His legacy was lying to cover up a sex scandal that pushed presidential decency so low it reached the subzero morality of Larry Flynt. The Smut King himself played Grand Inquisitor to judge and condemn the nation's most powerful leaders.

Between 1900 and 1970, Washington sex scandals were *unheard of*—meaning they existed (FDR, JFK, LBJ) but were almost never reported. Since they were weaponized by Larry Flynt to save Clinton, they have exploded to an average of two dozen per decade. In March 2022, a rookie congressman said that the sex-drenched Netflix series about Washington, *House of Cards*, was "closer to a documentary" than it was to fiction. The media yawned.

The press used to get aroused by sex scandals, Politico reported. "But then came Bill Clinton, who had at least one affair (and probably many more), lied about it, got caught lying, was impeached, and then saw his approval ratings rise and crest like a wave at Honolua Bay. We care so little about peccadillos nowadays since sexual expression has been decriminalized."[180]

More likely, the media care so little nowadays because the same Washington press corps that salivated over sex accusations by porn star Stormy Daniels against Republican President Donald Trump, covered their eyes to ignore credible accusations that Democrat President Joe Biden shoved his hands up a woman's skirt and has a creepy attraction to sniffing little girls and groping women. Even sexual assault has become partisan—another Clinton legacy. Allegations against Republicans are front-page news; credible victims of Democrats are mocked, shamed and ridiculed or simply ignored.

Flynt wriggled off the hook like his idol Clinton. He paid some informants up to six figures, but nobody was able to claim the $1 million bounty. Livingston's mistress honorably refused a reward from Flynt. And Flynt paid his lawyers to weasel out of paying others what he promised.

---

180 "Why Nobody Believed Madison Cawthorn – and Nobody Would Have Cared if it Was True," Jack Shafer, *Politico*, March 31, 2022.

Like most modern politicians whose wax wings were melted by scandal, Livingston did not fall far. He landed softly with a lobbyist parachute. When Flynt died in 2021, a reporter asked Livingston for a comment. He replied, "I don't have anything to say, because I'm too busy partying."

20

Serpent's Tooth

THE CINCINNATI ENQUIRER, JANUARY 10, 1997—"Hey, Judy, get a load of this," Jake said. "That fringy Act Out Theater Company in Over-the-Rhine has announced a new play in their Urban Shakespeare series. *Much Ado About Booty*. The press release calls it 'A hip-hop tragedy about Larry Flynt and the death of free speech.' As Dave Barry says, you can't make this stuff up."

Judy laughed. "I wonder if they realized that their press release is funnier than Bennie Hill. If Shakespeare could write a play about Larry Flynt it would have to be a comedy called 'King Leer' with two E's."

"'Hell is empty and all the devils are here,'" Punch quoted from *The Tempest*.

Judy replied with one from *Hamlet*: "'There is nothing either good or bad, but thinking makes it so.'"

"'The evil that men do lives after them,'" Punch retorted.

"That's from *Othello*, right?" Jake asked.

"*Julius Caesar*," Judy corrected. "Shakespeare was talking about Larry Flynt."

Jake was learning. Copyeditors are always right. But Jim probably would have known it was not *Othello*. Sitting at Jim's desk made him feel like an impostor, as if any minute someone would come along and say, "Who is this guy pretending to be the city editor—and where's Jim Gardner?"

Gardner was gone. He had retired after the Chiquita debacle. He said he felt like it was time to go. But Jake knew the exact day when Jim made up his mind. They were in a staff meeting to discuss the latest reader survey. Two-thirds of the readers had said the newspaper was "too liberal." And Clarabell had responded, "We need a new survey. We asked the wrong people."

Jim replied, "I thought you quit smokin' that devil's lettuce last year. Those 'wrong people' are the subscribers who pay the bills around here. They are the loyal readers who keep us in business. And they're right."

After the meeting, Jim was summoned to the "principal's office," where the latest Gannetoid "man upstairs" told him his remarks were inappropriate and insensitive, and a reprimand would be added to his next performance evaluation for referral to HR. He was ordered to apologize to Karen for making her cry. And the woodshed treatment continued with some pointed remarks about how the *Enquirer* needed to appeal to *younger* readers to keep up with the new digital media revolution, blah, blah, blah. Cincinnati, meaning Jim, needed to accept changes and get with it. The old rules no longer applied, times have changed, smell the coffee....

Jim realized it was a waste of breath to point out that nobody buys a newspaper subscription in their 20s. Catering to those readers was like selling TVs to the blind.

That was the last straw, Jake thought when Jim told him about it later. Besides, Jim never liked the transition to the new newsroom on the nineteenth floor of the new Enquirer Building at 312 Elm Street. Most of the younger staff thought the glitzy glass and chrome newsroom overlooking the river was cool, but Jim had quipped, "I guess this makes it official: Now we can look down on everyone."

Veterans like Punch and Judy called it the "Nightmare on Elm Street." They had a point, Jake thought.

The newsroom looked like a telemarketing call center or an insurance office. Instead of desks scattered around, everyone was subdivided in a geometrical gopher-town maze of cloth-paneled dividers. Heads popped up like prairie dogs when people wanted to talk or look around to see who was there. And to go with the new offices, the paper had a new publisher, then a new editor, both "Gannetoids" who were transplanted like bioengineered hydroponic tomatoes: they looked like the real thing but their roots never touched the ground and they had no flavor.

CHAPTER 20 • SERPENT'S TOOTH

The new Gannett bosses didn't know or care much about Cincinnati; they could barely conceal their scorn to be stuck in such a backward whistlestop town on their express train to success and promotion.

And then the Chiquita car-wreck was planned behind Jim's back. Nobody who was not in on the secretive project knew about it until it was published one Sunday morning. Jim's phone rang at home all day, and he was humiliated to have to admit that the city editor was kept in the dark by a "black box" squad of editors and reporters who worked out of a locked room, like some CIA plot to kidnap a Pulitzer Prize.

Of course, the new editor and publisher knew all about it, and so did the Gannett corporate executives who reviewed every comma and quote with their expensive lawyers. None of them noticed that hacking voice mails was illegal. So when it blew up in their faces, the people at the top followed the *Mission Impossible* TV script: "The secretary will disavow any knowledge of your actions."

They ran for cover and blamed the *Enquirer*, which was now treated like a stepchild with measels. The editor and publisher were contagious with shame, crippled in the community, mocked by the staff, walking dead men in the corporate career universe. And the paper had squandered its only coin of credibility on some counterfeit magic beans.

Morale was in the dumpster, somewhere among the swaybacked, nicotine-stained chairs and cigarette-burned desks from the old Vine Street newsroom. Suddenly, budget cuts were as predictable as seasonal orange traffic cones on I-71. Everyone was waiting for the next ax to fall.

Jake turned to Punch and Judy, "Here's one that would fit like Flynt's gold-plated wheelchair: 'How sharper than a serpent's tooth it is to have a thankless child.' *King Lear*, without two Es."

"Perfect," Judy said. "That story about his daughter the other day was amazing."

"Too bad they won't be making a movie about her," Punch nodded. "'Though she be but little, she is fierce.'"

"I think that's from *Romeo and Booty-ette*," Judy said.

Punch shook his head and muttered, "All the world's a stage."

Flynt vs. Cincinnati, the sequel

When *The People Vs. Larry Flynt* movie came out in 1996, the porn king was enshrined as a First Amendment martyr—a genuine "American patriot," the media said. The movie was nominated for Oscars and won numerous awards. Billboards showed the Hollywood version of Flynt, actor Woody Harrelson, posing with outstretched arms like Christ on the cross, crucified on a woman's crotch.

Hollywood, the media, TV pundits, college professors, suburban moms... *everyone* agreed that Larry Flynt was redeemed. Except his daughter, Tonya Flynt-Vega.

"When we start, as a country, worshipping a man like Larry Flynt, we're in trouble," she said. "I don't believe he deserves a respectable place in history."[181]

She reacted to the glorified, sanitized movie version of her father by embracing a new mission as an anti-porn activist. She joined the American Family Association—Flynt's nemesis—at press conferences to set the record straight.

"I don't have the words to tell you how much damage is being done to our society because of pornography. I believe God has called me and prepared me to do something about this," she said to Religion News Service.

Flynt accused her of seeking attention. The irony.

No doubt she did want attention from her father back in 1965, when he deserted her and her mother. She seldom saw him when she was a child, but did receive $500 one Christmas—enclosed in a card showing a pornographic Santa Claus.

She accused him of sexually abusing her as a child and exposing her to porn that gave her nightmares during visits to his home in California. "When you expose young children to sexuality at a very young age, you ruin your children," she said, speaking from personal experience.[182]

---

[181] "Tonya Flynt-Vega Vs. Larry Flynt: Daughter is Anti-Porn Crusader," *Orlando Sentinel*, January 13, 1997.

[182] Ibid.

CHAPTER 20 • SERPENT'S TOOTH

"My father began sexually abusing me before I was ten years old. He told me he was doing it because he was sorry for beating me the same day." What she described echoed testimony from victims in the anti-pornography Meese Report.

He showed her *Hustler Magazines* to "break down my inhibitions," she said. "He said he wasn't allowed to publish lies in his magazine so whatever was in there was okay."[183]

She hoped her battle against porn would inspire other victims. "I want people to know that they have a voice and they need to speak out if they are being abused," she said. "If I can do it with all the wealth and power my father has, they can do it, too."

Flynt denied the abuse accusations. But his FBI file includes an April 1989 memo from the Special Agent in Charge in Los Angeles. The subject line: "Sexual Exploitation of Children." The redacted file was marked for destruction and nothing more was released.

The story his daughter told was lost in the shadows while all the spotlights were turned on Larry. He schmoozed with the Hollywood elites and gave interviews. He was treated like a star. He relished playing the movie role of Judge William Morrisey, who sentenced him in 1978. He was even invited to the White House Correspondents Dinner as the guest of John F. Kennedy Jr. in 1999.

The People vs. Larry Flynt airbrushed the dark side of porn. It premiered in Cincinnati, of course. Flynt was the star of that, too. And when the movie ended, a cheering crowd begged for autographs.

"LARRY! LARRY!" they chanted. "You're a god, man!"[184]

"They rekindled the flame," said his lawyer, Louis Sirkin. "It energized him."

Like a publicity version of Viagra (approved by the FDA in 1998),[185] it gave him ideas. Suddenly, Flynt lusted for another chance to do to Cincinnati what was being done to women in his new line of XXX-rated videos.

---

183 "Porn Publisher's Daughter Decries Smut, Abuse," *Religion News Service*, January 1, 1997.
184 "Flynt: Sequel to a blockbuster trial arrives," *The Cincinnati Enquirer*, May 2, 1999.
185 "New Pill Thrill for Impotent Men," Lee Bowman, *Scripps News Service*, March 28, 1998.

In 1997 he loaded a limo with *Hustler Magazines,* drove to Fountain Square in the civic heart of Cincinnati, and handed them out like he was campaigning for a jail term. The magazine had not been sold in the city for twenty years, since Flynt was convicted and jailed on obscenity charges in 1978. Surely the Cincinnati Police vice squad would handcuff him and drag him to jail while the TV cameras spread the news from coast-to-coast.

But much to his dismay, Hamilton County Prosecutor Joe Deters declined to bring charges.

So Flynt escalated and opened a Hustler store downtown later that year. Nothing happened.

Determined to poke the bear until he got the media mauling he craved, he went on Court TV in January 1998 and told Cincinnati Councilman Phil Heimlich and Citizens for Community Values leader Phil Burress, "I'm ready to go to the mat again. ... Why don't you go to Joe Deters, who's the prosecutor, and say, 'Let's indict this guy'?"

Again, Cincinnati refused to take the bait. Instead, Heimlich and others on City Council outflanked the smut gangsters with a Sexually Oriented Business (SOB) law to zone porn shops out of downtown. "It worked fantastic," Heimlich said twenty-four years later. "Phil Burress brought it to me. It was a brilliant strategy."

The local media treated Burress as if he had Old Testament cooties, but his plan was a great success. "Don't make them illegal," Heimlich explained, "just put them in a separate zoning category and make it so difficult to exist they could not set up shop. We required them to get a license, which eliminated 95 percent of them because most are criminal operators. We zoned them away from downtown, next to junkyards, far away from retail.

"It's why we don't have sex businesses, massage parlors and peep shows in Cincinnati today."

But in 1998, Flynt was desperate to reenact his 1978 trial. He craved a rematch, certain he would win. Surely he was now so famous and beloved by the press and Hollywood, Cincinnati wouldn't dare to put him in jail again. So in March he put XXX-rated videos on sale in his

CHAPTER 20 • SERPENT'S TOOTH

In 1998, Larry Flynt returned to Cincinnati to provoke a rematch of his 1978 trial (left), sure that he would win. He had played Judge William Morrissey in his movie; he was a star. Surely Cincinnati would surrender. He was wrong. *The Cincinnati Enquirer*, 1978.

downtown Cincinnati store. "I think everybody is a bit more rational than they were then," he said. "Things are going to be different this time."[186] He was wrong again.

On April 4, he finally got his wish: The store was raided by more than a dozen Cincinnati Police vice squad officers.[187]

Flynt's lawyers pretended to be shocked. "I guess they are trying to make an allegation that it meets the definition of an adult bookstore," Sirkin said. Flynt's brother Jimmy, who ran the Cincinnati store, said it was like a raid by the Gestapo, "like you're some kind of criminal."

Deters and a grand jury replied: "Adult bookstore? Yes. Criminal? Exactly."

"If the jury doesn't find that this stuff is obscene, then nothing is obscene," Deters said. "The material sold here is the most vile and degrading—particularly degrading to women—that has ever been sold in Hamilton County."[188]

Nationally, most of the news reports made it sound as if those prudish rubes in uptight Cincinnati were picking on poor ol' Larry Flynt again. "Once again, it's The People vs. Larry Flynt," an AP story said, turning a national wire story into one of the biggest free movie promotions of all time.

---

186 "Flynt betting county 'more rational' now," Dan Horn, *The Cincinnati Post,* April 8, 1998.
187 "Police raid Hustler bookstore," Dan Horn, *The Cincinnati Post,* March 28, 1998
188 ibid

Larry Flynt leaves the Hamilton County Detention Center in his gold-plated wheelchair 1998, where he was booked and fingerprinted on a warrant for obscenity charges. Steven Herppich, *The Cincinnati Enquirer.*

But prosecutors knew what Flynt was doing and rejected the "1978 rematch" narrative. "There's no question that to a great extent, Hamilton County has changed," Deters said. "People have become desensitized by HBO, cable and the Playboy channel. But we're not talking about that kind of material here."

It was not about morals, he said. It was about the law: a 15-count indictment of Flynt for pandering obscenity, disseminating harmful material to juveniles (the Hustler store had sold a porn video to a 14-year-old boy),[189] conspiracy, and engaging in a pattern of corrupt activity. If convicted, Flynt faced up to twenty-four years in prison.

Even a Hustler store clerk described the videos as "degrading and extreme."

The case finally went to trial in May 1999. But the climax Flynt yearned for was not to be. It was settled out of court almost before it got started. Flynt agreed to remove all videos from his store and never sell them in Cincinnati again. He was fined $10,000. And he declared victory.

---

[189] When the 14-year-old witness was approached with a bribe, the county provided witness protection to keep the boy safe from Flynt.

"He didn't win anything" said Prosecutor Mike Allen, who had replaced Deters after Deters won election as Ohio Treasurer. "He turned tail and ran."

Once again, Flynt had played the press like a Magoffin County squeezebox. The title of his movie was repeated in countless headlines, news stories, editorials and broadcasts.

Freelance writer Rudy Maxa, who knew Flynt as well as anyone outside his inner circle, looked back in 2022 and said, "How would I describe Larry? Smart as a whip with little formal education. Tough on his employees. A master of getting press when he wanted it—very good on soundbites! And a very smart businessman who knew enough to diversify by buying casinos."

Cincinnati also declared victory. Burress said that the settlement would keep the city permanently clean by sending a message that porn videos would be prosecuted. The real winner was the SOB zoning law, which was crafted with help from Bruce Taylor of Citizens for Decency Through Law.

"In terms of sexually oriented businesses, we won," Heimlich said. Flynt's Hustler stores existed when the zoning rules were passed and could not be removed retroactively. "But we know it worked because we don't have those things in Cincinnati, and other cities have them all over the place."

Flynt claimed his magazine was now accepted and "normal" in Cincinnati.[190] As the prosecutors said, times had changed.

And one of the reasons was a case that made Cincinnati a target of national ridicule and scorn eight years earlier, in 1990.

'Is that Art?'

THE CINCINNATI ENQUIRER, APRIL 13, 1990—It was a busy Friday on the Copydesk as advance sections for the huge Sunday edition were jammed into the news funnel along with stories for Saturday. The comforting clack and ding of Royals and Underwoods had long ago been replaced by

---

[190] "Both sides proclaim 'total victory,'" Dan Horn, *The Cincinnati Enquirer*, May 13, 1999

the toylike plastic whisper-click of computer keyboards. Cyclops cathode ray terminals as big as ATMs glared at everybody with unblinking malevolence, waiting for the slip of a finger to vaporize an entire story with one careless keystroke.

Punch turned to Judy and said, "Did you ever wonder who draws the pictures on boxes of Rice Krispies?"

"I was awake half the night wondering," Judy said with sarcastic wide eyes behind her granny glasses.

"Finally, we have the answer from our fine arts reporter. 'Cerealist painters.' Check it out." He pointed to his terminal, where part of a story about the Contemporary Arts Center was highlighted: "…Salvador Dali, Renee Magritte and other cerealist painters…"

"Cheerio!" Judy laughed. "That's going into my collection." She kept a fat folder of what she called "serendipitously stupid" spelling blunders. It was labeled the "Ignoranus File," named after one of her favorites from the 1970s. "I think it's Latin for dumb-ass," she had told Punch when she clipped it.

"Send the cerealist to the printer," she told Punch, as thrilled as if he had just handed her a dozen roses. "I'll put that next to 'supersillyous.' Do you suppose there are also 'cerealist killers' who turn their victims into shredded wheat?"

"I'm still laughing about the 'buryem enema' in that story about cancer research," he said.

"Did you hear the one about the Mapplethorpe Exhibit?" she asked.

Punch raised one eyebrow skeptically and gave a reluctant nod to signal, *Okay, go ahead.*

"Si Leis sent two of his sheriff's deputies to check it out and see if it was obscene. The first one looks at photos of two naked guys doing—"

"You don't need to describe it," Punch interrupted.

"Okay, so the first one turns to the second one and says, 'Do you think that's art?' And the second one studies it for a minute and finally says, 'No, Art has a tattoo on his ass.'"

Punch blushed but had to laugh. "My sister-in-law went to that," he said. "She's very sophisticated and artsy, thinks of herself as an enlightened, open-minded progressive."

"So open-minded her brains fell out?"

"Sounds like you know her. She was thrilled that backward Cincinnati was chosen for such an exciting, *transgressive* art show. When I asked for details after she went, she was unusually quiet. Her comments were vague and I could tell she didn't want to talk about it. But I kept asking and she finally had to admit she was grossed out. Lots of beautiful photos of flowers and then, wham, it all went sideways into this kinky, perverted stuff that gave her bad dreams."

"I saw the contact sheet of pictures we could never publish and thought, 'Now that's a buryem enema...'"

"What do you think, Jim?" Punch asked to head off Judy.

Gardner, his head deep in copy, had been half listening. He looked up, "You mean about the so-called artsy pictures of guys with bullwhips shoved up where the sun don't shine—"

"Yes," Punch stopped him. "Do you think the obscenity charges will stick?"

"Look, I'm a First Amendment purist. If sickos want to pay to look at that stuff and call it art, have at it. But I don't recall being asked for permission to spend my tax dollars on crap like that. If they did, I'd say hell no along with most Americans. And it drives me nuts to listen to the arts crowd claim it's censorship if they don't get federal subsidies to put a crucifix in a jar of urine. Panhandling for tax money is not free speech. If you take my money, you play my tune."

"Where's my federal subsidy for copyeditors?" Judy asked in a whiney voice. "We're artists too."

"Like Jim said, that wouldn't be a free press at all," Punch said. "The way I see it, the news business is married to the First Amendment, and every time we defend obscenity as free speech we're putting the bride in bed with Larry Flynt. Readers see that and lose respect for us and for the First Amendment."

"Good point," Jim said. "As to your original question: No, I don't think a jury will buy it as misdemeanor obscenity. They would have to find no artistic value in the exhibit. It's not *Hustler*. In some ways it's a lot worse. But I think they have gamed the Supreme Court guidelines this time. Prosecute, and Cincinnati is the enemy of the arts. Don't prosecute, and we have lost whatever community standards we had. It's a clever trap. We can hardly even describe the pictures in print, much less show readers why they're obscene."

Judy said, "What's with these cultural missionaries who come to Cincinnati to stick a thumb in our eye and save us from our morals? Looks to me like the museum director was itching to embarrass the city as soon as he got here."

"You're probably right," Jim said. "We have more than a few of those cultural Crusaders here in the building." He rolled his eyes at the ceiling to indicate he was not talking about just the newsroom. "But I think there's another motive, too. The CAC has been struggling. They have that dumpy place on the skywalk and their support has been drying up. So this is how they save their jobs and stick it to Cincinnati at the same time. Provoke an obscenity battle and the contributions will pour in."

"That's almost as revolting as the pictures," Punch said.

Riders on the Storm

21
The Mapplethorpe Meltdown

"The Perfect Moment" was a 1990 exhibit of 165 photos by New York artist Robert Mapplethorpe, who had recently died of AIDS. The critics gushed over it like the fountains of Rome.

"Hailed by museum directors as one of the finest examples of twentieth century photography," said the *Cincinnati Post*.[191]

"One of the most important photographers working in the 1980s formalist mode," an art museum director from Philadelphia said.

Another arts expert from Los Angeles seemed appalled to even be asked if it was art. "If it is in an art museum, it is intended to be art, and that's why it's there," he sniffed.[192]

So, put a dead fish in a tank, or pee in a glass over a crucifix—and "voilà!"—it suddenly becomes art if someone puts it on display in a museum? *Yes!* said the experts. *Art is whatever we say it is, and you have to pay for it with tax subsidies or we will roll on the floor and scream "Censorship!"*

One art critic got it right. Martha Rosler told the *New York Times* that most contemporary art is "patently exclusionary in its appeal, culturally relative in its concerns, and indissolubly wedded to big money and 'upper class' life in general."

The reporter who quoted her translated that for hicks outside of New York: "Contemporary art is always on the edge of social acceptability and thus is vulnerable," he wrote after the dust settled in the Great

---

[191] "Mapplethorpe," Jerry Stein, *The Cincinnati Post*, March 6, 1990.

[192] "After the trial, questions of art," Andy Grundberg, *The New York Times*, October 21, 1990.

Mapplethorpe Meltdown of 1990. "Contemporary art is also linked in the public mind to a moneyed, urban elite."[193]

Call them MUELs – Moneyed Urban Elites.

And Dennis Barrie was the perfect MUEL spokesman. With his flowing, longish white hair, distinguished Dos Equis-guy beard, plummy baritone and impeccable suits, he was made for the role.

A native of Cleveland, Barrie graduated from Ohio's Oberlin College, a private school that adds an extra helping of "liberal" to the liberal arts. He started out in Detroit working for a branch of the Smithsonian Museum of Washington, DC—the national atom-smasher where political neutrons and arts-world electrons collide.

In 1983 Barrie was hired as the new director for Cincinnati's struggling Contemporary Arts Center (CAC). Among local museums, the CAC was a homely Nash Rambler dwarfed by the Big Three: the Cincinnati Art Museum (VanGogh), the Taft Museum of Art (Rembrandt); and the Cincinnati Museum Center (art deco architecture, murals and natural history). The CAC was parked in a back corner of downtown like an orphan stepchild, up a flight of escalators, above a Walgreen's drugstore. The old-money Cincinnati Art Museum on Mount Adams already had a fine collection of contemporary art. The upstart CAC was a dimly-lit stage for alienated fringe artists who were kept on life support by deep-pockets MUELs, whose favorite exhibit was a look-at-me plaque listing the names of the biggest donors.

But Barrie would soon let everyone know there was a new hustler in town.

In 1988 he visited the Mapplethorpe exhibit in New York City and seized the Perfect Moment. He had to bring it to Cincinnati. The city that banned adult bookstores and ran Larry Flynt out of town would love it. What could go wrong?

Better question: What was he thinking?

As they say in the arts world, context is key. It was a time of angst and histrionic drama for the arts. Congress was being scorched by

---

[193] Ibid.

CHAPTER 21 • THE MAPPLETHORPE MELTDOWN

angry voters for spending taxpayer money on offensive art such as "Piss Christ" (crucifix in urine) and "Madonna and Child" (sacred icon floating in "amber liquid," a.k.a. urine). Republicans wanted to strangle the National Endowment for the Arts (NEA) that urinated millions on carnival geek "art."

When the prestigious Corcoran Gallery of Art in Washington announced the Mapplethorpe exhibit, Congress vowed to cut off its NEA funds. The Corcoran quickly sold its artistic soul for tax dollars and canceled.

But by then Barrie had already scheduled the show in Cincinnati. When the Corcoran caved, he told the CAC board in an emergency meeting that he would resign if they flinched. He assured his nervous board members that Mapplethorpe would finally make Cincinnati "a progressive city."

"I did not set out to create a controversy" and "never expected" to be the target of protests, Barrie insisted thirty years later. In technical artists' terms, that was "amber liquid." Barrie and the CAC knew very well what would happen.

"If you wanted to stir up controversy," Barrie acknowledged in 2020, "the game had shifted from making art that was seemingly about nothing, to making art that was very much about something and about something controversial, such as homosexuality, gender identity, race, social class, police repression, or some other topic with a political punch."

The Mapplethorpe exhibit was a political gut-punch aimed to knock the wind out of unenlightened, conservative Cincinnati. It was cleverly designed to slip through the Supreme Court's key loophole for obscenity: "serious literary, artistic, political or scientific value."

But first, Barrie and the CAC board set the stage with a two-year PR campaign to groom business and opinion leaders. Although the museum was struggling with a $100,000 budget deficit, they spent $40,000 to hire a New York public relations firm to woo the national media. They used every opportunity at meetings, cocktail parties and arts events to cultivate local support, or at least tacit acceptance. They clearly expected controversy and welcomed it.

They also hired one of the top First Amendment lawyers in the nation, Louis Sirkin of Cincinnati, well known for his courtroom defense of porn kings like Larry Flynt and their adult bookstores. Before the exhibit opened, Sirkin and co-counsel Mark Mezibov filed a lawsuit to block enforcement of obscenity laws. It failed.

The New York PR budget was probably unnecessary. The press was unanimously enthusiastic. Reading newspaper previews of the show, it was hard to see why there could be any controversy at all.

The *Cincinnati Post* described "exotic flower studies, famous geometric wall reliefs and nudes in classical Greek poses." Oh, sure, there was unfortunate attention on "homosexual and sado-masochistic images" such as "a male couple kissing, another male couple in a romantic embrace and still another pair in leather regalia and chains." But the photos in question "elevate above erotic."[194]

Big deal, readers thought. It sounds like the annual Krohn Conservatory Flower Show on "Bring a Buddy Night."

The press was "burying the lede," like the old newsroom joke about the reporter who failed to call in the score of a basketball game. "What happened?" his editor asks the next day. "The team bus crashed and they all were killed, so there was no game," the clueless Jimmy Olsen replies.

But no matter how the media rolled out the red carpet, the lede on the CAC exhibit would not stay buried. Citizens for Community Values (CCV), the descendant of Citizens for Decency Through Law, sent up flares to launch thousands of protest phone calls to elected and business leaders. They were two years late and many dollars short of the slick CAC blitz. But the angry villagers who stormed Frankenstein's art museum were still effective.

Barrie complained that the CAC was the victim of "a very significant and well-orchestrated campaign against the exhibition." In the modern art of hypocrisy, that was a Kandinsky.

The show opened on April 6, 1990 with 4,000 lined up to see what the big noise was all about. Mingled among the crowd were nine

---

[194] "Mapplethorpe," Jerry Stein, *The Cincinnati Post,* March 6, 1990.

CHAPTER 21 • THE MAPPLETHORPE MELTDOWN

members of a Hamilton County grand jury. They admired the "voluptuously beautiful" flowers and the "compositionally balanced classic nudes." Then they strolled over past the "Adult content" warning signs to look at "X Portfolio." When they were able to breathe again, they looked at each other with wide eyes and agreed: "X Portfolio" was egregiously obscene.

When the local press tried to describe what the grand jury saw, readers spilled their coffee and did "spit takes" all over town:

"A study of buttocks with a hand and portion of the forearm inserted into the anus..."

"Additional images depicting the insertion of objects..."

"...one is urinating in another's mouth."

"...male genitalia, often aroused."

And the last straw for the grand jury: a little boy "posed frontally nude" and "a little girl sitting on a carved stone bench. Her dress is askew so as to reveal she is not wearing underwear."[195]

The reporter hastened to add, "Neither photo of the children intimates eroticism."

"Really!?" readers asked in letters to the editor. The children were captives in a homoerotic exhibit that was described as pornography by the CAC's own newsletter, by the artist's close friends and by the artist himself. How could it not be obscene to include images of innocent children in all that twisted "leather regalia"?

And who was the press to tell Cincinnati what was and was not obscene? Community standards were set by juries, not journalists.

The next day, museum visitors were ushered to the exits as twenty Cincinnati Police and vice squad officers moved in to collect evidence and take pictures of the photos (raising a question: were the police photos taken in a museum evidence or art?). Hamilton County Prosecutor Art Ney indicted Barrie and the museum for misdemeanor charges of pandering obscenity and illegal use of a child in nudity photos. The Mapplethorpe Meltdown began.

---

195 "Here's why Mapplethorpe show controversial," Jerry Stein, *The Cincinnati Post*, March 23, 1990.

A crowd of about fifty protesters outside the CAC gave mock Hitler salutes and chanted, "SAY NO TO SIMON LEIS, SAY NO TO THE ART POLICE."[196]

"SIMON LEIS IS THE ONE WHO'S WARPED, KEEP YOUR HANDS OFF MAPPLETHORPE," they yelled in unison.

The protests rhymed but missed the mark. The case was being prosecuted by the city. This time, Sheriff Si Leis was just a reluctant bystander. "Prosecutor Art Ney handed the case off to the city and they gave it to a prosecutor who had never handled an obscenity case in his life," he recalled. "They didn't know what they were doing."

It became a city case that had nothing to do with Sheriff Leis. But the protesters could not resist making him the boogieman of their nightmares.

"NOT THE CHURCH, NOT THE STATE, WE DECIDE WHAT ART IS GREAT," the crowd shouted on cue. It sounded too scripted for a spontaneous protest—more like a syncopated ad jingle for toothpaste, written by the CAC's expensive PR firm in New York?

"It's like a police state," the protesters said, parroting the same phrases. "Everyone is horrified." Most in Cincinnati were indeed horrified, but for very different reasons.

To the protesters, art critics and wealthy MUELs, art was on trial in a battle for artistic freedom and the First Amendment. For the other side it was no less than a battle of good and evil.

While opinions in the press were led by newspaper art critics—which was about as objective as asking sheriff's deputies to recognize "Art"—one local pastor with the Old Testament name of Gaston Dabney Cogdell called down fire and brimstone on the CAC Sodom.

"While being masqueraded as an art exhibit, the Mapplethorpe display is a propaganda effort to achieve the validation of and social acceptance for homosexual relationships," he wrote in a guest column.[197]

---

[196] "Vocal crowd protests police action," Jane Prendergast, *The Cincinnati Enquirer,* April 8, 1990.

[197] "Evil of Mapplethorpe's photos," Gaston Cogdell, *The Cincinnati Post,* May 25, 1990

CHAPTER 21 • THE MAPPLETHORPE MELTDOWN

To those who yearned for Cincinnati to be more sophisticated like New York, he quoted Mapplethorpe friend and artist Patti Smith, from the exhibit's own video: "New York produced me; New York seduced me. New York formed me; New York deformed me. New York converted me; New York perverted me. I love New York."

In the same video that accompanied the exhibit, a Princeton University expert on art and gay culture insisted, "Society has no right to protect itself against pornography." The Reverend Cogdell disagreed, pointing out that 10 percent of the CAC budget was paid by city taxpayers. "At this point in time, man as a moral being is an endangered species and the moral environment is only becoming more inhospitable and toxic to his existence." That was 1990.

As the Roman Emperor Trajan said, "Being right too soon is the same as being wrong."

The battle went national. It was free speech vs. censorship, good vs. evil, obscenity vs. community standards, Cincinnati vs. the civilized world. But there was another battle going on that most people missed: the moneyed urban elites vs. the peasants.

When the case finally came to trial in September 1990, jury selection took two days as both sides shuffled through the deck to find people from outside the city who had no opinions about the show, who lived blithely unaware of the controversy, working hard to raise their families and earn a living, untroubled by the sound and fury of the media circus.

Looking back, Barrie said, "Of the fifty people interviewed, other than three who had seen the Mapplethorpe show, none attended museums. Most of them had no contact with the arts at all. Not just the visual arts. They didn't go to the ballet. They didn't go to the symphony. It was a pretty stunning indication of the failure of our arts organizations, and it made the outcome of the trial pretty hard to predict."

As those hopelessly uncultured jurors were questioned, the arts crowd in the courtroom showed their scorn with loud groans at their answers. The jurors, dragged against their will into the spotlight of something they did not understand, got the message: They were not part of the "in crowd" at Downtown High School. They were white-socks nerds, to be ostracized and mocked.

Meanwhile, Cincinnati City Council was a reluctant warrior. Mayor Charlie Luken said he would not apologize for protecting community standards. But Councilman David Mann believed the case made Cincinnati "the laughingstock of more sophisticated communities."

So the city sent an assistant city solicitor, assigned to misdemeanors, to prosecute the case, facing off against Sirkin. It was a mismatch like Michael Jordan vs. Michael Moore in an ESPN dunk-a-thon. (Not donuts.)

The prosecution's fatal mistake was failure to rebut the CAC lineup of arts experts. The only prosecution arts expert, Judith Reisman, testified that the photographs were obscene, including carefully staged child pornography. She had ten pages of impressive credentials, but was mocked by the CAC lawyers because she had once produced music videos for *Captain Kangaroo*.

Reisman said, "We are, I think, putting at risk additional children, because many people see themselves as photographers and many people do use the technique of telling children this is appropriate because it's in a museum or a book." She called it "a standard technique that child sex abusers use to seduce vulnerable kids."[198]

Her testimony was not enough to stack-up against the defense parade of museum directors, artists, critics and professors from New York, Berkeley, Philadelphia, Cleveland and Los Angeles.

Once the case became "art on trial," not obscenity, it was over. The jury certainly knew what obscenity was, but they did not feel qualified to contradict all those highly educated cultural aristocrats. The four men and four women said not guilty. "I'm not an expert," one juror said. "I don't understand Picasso's art. But I assume the people who call it art know what they're talking about."

The MUELs finally had their icon for the arts: Saint Mapplethorpe, patron martyr of sadomasochism. Barrie bestowed his forgiveness and

---

[198] "Controversial Witness Says Five Mapplethorpe Works Are Not Art," Kim Masters, *Washington Post*, October 5, 1990.

CHAPTER 21 • THE MAPPLETHORPE MELTDOWN

Contemporary Arts Center Director Dennis Barrie hugs his lawyer, Louis Sirkin, as the verdict came in on October 5, 1990: Not guilty of misdemeanor pandering obscenity. Annette Pember, *The Cincinnati Enquirer*.

declared that Cincinnati was finally "normal." Cincinnati had been saved, blessed by the benediction of eye-bleach pictures.

City leaders were relieved. They could shake off the stigma that might "forever brand us as small-town bluenoses," in the words of *Cincinnati Magazine*—perfectly expressing the Queen City's neurotic insecurity as the girl with thick glasses who never gets invited to the prom.

But the jokes continued. "Media's verdict is in: Cincinnatians are hicks," was the headline on a facetious column by Leonard Larsen in the *Cincinnati Post*.

> "Cincinnati is a backwater, it's been written and broadcast, such an intellectual dump that town officials are blind to the artist's statement in a photograph of a man urinating into another man's mouth....
>
> "These appalling hicks in Cincinnati, those sad dolts and discards from holy roller ministries and catfish carnivals, haven't even the faintest appreciation (for) Mapplethorpe portrayals of sexual violence that wouldn't be tolerated if practiced on animals."[199]

When the verdict was announced, a crowd outside the courthouse chanted "BARRIE! BARRIE!"—which would be echoed nine years later at the end of the Flynt trial with "LARRY! LARRY"

Barrie thought he had won. But he still had a lot to learn about Cincinnati and how it works.

---

199 "Media's verdict is in: Cincinnatians are hicks," Leonard Larson, *Scripps Howard News Service*, April 20, 1990.

In 2003, long after the Mapplethorpe Meltdown had cooled, the CAC built a new museum on the same site once occupied by Larry Flynt's downtown Hustler Store, shown here during a protest at its opening in 1997. Glenn Hartong, *The Cincinnati Enquirer.*

The Contemporary Arts Center had to divorce from the local Fine Arts Fund for a while, to protect fundraising for all the arts from being scorched in the backlash. A CAC board member who led the campaign for Mapplethorpe had to resign as vice president of Central Trust Bank because business leaders threatened to pull twenty accounts in retaliation for the exhibit. The CAC made $445,000 from the show, but that was swallowed up by legal expenses.

And Barrie, the hero of MUELs, was radioactive. "It was clear I had to go," he said later. "While they had won the trial, the CAC had been cut from the art fund and had lost much of its corporate support. We had $350,000 in legal bills to pay off. It was time for wounds to heal. They wanted me out of the way."[200]

He was an awkward reminder of the kind of unpleasantness that nice Cincinnati hates. He resigned in 1993 for a job in Cleveland, to

---

200 "Thirty Years After the Perfect Moment," Henry Adams, *CAN Journal*, Cleveland, November 2020.

run the Rock And Roll Hall of Fame. It was spun as a promotion, but it was not. The new Cleveland museum was not even open and had almost no exhibits. He left the Rock museum three years later amid disputes and criticisms about fundraising. He was briefly director of a Cartoon Museum in Florida, and finally landed at the Mob Museum in Las Vegas.

Even Barrie had soured on the elitist arts. "The art world is often so petty," he said.

Once he was gone, Cincinnati began to mend fences. The CAC added a few token conservatives to its board for adult supervision, and announced "a clear-cut judgment not to engage in any exhibitions of such a controversial nature that would interfere with fundraising." It was invited to rejoin the Fine Arts Fund that claimed to have raised $5 million off the Mapplethorpe Meltdown.

In 2003, the CAC was reborn in a new $35 million museum designed by architect Zaha Hadid. Almost as remarkable: The names of Carl and

The new Contemporary Arts Center opened after Dennis Barrie was long gone. "It was clear I had to go," he said later. "The art world is often so petty."
The Cincinnati Enquirer.

Edyth Lindner were added to the list of donors. The most powerful conservative billionaire businessman in Cincinnati was now a supporter of the CAC.

And a wicked irony went unmentioned: The new CAC museum was built on Sixth Street, right where a Larry Flynt Hustler store used to stand.

The Queen City had been put in the stocks and severely chastised to abandon its intolerable morals—all in the name of *tolerance*, of course. The perimeter for artistic freedom under the First Amendment was pushed deeper into the darkness to include even the most offensive "art." Some said the Cincinnati verdict even saved the NEA—but couldn't say if that was a victory or an embarrassment. And the Mapplethorpe Meltdown spawned decades of shockingly ugly, crap-tastic "art."

There was a cow's head covered in flies. A child murderer's portrait in the handprints of children. A pornographic Virgin Mary painted in excrement. A nude woman who smeared herself in chocolate. Testicles cooked and served in tea. A naked man on a leash, barking like a dog....

"Transgressive" was the ticket to fame and NEA fortune, as artists competed to be the next Mapplethorpe by shocking the public right out of their loafers. And the best part was that those peasants actually were forced to pay to be insulted, with millions in NEA subsidies. The MUELs and the arts world pretended to love all that transgressive art. Everyone else found it revolting.

And the chasm between the arts and the public widened like the drift of continents. Why do the arts struggle for public support? Start with Mapplethorpe. As Barrie said, art had to be about something political and offensive. It had to punch the peasants in the face.

Most taxpayers could not punch back. But they could refuse to pay for it and stay as far as possible from anything that sounded like art.

Get Off of My Cloud

22
What Were Once Vices Now Are Habits

In 2005, Hamilton County Prosecutor Joe Deters packed his bags and flew to London, Paris and Brussels in five days. The one-week Grand Tour was not a vacation. It was all business. He went to Europe to track down witnesses who could help him convict a monster in the worst child abuse and pornography case in Cincinnati history.

In eight years as prosecutor, Deters had handled cases of rape, child abuse, pornography, obscenity, horrific murders and grisly beatings. He had prosecuted Larry Flynt for sex videos that even a Hustler store clerk said were disgusting. But this case was something else. A completely new basement crawlspace in hell.

"Just when you think that you've seen the lowest point of human depravity, someone like Paul Kraft comes along. It's worse than you can imagine," he said as he announced the indictments.[201] "Nobody around here has ever seen anything like this."

The grand jury agreed. They were shocked and sickened. Kraft was indicted on seventeen charges of rape and pandering sexually oriented videos of children being raped. And that was just the beginning.

Assistant Prosecutor Mark Piepmeier told the judge, "I hope you give him a sentence so long that when he leaves prison it'll be in a pine box."

And Judge Charles Kubicki said, "These images are some of the most disgusting and disturbing images I have ever seen. Unfortunately, they are images I will not soon forget."

Even Kraft agreed. When he confessed to detectives that he raped

---
[201] "Child rape suspect indicted," Kimball Perry, *The Cincinnati Post*, March 16, 2005.

his toddler daughter five times, he banged his head on the table and cried, "I'm a monster."[202]

His wife was a monster too. But the detectives did not find that out until months after the Winton Terrace couple was arrested. At first she said she didn't know anything about what her husband was doing to their children.

The pair were arrested in March 2005, when the Hamilton County Sheriff's Office was alerted by a Secret Service agent in Miami, Florida, who had been monitoring an online chat room called "Preteen, Baby and Toddler Sex."

The agent struck up a chat with Kraft, 31, who offered to share video of raping his 3-year-old daughter if the agent would also make a child rape video and swap it.

Deters recalled, "He said on a video cam, 'Is anyone out there willing to have sex with a three-year-old? I will do it with my daughter.' They traced the IP address to Cincinnati, recovered his computer and removed the kids."

When the sheriff's deputies arrived, they found a horror scene. "It was a squalor. The kids were hungry and dirty," Piepmeier said. There were no sheets on the beds. Rotting food was left out in the kitchen and the floors were littered with dirty clothes. The children had no language development and could not even communicate.

There were five kids: four boys, ages 1, 3, 5 and 6, and a 3-year-old girl who was a twin of the 3-year-old boy.

After a few months in foster care, the children learned to speak well enough to tell about what had gone on. "This went well beyond the initial internet case," Deters said. "They literally subjected their kids to a sexual circus." And the mother, Robin Kraft, 25, was one of the ringleaders.

"It was non-stop," Deters recalled. "Bring in the next kid. They both were involved. We got porn off his computer that included sex with infants."

---

[202] "Man found guilty of child rape," Tony Cook, *The Cincinnati Post,* January 27, 2006

CHAPTER 22 • WHAT WERE ONCE VICES NOW ARE HABITS

Kraft's defense lawyer insisted it was not real porn. It was only "virtual porn," he claimed, photoshopped or made with computer graphics to look real. And "virtual" kiddie porn that is created with computer graphics, like dinosaurs in *Jurassic Park*, is completely legal, no matter how it might incite child molesters and pedophiles or be used to groom children for sex with adults.

In 2002, the Supreme Court legalized "virtual porn" in *Ashcroft v. Free Speech Coalition*, overruling the Child Pornography Protection Act of 1996. The majority 6-3 opinion[203] said that outlawing virtual porn might also ban films that depict simulated teen sex, such as *Romeo and Juliet*. The dissenting justices[204] said that was nonsense. The CPPA had clearly defined hard-core virtual pornography in graphic terms. The law "was intended to target only a narrow class of images—visual depictions 'which are virtually indistinguishable to unsuspecting viewers from unretouched photographs of actual children engaging in identical sexual conduct.'" But once again, the porn industry pushed back the boundaries by waving the banner of the First Amendment.

The Free Speech Coalition was in fact another porn industry wolf hiding behind First Amendment sheepskin, described on its website as "the non-profit trade association of the adult industry."[205]

Given the unusual time and expense required to prove the children in the porn videos were real, most cities would have thrown up their hands and surrendered with a plea bargain for Kraft.

Not in Cincinnati. "Not in our town" was still the benchmark for Cincinnati's community standards.

"We had to rebut their expert," Deters said when reporters asked how the county could afford a trip to Europe. He sent porn from Kraft's computer—which contained more than 200 videos and photos of

---

203 Written by Associate Justice Anthony Kennedy

204 William Rehnquist, Antonin Scalia, Sandra Day-O'Connor

205 Winners of annual awards from the Free Speech Coalition include *Penthouse* Publisher Bob Guccione, porn stars, *Screw Magazine* pornographer Al Goldstein, *Deep Throat* director Gerard "Rocco" Damiano, strip clubs and pornography tycoon Harry Mahoney and Larry Flynt. Their attorney in the Supreme Court arguments was Flynt's former lawyer, H. Louis Sirkin of Cincinnati, who also defended the Contemporary Arts Center's Mapplethorpe exhibit.

extreme child porn—to a national clearing house that matched the faces of children to three real children who were raped for porn videos in Europe. Deters used his surplus campaign funds to pay for his trip to London, Paris and Brussels, where he obtained sworn testimony from police officers that the children in the videos were actual living, breathing, suffering, crying victims.

Kraft waived his right to a trial by a jury—which might have demanded a hanging on Fountain Square. He was sentenced by Kubicki, who did the next closest thing: five life sentences plus another ninety-six years, with no chance of parole.

"It was 181 years to life. The largest sentence in Hamilton County history," Deters said.

Robin Kraft was sentenced to forty years in prison—long enough to make sure she would be over 65, no longer be able to have children when she was released in 2046.

Kraft apparently decided he was not such a monster and protested that he was the victim of "injustice."

Deters replied that the children were damaged for life. "It rips your heart out. These were innocent babies."

The videos and child-molesting chat room used by Kraft had been provided by Yahoo.com and Time-Warner internet service. "I'm very disturbed about the ability for some of these internet carriers to be complicit in this activity," Deters said at the time.

His instincts were on target. The internet, the Dark Web and social media have done for the porn industry what *Deep Throat* did for the Mob in the 1970s—they opened a new frontier for obscene profits from porn. As the Meese Commission warned in 1980, technology had overwhelmed law enforcement like a tsunami rolling over a picket fence.

"Now people are totally desensitized to it," Deters said in 2022. "The chances of us getting a conviction in an old-style obscenity prosecution are nonexistent unless there are kids involved. People's entire perspective on what's moral has shifted dramatically. And it's not just pornography. Crimes we used to prosecute are now legalized. The attitude is 'Just legalize it so there's no crime.'"

CHAPTER 22 • WHAT WERE ONCE VICES NOW ARE HABITS

Gambling, which replaced bootleg liquor as the Mob's major source of income after Prohibition was repealed, was legalized by voters and appropriated in a hostile takeover by the states. First came lotteries "for the schools," then casinos "for tax revenue." Now even sports betting that got Cincinnati Reds player Pete Rose[206] banned from baseball has been legalized in most states, including Ohio.

The war on drugs is over. Drugs won. Marijuana was legal in eighteen states by 2022 and more were joining the gold rush, blinded by hash-pipe dreams of tax revenues.[207] Even heroin, meth, LSD and opioids have been legalized in Oregon.[208]

The Mob's loan sharks have been put out of business by payday lenders. The numbers racket is now run by convenience stores that sell $1 lottery tickets. Poker machines in bars, online gambling, Dark Web drug sales, massage parlors that are fronts for sex trafficking, small towns littered with "gaming" parlors where gamblers leak away hard-earned wages, college funds and mortgage payments on video poker....

---

206 In 2017, Rose was accused in sworn testimony of also having sex with underage girls who were brought to him by his bookie. "Baseball Legend Pete Rose, Accused of Sex With Minor in 1970s, Faces Tainted Legacy – Again," Erik Ortiz, *NBC News*, August 1, 2017.

207 California sold $4.4 billion in legal marijuana in 2021, but black market sales remain and are probably twice that much, according to the *Times of San Diego* ("Gov. Newsom Under Fire as Problems Grow for Legal Marijuana in California, Alexei Koseff, February 6, 2022). In Colorado, cartels from China, Columbia, Mexico, Cuba and Russia have moved in. Advocates promised legalization would drive out crime. The opposite has occurred. From a report by the Hudson Institute ("The 'Colorado Experiment': Legalized Marijuana's Impact on Colorado, David W. Murray, June 20, 2021): "By now, however, we have enough accumulated data in 2020 to see the actual effects of this experiment in drug policy. And they are not comforting. Not only did the promised benefits, both financial and on behalf of public safety, not come to pass, but in multiple areas of daily life the metrics have worsened. Moreover, the data from Colorado have been accompanied by several years of greater medical science awareness of the health risks from marijuana exposure. Easier access, greater prevalence, higher psychoactive potency from increased THC, a continued criminal element, and more intensive daily use have all occurred since the experiment began. Maybe the sky hasn't fallen, but a great deal of damage has rained down on Colorado, as measured across several indicators."

208 "Portland, Oregon has suffered an explosion in violence following the legalization of cannabis. Portland had 16 murders in 2013, the year before voters in Oregon approved full legalization. Last year it had 90. It's on pace to have even more in 2022. It has gone from being one of the safest medium-sized cities in the United States to one of the most dangerous. Denver has seen a similar trend." ("Cannabis causes psychosis. Psychosis causes violence." Alex Berenson, *Unreported Truths*, May 26, 2022.)

The "walk of shame" in 1961: five people were arrested by U.S. Marshals for illegal gambling in cafes and bars in New Richmond and Norwood. Now the government has replaced the Mob with lotteries and casinos.
Herb Heise, *The Cincinnati Enquirer*, 1961.

The old gangsters in Newport would shake their heads and say, "Boys, we was born too soon."

Even Nostradamus did not predict all of this. But the Doobie Brothers did. Their 1974 album was called, "What Were Once Vices Are Now Habits."

And one of the most insidious of those modern habits is porn.

In the 1990s, Ohio had a law called the "Display Statute" that required magazines with nudity or porn on their covers to be kept under the counter or behind pieces of cardboard to protect children.

Today, that has joined the list of archaic "blue laws," ranked somewhere below spitting on the sidewalk, cursing in public or selling alcohol on Sunday.

"No one goes to a bookstore for dirty books anymore," Deters said. No more furtive, red-faced visits to buy skin magazines in brown paper bags. No more guilt. "It's all available on their computer. They can do that in the privacy of their own home."

In just three generations, porn has evolved from grainy "French postcards" passed like contraband in locker rooms, to an international

CHAPTER 22 • WHAT WERE ONCE VICES NOW ARE HABITS

industry that makes billions by peddling the most extreme hard-core videos on social media, available to anyone, regardless of age.

There's already growing concern about the way social media can isolate and manipulate users. Add another concern: Porn is literally in the palm of your hand—by phone.

"The old porn business is all gone," said Benjamin Bull, a veteran of the porn wars who traveled from city to city in the 1980s as a courtroom attorney representing Citizens for Decency through Law. "The old sex trafficking industry you saw in *Taxi Driver*, with the pimp on the sidewalk, that's gone. Now the money is online."

Bull prosecuted pornographers in fourteen jury trials without a loss, including a case in the U.S. Supreme Court. After leaving CDL, he became senior vice president, general counsel and director of the National Center on Sexual Exploitation.

"Women are being trafficked—forced to make porn videos through force, fraud or coercion," he said.

It's a new marketing twist. Street pimps were retail: one customer at a time. Online videos are wholesale, reaching millions through social media and the internet.

Bull uses the example of a 16-year-old girl who went on a date with an older guy. "She was given a pill in her drink and raped all night. They videotaped it. Two months later she's in school and finds out the guy uploaded it to Pornhub to make money.

"In another case, a 14-year-old girl was abducted, raped all night by three guys, beaten, abused and thrown out of a car like a dead cat, totally naked. Six months later she was back in school and found out they had made videos that were uploaded to Pornhub for everyone to watch."

New York Times columnist Nicholas Kristof told similar stories in a series of columns in 2020.[209] The tales of destroyed young women are heartbreaking—almost identical to the testimony women victims gave to the Meese Commission in 1980—but with damage, suffering and profits multiplied by millions.

---

[209] "Children of Pornhub," Nicholas Kristoff, *The New York Times,* December 4, 2020. "Why Do We Let Corporations Profit from Rape Videos," Kristoff, *New York Times,* April 16, 2021.

Some young women and their families tried to move from town to town to escape the shame and invasion of privacy. Some victims committed suicide. "How do you get your mind around 200,000 guys masturbating as you're being assaulted?" one of them asked.

"I know this is hard to read," Kristoff wrote. "But it's nothing compared with what the children in the videos endure."

Bull reported, "Today, exponentially wealthy, international companies like MindGeek (which owns Pornhub), XHamster, and Xvideos dominate the online pornography industry and make hundreds of millions in profit. Their online videos are violent, racist and incest-themed. They also feature actual sexual assaults, sex trafficking and massive quantities of child pornography."

The users are degraded and damaged too, he said. "There is recognition now that online porn is doing really, really bad things to people, especially young people. It can lead to a form of addiction like alcohol or gambling. You can see on an MRI how it changes the brains.

"A huge number of men have told therapists they can't have sex with their wives unless they're looking at pixels on a screen because they've been using porn since they were ten. It's available on every child's phone and laptop in America."

The companies that produce it are elusive and powerful, based in Thailand, the Czech Republic, Paris, Prague, Cypress, Luxemborg, Ireland....

In some cases, class-action lawsuits have been successful, Bull said. "We win some battles, but lose the war. It's a chicken and egg thing. Which came first, losing the will to take them on or the culture that decided to tolerate it?"

What once were vices....

As usual, the politicians don't lead—they follow the culture. Prosecutions of the porn industry that began under President Reagan in the 1980s had a 90 percent victory rate for major cases, Bull said. "Under Obama, the Department of Justice stopped prosecuting any adult porn. When Trump came in we thought he would revive it, but he did nothing. Biden has done nothing."

CHAPTER 22 • WHAT WERE ONCE VICES NOW ARE HABITS

Bull hopes the culture may be changed by recent protests over the way women have been exploited by powerful men such as Jeffrey Epstein, Harvey Weinstien, Bill Cosby, Matt Lauer and others. But the "Me Too" protesters are selective. They are deafeningly silent about exploitation of women and children by online pornographers.

And if entertainment on streaming platforms such as Netflix, Amazon and HBO is any indication, the public demand for graphic, often gratuitous sex is as insatiable as the fictional characters in *Desperate Housewives*.

Porn was once a vice. It's now a lazy habit—the easy answer for every scriptwriter's stunted imagination or creative block. The demand for forbidden fruit is inelastic.

The Denmark Model of legal, anything-goes porn that was scorned and repudiated in the 1970 is now ho-hum reality. The *Playboy* Philosophy is everyone's philosophy: whatever consenting adults want, when they want it, and who cares what it does to children. As they said in the 1970s, "Let it all hang out."

On April 8, 2022, a 15-year-old girl who was at a Dallas Mavericks NBA game with her father went to the restroom and didn't come back. She was found 11 days later in a motel room where she had been abducted, sold, raped and sexually abused. She was found through ads for a sex-trafficking website.

That girl was not assaulted by the ghost of Larry Flynt. But the dots are not hard to connect. His Hustler empire was a plague ship, spreading the contagion of smut through infected blankets called porn magazines. His grubby handprints are on those children raped by the Krafts, and on all the countless women exploited, abused and assaulted for profit. When he died in 2021, he left a legacy that moved back the fences of decency and made pornography a mainstream merry-go-round on the adult playground.

But through it all, one city said no. In spite of the lawyers, the trials, the publicity stunts, the caustic contempt from the sophisticated elites and the scornful media insults, a few leaders in Cincinnati had the guts to say, "Not in our town."

Newport Madam Hattie Jackson exposed a scandal in Newport when she testified in 1961 about payoffs to local police and court officials. Mob corruption had deep roots in Northern Kentucky, but mostly stayed south of the Ohio River. Newport Police Chief George Gugel (in dark glasses at left), swore under oath he knew nothing about any Mob gambling or prostitution. Ran Cochran, *The Cincinnati Enquirer*, 1961.

Robert Meldon, Charlie Keating, Carl Lindner, Si Leis, Joe Deters, Ben Bull, Bruce Taylor, Mike Allen, Tom Streicher Sr. and Tom Streicher Jr., Phil Burress, Jerry Kirk and others who supported them were all that stood between Cincinnati and Newport, which was a lot closer than a bridge across the Ohio River.

The Cleveland Mob that ran Newport, with 300 prostitutes per mile in the 1950s and seventeen strip clubs in the 1970s, found no place to hang their fedoras in Cincinnati. The Queen City drew the line: The numbers racket was prosecuted in the 1960s; adult bookstores were harassed and prosecuted in the 1970s; Larry Flynt and the porn Mob were run out of town in the 1980s and again in the 1990s. The lonesome Hustler store that remains on Seventh Street downtown is the exception that proves the rule, kept open as a defiant, middle-finger insult.

Even Playboy failed in Cincinnati. In 1965, Publisher Hugh Hefner ran a big ad in local papers saying "Thank You!" to "the gentlemen of Cincinnati" for supporting his new Playboy Club at 35 East 7th Street. He claimed there were 10,000 Playboy Club "Keyholders" in Cincinnati.

CHAPTER 22 • WHAT WERE ONCE VICES NOW ARE HABITS

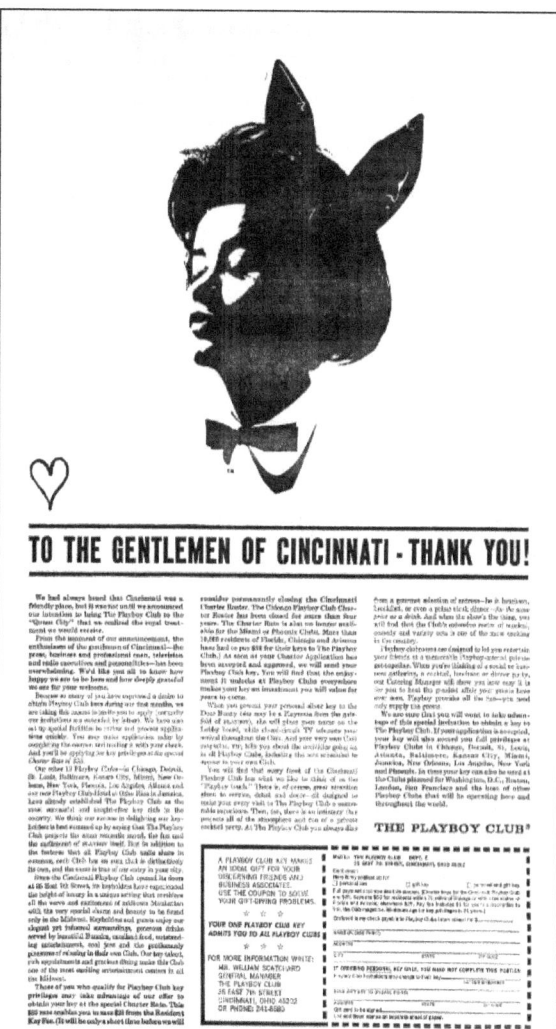

An ad announced the new Playboy Club in Cincinnati in 1965.

The club catered mainly to salesmen who used it to entertain customers. But in 1982 it was losing its charm. A "Bunny Hunt" to find young women who would wear the signature Playboy fluffy tail, ears and shrink-wrapped costume, was protested as "sexist." In 1983 the club closed for lack of business.[210]

---

210 By 1988, the last Playboy Club in America closed near a highway interchange of low-rent motels in Lansing, Michigan. "Tails droop as last Playboy Club closes," Nathan Cobb, *The Boston Globe*, July 28, 1988.

A story looking back twenty-eight years later was headlined: "Playboy Club Failed to Transform City's Culture."[211] It was a fitting epitaph.

But meanwhile, the men who stood up for decency paid a price. For some it was at great personal and family cost. For others it was scorn and ridicule, nationally and locally.

Prosecutor Si Leis felt the hostility when he prosecuted Larry Flynt for obscene magazines in 1976. "A lot of people didn't like that. They didn't want Cincinnati to be known as such a conservative city. But personally, I believed in what I was doing. I was not drawing the line. Members of the jury, representing the public, did that. It's BS that obscenity doesn't cause problems."

Joe Deters took the same abuse when he prosecuted Flynt for X-rated videos in 1998. "I constantly feel at the national level the distaste some of the elites have for Cincinnati," he said. "But I am also constantly asked by law enforcement in other cities how we did it. That is our reputation. Larry Flynt vs. Cincinnati was our reputation because we had people in our community like Charlie Keating and Carl Lindner who were hellbent on not letting it happen, and we had Si Leis who would prosecute it.

"Law enforcement was willing to take a stand where no other place would. Times Square and other big cities had this stuff running rampant. But we had a prosecutor who was saying, 'Not here.'"

THE CINCINNATI ENQUIRER, APRIL 1, 2014—Charlie Keating was America's favorite bad guy in the media. But he's still a hero to many in Cincinnati. His passing yesterday at age 90 reminded those who knew him and admired him of the man who left deep footprints in the Queen City.

I will leave it to the rest of the press to rehash how he was collared with the albatross of the S&L scandal and the ethically crippled senators known as "the Keating Five." What those reporters won't tell you is that he was also a generous philanthropist, a champion athlete, a leader who put Cincinnati on the map for Olympic swimming and a fearless warrior for

---

211 Jim Rohrer, *The Cincinnati Enquirer,* September 11, 2011.

something that seems almost like an archaeological artifact from the Old Testament: Decency.

Jake paused. "I'll probably get in trouble with the diversity committee for using 'cripple,'" he thought. "I wish Jim were here. Even Punch and Judy."

He wanted to lean on the Copydesk and tell Judy about the TV news reporter he saw last night. A tornado had touched down in a two-stoplight village east of the city, and ripped the roof off a biker bar. The mangled sign called it "Ben Dover Lounge," with a mudflap silhouette of a shapely, naked dancer touching her toes to make sure there was no doubt about the name.

A cute young Eyewitness News TV reporter was doing her best to avoid mentioning the racy name as she interviewed a longhaired, grizzled guy covered in tattoos, scars and leather. His tee-shirt said, "Working Like Crazy to Support the Lazy." The reporter looked at it and visibly winced.

"Like, looking around at the destruction, like, how did you feel when the roof was ripped off the… umm… like, this bar?" she asked.

"I had just ordered a beer so I felt like thirsty," he replied with a grin.

"But it must be, like, devastating to see what this storm has done to your community. What emotions are you going through right now, like, what are you experiencing?"

"I'm very sad," he nodded, picking up her cue for a sober tragedy face. "I never got that beer."

"I can only imagine, like, the devastation," she plowed on. "What was it like when the tornado hit… like, being right there in this bar you were in? It must have been, like, terrifying. I would be scared. I've never seen anything like this. Were you afraid? I wonder how the community will recover from this?"

"We always wanted a topless bar," he answered with a twinkle in his eye. "I didn't have no time to be scared. Not sure what community you're talkin' about, but we'll get by. It's just a pole barn. My guys can put a roof on that before you, like, put on your make-up. I hope y'all come back to Ben Dover."

It went clean over her head like a flying roof. Jake could almost hear Judy laughing. It was hard to say what was more hilarious, the eager reporter desperately mining sensational drama from a damaged biker bar, or the biker's subtle wit. Judy would have yelled at the TV, "Quit putting yourself in the story and just ask what happened! And, like, quit saying LIKE!"

But Judy and Punch were gone—casualties of retirement and staff cuts as corporate headquarters ordered a purge of high-salary veterans. "Just as well," Jake thought. "They wouldn't recognize the newsroom now, with 'content providers' chasing web clicks, empty chairs where editors used to sit, and reporters who injected their 'woke' ideology into everything, even sports."

Jerry and Clarabelle were gone too, off to climb the greasy pole of Gannett corporate promotions. He could picture them yammering away in marathon meetings, busy ruining newspapers in other cities.

He went back to his column.

The battles Charlie Keating fought were not pretty and made Cincinnati more uncomfortable than a priest at a stag party. There have always been plenty of people in this town who would gladly sacrifice decency for a condescending pat on the head from the New York Times. They are the neurotics who lie awake at night, worrying about what New York and Boston and even Chicago think of Cincinnati.

I can tell you what they think: Nothing at all.

But those neurotics have a voice in our media and politics and they made life pretty tough for Keating and the others who fought for decency. They called them "prudes," "bluenoses," "Puritans," "backward Baptists," "Nazis," "squares" and "uptight, guilty Catholics."

But there's a flipside to that record: All that name-calling offended about 60 percent of the decent people who vote in this town. So those "backward" prosecutors, judges and sheriffs kept getting re-elected for life because they were not afraid to step on the cockroaches who peddle smut.

CHAPTER 22 • WHAT WERE ONCE VICES NOW ARE HABITS

The people like Keating who fought the good fight can look back with pride at their victory. Yes, it looks like they lost the war every time we turn on the television. But in all the ways that matter, they won.

The city's Sexually Oriented Business zoning law acted like skunk repellent to keep the porn Mob away. But it took strong leaders to back it up.

Unfortunately, those kinds of leaders are all but gone.

Jake wrote several more inches of copy about the court victories, legislation to protect women and children, and the poison of porn in social media. He could almost see heads exploding in the newsroom when his column ran tomorrow. "*If* it runs tomorrow," he corrected himself.

He continued with the closer:

Whatever Charlie Keating left as a legacy, he gave us this warning to remember. Forty-four years ago, in 1970, he described what would happen if the battle for decency was lost. It looks a lot like the world we see around us today:

"First of all, there will be a loss of creativity, of a sense of destiny, and a subsequent decline in the family life, which is already beginning to occur. And with that, the crumbling of the basis of our culture."

Jake read it again and had no doubt: It would be spiked. "Too polarizing," he would be told, meaning someone in the newsroom would complain about hurt feelings or "hate speech." But he wished he could at least show it to Punch and Judy or Jim.

He could picture Jim with that inscrutable smile looking up from the copy to ask, "Jake, have you been sampling the cooking sherry again?"

He looked around at all the empty chairs. Almost nobody was left from the old days, and Jake would be gone in two weeks—or maybe sooner. Management had asked everyone to re-apply for their jobs, an idea so insulting and demoralizing it could only come from the geniuses at Gannett.

Jake had replied in writing with General Anthony McAuliff's answer to the Nazis who demanded his surrender at Bastogne: "Nuts!"

So far, there had been no response. Just cold, hostile silence. He shook his head and laughed, thinking, "When I turn this in, they will probably lock me out of the network and cancel my keycard so I can't get in the building. But I'll put a headline on it anyhow."

He keyed bold type and wrote:

"Not in Our Town."

Then for Jim's sake, he went to the bottom of the column and added the old command that told typesetters it was the end:

--30--

Last Word: Broken News

As a career newsman, editor, reporter, columnist, magazine writer, author and publisher, I can't resist a final comment on the media.

In my 2005 book, *Behind the Lines: The Untold Stories of the Cincinnati Riots*,[212] I revealed how sensationalized reporting of police confrontations with violent black suspects incited and aggravated race riots that broke out in 2001. They came just ten years after the same thing happened in Los Angeles in the Rodney King riots.

Now the pattern has accelerated. Trayvon Martin in Florida. "Hands up, don't shoot!" in Ferguson, Missouri. Kyle Rittenhouse in Kenosha. A litany of fake news that has incited deadly violence and torn our country apart along racial fault lines.

And the fake news factory just keeps on shouting at us from headlines and the creepy "crawlers" at the bottom of our TV screens. The news is broken. And it has been that way for a long time. Watergate was just the watershed.[213] Fifty years later, the scandal that launched a

---

212 Chilidog Press, 2005, chilidogpress.com and Amazon.

213 See "Exploding the Watergate Myth," Bruce Bawer, *Frontpage Mag*, July 20, 2022. From his review of *The Mysteries of Watergate* by John O'Connor, and *The Nixon Conspiracy: Watergate and the Plot to Remove the President*, by Geoff Shepard:

"... there are plenty of scoundrels in the annals of Watergate. But when it comes to long-term impact, none of them compare to Woodward and Bernstein. To revisit the movie *All the President's Men* after reading these two recent books is to appreciate anew the genius (of the movie). For all the cloak-and-dagger drama of the film, in real life the *Washington Post*'s big Watergate headlines were almost entirely based on leaks from Mark Felt at the FBI, and had no influence on the proceedings that ultimately brought down the Nixon presidency.

"Which is not to dismiss the massive influence of Woodward and Bernstein. Thanks to their selective, slanted reporting, Americans started revering journalists, of all people - a habit that they began to shake off only a few years ago.

"Woodward and Bernstein didn't just destroy Nixon. They radically altered the course of

thousand "(fill in the blank)-gates" has aged about as well as Dorian Gray's picture. Recent books and unsealed documents are also exposing the self-aggrandizing reporters who claimed credit—at least for anyone willing to take a fresh look with an open mind.[214]

But don't hold your breath to read about it in the news. The press protects is "narratives" like Teruo Nakamura, the last Japanese soldier who surrendered on a Pacific island in 1974—thirty years after he and his "narrative" were declared dead.

As I found in researching this book, the press defended and celebrated the narrative about Larry Flynt and others like him for more than thirty years, as the porn Mob destroyed decency like termites in the woodwork of America. The coarse culture we suffer today is the direct result.

And now the fake news factory works 24/7—cable news headlines sensationalize fear and panic to agitate and divide us into Red and Blue America. Truth, accuracy, fairness and context are all but irrelevant. The media business model is not about trust anymore, it's clicks. Fake news sells.

If the stories, distortions and coverups about Nicholas Sandmann, Ferguson, Kenosha, the Russia Hoax, Hunter Biden's laptop, etc. were

---

American history. By bringing down Nixon, they gave us Jimmy Carter. They revealed to their colleagues in the American news media just how much power they all had to shape public opinion - and how much wealth and prestige they could accrue by bending the facts to fit a partisan narrative."

"Woodward and Bernstein didn't just destroy Nixon. They radically altered the course of American history. By bringing down Nixon, they gave us Jimmy Carter. They revealed to their colleagues in the American news media just how much power they all had to shape public opinion - and how much wealth and prestige they could accrue by bending the facts to fit a partisan narrative."

214 "Due largely to the fame and fortune of Woodward and Bernstein, thousands of aspiring writers have sought to uncover or sensationalize some event as the capstone to their career as an investigative journalist. With each new graduating class, however, journalism schools pushed newsrooms to the left. The new recruits all too often reflected the bias of the increasingly liberal institutions from which they graduated. If the bias was real even when Nixon was president—the *Washington Post*'s Ben Bradlee, after all, was an uncomfortably close friend of JFK—by the time Trump became president, the bias had yielded to endemic corruption. It has become that overt and aggressive. The historic separation between news and opinion has ceased to be. What arguably began during Watergate has resulted in a situation where thinking citizens simply cannot trust the media as a reliable source for straight news." *The Nixon Conspiracy: Watergate and the Plot to Remove the President*, Geoff Shepard, Bombardier Books, 2021.

wrong and dishonest, no matter. The reporters had their starring role in the "real time" drama and their media platforms hauled in their "clickbait" headline jackpots, ignoring the ruined lives, poisoned politics and burning cities they left in their wake.

Almost nobody trusts the press anymore.[215] Yet most of the "journos" stay hooked on their crack-pipe narratives like addicts in denial, panhandling for another hit of social media fentanyl.

An intervention is needed. A reckoning. Accountability.

I don't know where that will come from, but there are encouraging signs, such as U.S. Supreme Court justices who are finally questioning why the press, alone, has immunity from libel.

I'm optimistic that consumers are abandoning broken traditional media and finding alternative sources. I hope there's a reverse "Gresham's law" for media, that good reporting and honesty will drive out the hacks and counterfeit reporters who are political activists.

And I hope that some of the many good people in the news business read this or something like it and do some soul searching about where this road they have taken will end.

---

215 A Gallup Poll on trust in media, conducted June 1-20, 2022, found 16 percent trust in newspapers; 11 percent trust TV news. Both are record lows.

Selected Reading

Fonzi, Gaeton. *The Last Investigation*. Simon and Schuster, 2018.

Goldfarb, Ronald L. *Perfect Villains, Imperfect Heroes*. Capital Books, 2002.

(Ohio), Law Enforcement Consulting Committee. *Organized Crime*. 1982.

O'Reilly, Bill, and Martin Dugard. *Killing the Mob*. St. Martin's Press, 2021.

Pornography, United States. *Final Report of the Attorney General's Commission on Pornography - United States*. Rutledge Hill Press, 1986.

Rappleye, Charles. *All American Mafioso: The Johnny Rosselli Story*. Houdini Publishing, 2014.

Shepard, Geoff. *The Nixon Conspiracy*. Bombardier Books, 2021.

Thanks to...

Craig Ramsdell, for a great design, inside and out; media attorney Jack Greiner, for his thorough legal review; Jeff Suess and *The Cincinnati Enquirer*, for permission to use some fantastic photos; the great team at the Kenton County Library, which provided pictures from *The Cincinnati Post*; Steve Kramer and the Cincinnati Police Museum, for help with research and pictures; the gracious family of the *Enquirer*'s best publisher, the late Bill Keating; John Kiesewetter, for sharing memories of the old Enquirer building on Vine; Marti Flanagan, for sharing memories and her legendary contacts; my daughter Liz and wife, Kathy, for advice and help with proofing; Judge Melissa Powers, private detective James Simon, former Police Chief Tom Streicher, Prosecutor Joe Deters, Assistant U.S. Attorney Karl Kadon and former Sheriff Si Leis; all the readers who asked for a sequel to *Forbidden Fruit*; and anyone else I missed. As always, any errors are mine alone.

www.ingramcontent.com/pod-product-compliance
Lightning Source LLC
Chambersburg PA
CBHW070504120526
44590CB00013B/744